Ellen Wilkinson

Ellen Wilkinson

1891 – 1947

Betty D. Vernon

CROOM HELM LONDON

©1982 Betty D. Vernon
Croom Helm Ltd, 2–10 St John's Road, London SW11

British Library Cataloguing in Publication Data

Vernon, Betty D.
  Ellen Wilkinson.
  1. Wilkinson, Ellen
  2. Politicians — Great Britain — Biography
  I. Title
  941.082'092'4   DA566.9.W/

ISBN 0-85664-984-8

Printed and bound in Great Britain by
Biddles Ltd, Guildford and King's Lynn

CONTENTS

Preface

Acknowledgements

List of Abbreviations

Dedicated to the memory of Dame Margaret Cole — socialist, teacher and friend.

PREFACE

A biography of Ellen Wilkinson should have been written when recollections of the 'elfin fury' were fresh, but for personal reasons that could not be. This belated attempt may now seem presumptuous, particularly as personal papers were destroyed soon after her death. Research, however, revealed that the shades of Ellen's vivid personality are evergreen and so, encouraged by the late Dame Margaret Cole, I made that attempt. I am deeply indebted to Ellen's family, friends and former colleagues in Great Britain and overseas — some now no longer alive — who encouraged me by answering innumerable questions and who dredged up history from their memories.

To my husband, above all, my gratitude is infinite. Always he sustained me with unlimited patience and continuous practical help through the doldrums of despair when Ellen invaded our lives. I hope my readers may feel that so much co-operative effort has been justified.

ACKNOWLEDGEMENTS

Many people have helped me in a variety of ways, especially Professor Harold Dent, Ernest Fernyhough, R. Neville Heaton, Beryl Hughes, H.D. (Billy) Hughes, Fred Johnson, John Parker, MP, Lord Redcliffe-Maud and Dr Richard Wilkinson. They have provided facts and anecdotes and have read chapters in draft, but the conclusions I have reached are wholly my own.

Among the many others who generously assisted were: Lord Alexander of Potterhill, Ambrose Appelbe, Betty Archdale, Vernon Bartlett, Nora Beloff, Maud Bickford, Sir George Bishop, Arthur Blenkinsop, Lord Robert Boothby, Mrs M. Bowrie-Mensler, Noreen Branson, Lord Fenner Brockway, Isabel Brown, Lord Ritchie-Calder, Professor W.H. Chaloner, Tudor David (Editor, *Education*), Dame Evelyn Denington, Bernard Donoughue, David Doughan, Roland Earl, Dorothy Elliott (Mrs Jones), Jack Feeney and Mrs Feeney, Maria Fischer, Sir Gilbert Flemming, Rt Hon. Michael Foot, MP, Heinrich Fraenkel, Eddie Frow, Margaret Gibb, Alex Glasgow, Mrs Godfrey, Dennis Gordon, Sir Ronald Gould, Dame Mary Green, Kenneth Harris, Mavis Hill, Sheila Hodges, Myra Hutchings, Professor George Jones, Judge Neil Lawson, Connie Lewcock, Arthur Logan-Petch, Helen Lord, Archibald McLeish, Edward MacLellan, Duncan Macrae Taylor, James Margach, A.R. Maxwell-Hyslop, Fred Meadowcroft, Amy Mitchell, Helen and Ivor Montagu, Muriel Nichol, Rt Hon. Philip Noel-Baker, Dame Kathleen Ollerenshaw, Dr Robin Page Arnot, Sir Antony Part, John Platts-Mills, QC, Maurice Reckitt, Jo Richardson, MP, Mrs Frances Robinson, Lord Goronwy Roberts, Paul Rotha, Sammy Rowan, Dr Rene Saran, William Sedley, Lord Shinwell, George and Phyllis Short, Margaret Simey, Rev. Lord Donald Soper, Mary Stott, Lord George and Lady Strauss, Paddy Scullion, Dame Mabel Tylecote, USDAW (T. Callinan, Ken Edwards, Patrick Jones, Jean Wood), Professor Ross Waller, Maud Warwick, Mr and Mrs Harold Weate, Sir Toby Weaver, Mrs Doris Wilkinson, Mrs Muriel Wilkinson, Dr and Mrs Richard Wilkinson, Kenneth Witney, Mr and Mrs George Woods.

Librarians and archivists have been untiringly helpful. Pre-eminently, Irene Wagner, chief librarian of the Labour Party Library, and her staff, who helped me immeasurably, and Miss Jean Ayton, archivist of Manchester City Library. Other sources were: Beamish (North of England Open Air) Museum, Bede Gallery, British Library (Newspaper Library) Colindale, British Library of Political and Economic Science, Department of Employment Library, Department of Education and Science Library, Electrical Association for Women, Fabian Society, Fawcett Library (City of London Polytechnic), House of Commons Library, House of Lords Record Office, Labour Research Department, Manchester Literary and Philosophical Society, Marx Memorial Library, National Union of Teachers Library, Nuffield College Library, Public Records Office, The John Rylands University Library of Manchester, South Tyneside Borough Council, Tyne and Wear County Council, University Library of Newcastle on Tyne, University of Reading Archives, University of Warwick Modern Records Centre, USDAW Library and Records (Headquarters and East Regional Office), Westminster City Libraries (Charing Cross and Central Reference).

To Roy Smith, Chief Librarian of the London Borough of Sutton and his staff go my special thanks for assistance both swift and constant. Colleen Saunders and Jeanne Williams performed miracles in typing my indecipherable handwriting. Without so much collective help from those who knew Ellen, or proudly remembered her, this book could never have materialised.

The author and publishers thank the following for permission to reprint excerpts from copyright material — Victor Gollancz Ltd: Ellen Wilkinson, *The Town That Was Murdered*. Harrap Ltd: Ellen Wilkinson, *Clash*. Longmans Green Ltd: Margaret Cole, *Growing Up Into Revolution*. Methuen & Co. Ltd: Margaret Cole (ed.), *The Road to Success*; G.D.H. Cole and R. Postgate, *The Common People (1746–1938)*; C.L. Mowat, *Britain Between the Wars (1918–1940)*. Frederick Muller Ltd, Margot Oxford (ed.), *Myself When Young*; Hugh Dalton, *The Fateful Years, Memoirs (1931–1945)*. The British Library of Political and Economic Science, extracts from unpublished diaries and papers in the Dalton collection. The Trevelyan family, Trevelyan Family Papers (Newcastle University Library). Mrs Helen Wilson, family papers of Annot Robinson. Marx House Library, unpublished papers of D.N. Pritt.

ABBREVIATIONS

AUCE	Amalgamated Union of Co-operative Employees
ETS	Emergency Training Scheme
FRD	Fabian Research Department
ILP	Independent Labour Party
LEAs	Local Education Authorities
LRD	Labour Research Department
LRC	Labour Representation Committee
NCLC	National Council of Labour Colleges
NEC	National Executive Committee (of the Labour Party)
NFS	National Fire Service
NSS	National Shipbuilders' Security Limited
NUDAW	National Union of Distributive and Allied Workers
NUT	National Union of Teachers
NUWM	National Unemployed Workers' Movement
NUWSS	National Union of Women's Suffrage Societies
PLP	Parliamentary Labour Party
PPS	Parliamentary Private Secretary
ROSLA	Raising of the School Leaving Age
UNESCO	United Nations Educational Scientific and Cultural Organisation
USF	University Socialist Federation
WIL	Women's International League for Peace and Freedom
WTUL	Women's Trade Union League

'It is absurd to imagine that a party could do without its left wing as it is to imagine that without one a bird could fly' — Arthur Henderson

'Ellen Wilkinson illustrated not unfairly in her political career, which was her life, the broad evolution of Labour views and attitudes over the past quarter century' — Times Educational Supplement

1 AWAKENING — 'RED NELLIE WILKINSON'

Childhood

On the wall outside the old Jarrow Town Hall is a metal plaque. It commemorates those who marched from Tyneside to Westminster on the Jarrow Crusade, protesting at the tidal wave of unemployment that engulfed their town. It states: 'These people brought to a nation's distress, courage and dignity and honour.' Words that could serve as an epitaph for the town's best known MP, Ellen Wilkinson. An active participant in the Crusade, her entire political life personified protest against poverty and inequality, expressed with courageous determination. 'Our Ellen', as she was affectionately known throughout Jarrow, was a passionate advocate of social justice.

Although, as Beatrice Webb noted, she was not an original thinker, there was little new or exciting in socialist theory during the 20s and 30s with which Ellen was not associated. She was no intellectual, but she was a marvellously alert and vivid interpreter of other people's thoughts and intentions.[1] With a power of speech rivalled only by Mrs Pankhurst[2] and a scalding pen, she argued, worked and fought for socialism with an intensity of conviction that, combined with ill health, burnt her out. Death snatched her away early, yet she remains in the memory as 'a flame of inspiration'.[3]

'I was born', Ellen used to boast 'into the proletarian purple.'[4] Her birth on 8 October 1891 was in an auspicious year for the Labour Movement. It saw the first edition of Robert Blatchford's *Clarion* (a paper which 'made socialism seem as simple and as universal as a pint of bitter'[5]), and the foundation of the Amalgamated Union of Co-operative Employees, which became the springboard for Ellen's political career.

Her Manchester based family life at Ardwick Chorlton-on-Medlock was secure, upper working class, respectable and undramatic. 'The Wilkinsons managed nicely, appreciated what hunger was, but never went without a meal.'[6] Ellen's parents, Richard Wilkinson, cotton operative turned insurance clerk, and Ellen Wood from Carnforth, Lancashire, were sensible citizens, whose practising Methodism influenced the lives of their four children — Anne (1881–1964), Richard Arthur (1883–1975), Ellen (1891–1947) and Harold (1899–1970). Her father had had a hard childhood. His Irish parents were heavy drinkers, and he, the eldest of nine, had to assume responsibility for the family. This may well explain his becoming a strict teetotaller, and it is likely that the tenet of abstinence drew him to Methodism, to which a certain Miss Wood was already a faithful adherent at the time of their first meeting. From her maternal grandmother Ellen inherited her most arresting attribute: a burnished head of red hair, which later proved a godsend to political journalists and became Ellen's hallmark. Her fiery temper was less of an asset.

The Wilkinsons lived at 41 Coral Street, Ardwick, Chorlton-on-Medlock, a respectable street of long terraced houses. The home now demolished and replaced by Balsam Close, is commemorated by a blue ceramic plaque recording Ellen's birth-place.[7] Chorlton-on-Medlock is notable as the parish of two Cabinet Ministers (Lloyd George was born nearby), and as an area where the Pankhurst family lived — for a while, Mrs Emmeline Pankhurst served it as an elected Poor Law Guardian.

It was a grimy district, and each house, two up and two down, had a little back yard with a privy.[8] Years later, Ellen described Ardwick in a nostalgic broadcast 'as part of Manchester's acres of narrow streets and brick boxes with slate roofs . . . where the weather was a mixture of soot and rain, and a typical Monday morning is the smell of wet mackintoshes and shawls tightly packed in a tram', but the grime was redeemed by the cleanliness of the housewife.[9] And in this Mrs Wilkinson was no exception. For she shared in the 'personal revolt against . . . industrial dirt and ugliness and in the individual passion for cleanliness of house and person'. The front doorstep at No. 41 was kept bright by regular 'stoning' — whitening to Southerners — a process as likely as not extended to window sills.

As this was done at least weekly, having to be at its pristine freshness for the weekend, the doorsteps of the old and handicapped were done by neighbours, for an unstoned doorstep indicated a feckless family. Moreover poverty did not excuse, as 'stones' could be obtained from the rag and bone man in exchange for rags.[10]

To the ugliness of her early life Ellen attributed her love of colour.

'There was so little in the street where we lived. Nearby was our green [Ardwick Green], though the leaves were always sooty.' But it was not all aridity. Professor Ross Waller, who lived next door to the Wilkinsons, recalls a neighbour who to everyone's amazement grew a small magnolia and sweet peas.[11] Internally however the houses were colour starved, and Ellen recollected that the favourite decoration for walls was brown paint and darkish red or green paper. 'We always had that at home because it did not show the dirt.' To this she added a human postscript:

One of the best men who ever came from the north, John Jagger MP, once confessed to me that his favourite dream as a boy was when he grew up to build a house entirely of white tiles and be able to wash it down morning and evening with hot water, just by turning on a tap.[12]

If the environment was begrimed and ugly, the Wilkinson's home life was warmly caring and clean. Mrs Wilkinson was able to employ a weekly washerwoman and Ellen once wrote a tear-jerker about the 'sad damp lives' of washerwomen, which must have been one of her earliest pieces of 'scribbling'. Family life centred round the big kitchen, with Mrs Wilkinson, whom Ellen judged the 'goodest mother that ever was', at the heart of things.[13] 'Mother was rather advanced for her day, a round sweet soul with long hair she could sit on. It was always my ambition to achieve hair like that, but when I did I had it cut short as a nuisance.'[14] Mrs Wilkinson's sister-in-law recalls her as being quiet, charming and capable. She had cancer, with bouts in bed, but when she got up was always active. Ellen remembers her childhood as being dominated by her mother's illness:

She had operation after operation. Father had been out of work a long time when I was coming. There was no unemployment benefit or maternity or child welfare schemes. Mother kept going by dressmaking. She couldn't afford proper attendance at my birth and was badly handled. The result was a life of agonising suffering. But she had the most marvellous recuperative power and would not be an invalid. Once the awful pain was still, she was up and around.

Mrs Wilkinson made every stitch that she and her children wore.

'She even made some of father's suits until my sister Annie grew old enough to help her.' (Skill with her hands was something that Ellen in no way inherited.)

> The maddening thing was that I had only been earning the money to give mother little luxuries for a year and a half before she died . . . yet across the years there comes to me no sense of the suffering martyr, but of a woman greatly in love with life.[15]

She died in 1916.

Living in a small crowded home, with two brothers and a sister Ellen acquired a penchant for privacy. Although essentially gregarious — an occupational characteristic of politicians — she never lost an occasional desire for solitude. In her semi-autobiographical novel *Clash* (published in 1929), Joan, the heroine, who had much in common with her creator, expresses just that feeling as 'she crept fully dressed between the sheets and pulled the bed clothes over her head. It was an old habit — dating from childhood in her crowded little home. . . . The only chance of any privacy was to slip between the sheets in the dark cold little room and hope that people would forget her.'[16]

Tiny, fiery and vivid, Ellen early evinced qualities of determination and directness. There is a tale, probably apocryphal, recounted by her childhood friend Stella Davies that at the age of ten Ellen was taking out baby Harold whose advent she had much resented. And pram-pushing she detested. So Harold was deposited on the pavement and left. 'Though it was typical that he had been made comfortable, snugly wrapped up, and placed on the side walk, out of harm's way. Ellen was not without ruth, even when determined on a course of action!' She returned home, reported the incident to her mother, and threatened repeated defiance if she were sent on a similar outing.[17] According to Ellen's aunt, however, it is more likely that Mrs Wilkinson, who was firm with all her children, was only too aware of a certain wilfulness which she had been trying to curb, and rather than giving in to Ellen she was probably making a concession in allowing her to take the baby at all![18]

If mother was firm, father spoilt all his children and cherished Ellen in particular. She in her turn regarded him as a 'tremendous figure', and proudly wrote of his having been a half-timer in a cotton mill at the age of eight, and head of the household, living in a cellar, at twelve. He learned to read and write at the local Sunday School, which was all the formal education he ever had, yet of his four children, three went to college, and two had university degrees.

Her father's extraordinary physical strength was not bestowed on Ellen, but 'the ruthless driving power with which he did everything' certainly was. Even more importantly, she learnt her first lessons about trade unionism and acquired an awareness of social conditions from Mr Wilkinson.

> I remember my father speaking bitterly of the life of undernourished idle men, wanting to work, but who were caught up in the realities of the over specialised, under organised cotton trade of pre-war days . . . and of the days when he tramped from one mill to another trying to get a job.[19]

As work was difficult to obtain and Mr Wilkinson had a growing family to support, he became an insurance agent. He is remembered as a 'rather fat man riding a bicycle on his insurance collecting rounds'.[20] In time he became more than a mere collector to his clients for he developed a real concern for their welfare. So much so that years later Ellen wrote to a constituent, 'I'm the daughter of an insurance agent, and I know how often they are the friends, general adviser and family lawyers to the poor.'[21]

Mr Wilkinson worked on his job well into his seventy-fifth year. Then one day 'he went to bed with a newspaper in his hands, and fell into his last sleep smiling over the headlines that his daughter had had a row with the Deputy Speaker in the House of Commons', Ellen wrote in a charming if suspect piece of family biography.[22]

Like all good 'Methodies', the family valued education and their house was not without books. 'I should assume it was probably like my own', Professor Ross Waller has written, 'some Dickens, Shakespeare and a scatter of popular novels . . . The children no doubt (as I did) used the excellent public library at Longsight.'[23]

At the age of six Ellen went to school — 'a filthy elementary school with the five classes in one room,'[24] — though whether this was St Paul's or St Luke's Church Elementary School is obscure. Both were close to Coral Street: both no longer exist.[25] Even then she was a rebel — 'Perhaps it was because they called me "ginger" ' — but she did not stay there long.

> I caught the inevitable germs in one of the epidemics that raged almost unchecked through the crowded insanitary schools and

had all the childish diseases in one swoop. I would certainly have died but for a devoted and intelligent mother . . . I didn't go back till I was eight, being taught to read at home.[26]

It has been suggested by the family that these various illnesses affected Ellen's physique. For although she had been a big baby she never grew tall[27] and even the arresting phrase 'five foot of dynamite' is inaccurate. Ellen, at her full height, was 4ft 10 ins, but she rarely found this a disadvantage. On the contrary, her tiny frame evoked waves of protective masculine sympathy[28] and attracted many distinctive epithets, from 'Elfin Fury' to 'Fiery Particle'.

Returning to school, Ellen continued 'along the broad highway of state education', and entered Ardwick Higher Elementary Grade (later Ardwick Central, now Nicholls-Ardwick High School) in 1902, to which at eleven she won her first scholarship. From that time, 'I paid for my own education by scholarship until I left university.'[29]

In retrospect Ellen disliked her school days, and was 'surprised by the sheer hate that surged up in my mind. Technically I was a "naughty" child. I was always top of the class in every subject other than drawing and maths — the subjects I hated and simply refused to do.' Years later one of her teachers visited her in the House of Commons:

The woman I had hated seemed kindly and reasonable . . . 'Why were you all down on me in class?' I asked. 'We were not. But you never behaved according to your marks. . . . You worked like a nigger at the subjects you liked and then refused to behave as a head girl should.'[30]

The school failed to tame Ellen. She readily admitted that someone should have made her do things she hated: 'I had never been made to do things I couldn't. I had been allowed to go on shining at the things I could do easily. It has never occurred to me since that there is anything — except of course maths and anything with my hands — that I couldn't do.' So it was Ellen left school 'with a boundless self confidence that my brains certainly did not warrant'. In retrospect Ellen made a shrewd appraisal of her schooltime difficulties:

The top few pupils were intelligent and could mop up facts like blotting paper . . . but we were made to wait for the rest of the huge classes . . . We wanted to stretch our minds but were merely a nuisance. The boy rebels fared better . . . The masters would often give them extra time and lend books to a bright lad. I never remember such encouragement. I was only a girl anyway.[31]

At the time boys and girls were taught in separate classes and not infrequently as a punishment Ellen was sent to join the boys. This was more of a pleasure than a punishment to her and something she did not forget. For reminiscing in a talk to the pupils of Ardwick Central, when as Minister of Education she visited officially in March 1946, she added a characteristic embellishment: 'When I am asked whether I feel embarrassed at being the only woman in the Cabinet I reply, "not at all, Ardwick prepared me for anything".' Behind her criticisms of school Ellen retained warm if ambivalent feelings and during that official visit, accompanied by the senior mistress, Miss Turner, she went into every room. When some time later Helen Lord, another teacher, burst into the staff room: 'I found her sitting at the table crying quietly, overcome by the memories of her childhood. At that moment she was no longer Ellen Wilkinson, Minister of Education, but little Nellie, a lively, happy and often rebellious school girl.'[32]

According to the school Log Book, in 1906 Ellen won a £25 pupil teaching bursary under the Ardwick Higher Elementary Scheme. This meant she would attend the Manchester Day Training College, then at Princess Street in the City Centre for half the week, and would teach during the other half for two years to qualify as a teacher. She taught first at Oswald Road Elementary School, close to Coral Street, then a 'beautiful new elementary school of the latest pattern . . . each class had its own classroom built round a light airy hall with fine mural paintings'. In those days 'elementary' schools embraced pupils up to the age of fourteen, so Ellen was teaching young people only slightly her junior.

Concern over her young pupils soon brought Ellen into conflict with authority. On one occasion she was left to take a lesson in History with Standard Seven boys: 'These boys were filling in time, bored stiff until they reached 14 years and could leave. I was an undersized girl . . . They all towered above me. My only hope was to interest them sufficiently to keep them reasonably quiet.' This she did by talking to them about J. Addington Symonds's *The Renaissance*, which 'I was reading for my own examination.' She and her pupils were absorbed until interrupted by the Headmaster who demanded to know why the boys were not all sitting upright with their arms folded. 'They are sitting that way because I am interesting them,' Ellen replied. To which the Headmaster responded by caning almost everyone:

> We had a grand row, and I was sent home [to be] reprimanded by an Inspector. But my temper had not calmed . . . The surging hate of all the silly punishment I had endured in my school days . . . prevented any awe of the Inspector. I whirled all this out at the unfortunate man, who listened quietly . . . and advised 'Don't do any more teaching when you have finished your two years here. Take my advice. Go and be a missionary in China.'[33]

Not without reason had the neighbours of Coral Street already dubbed her 'Red Nellie Wilkinson.'[34]

This experience, which, amongst others, helped Ellen decide that teaching was not to be her life's work, had an ironic twist. During the time at Princess Street she met Fred Marquis — a fellow trainee — later Lord Woolton, the wartime Minister of Food. According to her sister Anne, 'nothing gave Ellen greater impish pleasure than to remind him of their common experience in pupil teaching. It used to make him furious. He didn't want to be worried by such plebian antecedents.'[35] Years later, however, when Ellen and Sir Frank Whittle received honorary degrees from Manchester University, it was Lord Woolton, the Chancellor of the University, who made the presentation!

All, however, was not despondency and anger. Ellen began to find that education could offer her a meaning beyond 'restraint on everything I wanted to do.' This was largely due to the French mistress, who 'persuaded us to read French as if it were human', and to W.E. Elliott, later at the Board of Education, 'who seemed to understand that I was starving for some intelligent direction in study, and also encouraged me to write articles.'

At this time something even more important occurred — the advent of 'school politics'. When Mr Elliott suggested that she might stand in the school election, Ellen jumped enthusiastically into the great unknown. Previously there had been only two candidates, but 'as you are the only girl who talks in school debates you had better be the socialist candidate', the head boy of the Centre persisted. 'It never occurred to me not to be the candidate, just because socialism was a word I had barely heard.'

Typically, Ellen set to and worked hard to meet the challenge. She borrowed books, including Robert Blatchford's *Britain for the British* and *Merrie England*:

> Here was . . . the answer to the chaotic rebellion of my school years. My mother's illness fitted into this protest against the treatment of the sick who could not pay, the inefficiency of commercialism, the waste, and extravagance, and the poverty. It was all very elementary but Blatchford made socialists in those days by the sheer simplicity of his argument. I went into that election an ardent, in fact a flaming, socialist.

About 500 students and staff gathered at the Centre. Ellen had carefully prepared her speech, though no one had mentioned heckling — and 'the foundations of my new faith were slender'. Because she was the first socialist ever to stand she received most of the questions, but sheer rudeness and laughter saved the day and she won the election by a narrow margin.

This episode not only showed that she never hesitated to undertake any job that she wanted, but it also taught Ellen a useful lesson:

> I learnt all too early that a clear decisive voice and a confident manner could get one through 90 per cent of life's difficulties. And the awful 10 per cent are thrust down so deep into my thoughts by a fierce will that the consequent agony of spirit has remained my own.[36]

But something more than increased self confidence emerged from that election. Her moral indignation over the social evils she was beginning to recognise, and a desire to 'enter the magic sphere of politics', directed Ellen into joining the Independent Labour Party when she was sixteen. 'It was a tremendous moment for me.'[37]

Ellen's capacity for concentrated hard work, for achieving goals upon which she was determined, was beginning to prove itself. In the summer of 1909 she passed matriculation in the Second Division. Since far fewer than half of those qualifying under the Joint Board of Manchester, Liverpool, Leeds and Sheffield Universities were women, this was no mean achievement. She was also working for the Jones Scholarship in History, a national award for which competition was keen. Winning it meant everything to Ellen's future. At this time opportunity for entering university was mainly open to men of money — with or without ability. For women without money, however talented, the going was hard. And for those from working-class homes access was almost impossible. Ellen knew that if she did not gain the award a government grant for teacher training would be her only academic option, and that she would be obliged to teach after qualifying. 'With my recent experience of elementary teaching the last thing that I wanted to do was to promise to teach for a period of five years — which at eighteen looks a lifetime away.'[38]

After sitting the exam, with the end of term excitement, the thought of the scholarship got pushed (so Ellen says) to the back of her mind, then something queer occurred:

> One Saturday morning . . . suddenly there came . . . into my mind . . . the complete certainty that I had won the scholarship. I stood perfectly still, and I knew. Never before or since have I had such an experience. There were still several days before the results were announced . . . But I knew with my whole being that I had got that scholarship.[39]

And so she had — an exceptional triumph for any woman and for a girl of Ellen's background outstanding.

The Voiceless Many

Disraeli's Two Nations still existed in Ellen's childhood, when working-class conditions were still Dickensian. However, as Victorian complacency receded before the evidence of poverty and social distress, fresh attitudes evolved — attitudes of determination to effect changes in society, which both emanated from and helped to encourage the growing trade union movement and new political organisations. The consciences of those far less observant and compassionate than Ellen were stirring, and against such a background her awareness of the national picture matured into real concern for the needs of *people*.

The meticulous, disturbing investigations of William Booth (made between 1889 and 1900) published in his *Life and Labour of the People of London* and of Seebohm Rowntree in his study of *Poverty in York* (1901) revealed the depths of deprivation and hardship into which unemployment could suck the helpless.

These conditions were as common in Manchester as elsewhere, for Rowntree calculated that 25 to 30 per cent of the town population in the United Kingdom lived in poverty — an estimate based on figures collected in 1899, 'when trade was unusually prosperous'. Rowntree's definition of poverty was in no way 'soft', but covered families

> whose total earnings were insufficient to obtain the minimum necessaries for the maintenance of merely *physical efficiency*, allowed only for a diet so basic as to be less generous in variety than that for able bodied people in the workhouse, and assumed that no clothing was purchased unless absolutely necessary for health, and then of the most economical description.[40]

Behind this general definition lay the hard facts of low wages, insecurity of employment, ramshackle housing, ill health, poor diet and minimal education, set against a stark and hopeless background. For unless family or neighbourly support was forthcoming, or a family had a life insurance policy, belonged to a Friendly Society, or father was in a trade union, no state assistance whatsoever existed (until 1910) to aid those facing unemployment, ill health or old age. There was only patchy charitable provision, local parish relief or the workhouse — a heartrending sight, where after a life of hard work the poor and the old who were left destitute finished up. Where husbands and wives were separated and let out together for a few hours on Tuesdays and Thursdays.

The surveys which Booth and Rowntree produced related only to London and York. But there is no doubt that their results were wholly comparable, and as Booth assured Rowntree, 'I have long thought that other cities if similarly tested would show a percentage of poverty not differing greatly from that existing in London. Your most valuable inquiry confirms me in this opinion.'[41] Young Ellen in working-class Manchester would certainly have seen such poverty at first hand. Rowntree was no politician, but his researches prompted him to pose questions. How, he asked, could a land abounding in wealth countenance probably more than one fourth of its population living in poverty? No civilisation could be sound or stable when based on such a mass of stunted human life. 'The suffering may be all but voiceless . . . but once we realise it we see that social questions of profound importance await solution.'[42]

A further dimension to the understanding of human exploitation was added by the *Daily News's* Sweated Industries Exhibition in 1906. This reproduced in a series of living tableaux the actual conditions under which women worked in their own homes, on trades ranging from fur sewing to coffin tassel-making, toiling for a pittance often in cramped and unhygienic accommodation. Such revelations shocked the complacent — as they were meant to do.

Legislative interference with conditions in industry was then highly suspect, and the exhibition had been assembled with the professed intent of 'cultivating an opinion which would compel legislation to mitigate the evils of sweating'. 'Co-operation', wrote Richard Mudie Smith in his introduction to the Handbook of the Exhibition, 'must be substituted for competition . . . The attitude of "each for all and all for each" will have to supplant "each for himself and the Workhouse take the hindmost", before sweating is abolished.'[43] The Exhibition proved to be an important factor in public support for the Trade Boards Act, 1909.

Such, in Ellen's youth, were the conditions of employment and poverty and change came slowly. For even in 1924, John Scurr, pacifist MP for Stepney from 1923–32, was writing bitterly of life in the slums which

> drew one's admiration to the great struggle put up against the environment by thousands of men and women . . . cramped together . . . overcrowded, in dark mean alleys, overworked at miserable wages — never enough to eat — subject to disease from bad conditions of work, and of living . . . They have been cast into the abyss of ignorance and our society passes them by.[44]

Because Ellen was to become so closely involved with the trade union movement it is important to understand their role and development during this 'seeding time of socialism'. Her childhood ran broadly parallel with the rise of the new unionism. Until the 1890s trade union organisation had embraced mainly skilled craftsmen — engineers, miners and building workers. However, a series of dramatic strikes among the matchgirls, the gas workers and the dockers (led by John Burns and Tom Mann) resulted in improved rates of pay (the dockers won their 'tanner an hour'), and in the formation of general unions for various categories of unskilled workers, including women.

Even so, women were extremely difficult to organise. Scattered and isolated in home industries, they received low rates of pay, yet were suspicious of trade unionism. Leaders of the women's trade union movement, Margaret Bondfield, Mary MacArthur and later Ellen had, therefore, to overcome immense resistance. But with the creation of Emma Paterson's Women's Trade Union League (WTVL), which aimed to convince women of their need to co-operate, and to persuade men to see them as colleagues rather than competitors, the situation improved. Unions began to affiliate to the League and the men, rather than seeking to expel women workers from their branches, used the League to organise them — though sometimes this was undertaken with more determination than tact. A document addressed to the League urgently requesting that an organiser be sent to a particular town, added, 'we have decided that if women here cannot be organised they must be exterminated', which says perhaps more for fraternal solidarity than for clarity of thought![45]

Although trade union activity often brought political work in its wake, unionism in Ellen's youth was certainly not synonymous with socialism. For even when a decision was taken to nominate a Labour candidate for Parliament (as in Jarrow in 1892[46]) many working men supported the employer's nominee. Ellen's own father was one of thousands of working-class trade unionists who voted Conservative — an ardent worker for A.J. Balfour in the old north-west Division of Manchester at election time, he took no other part in politics.[47] He did not vote Labour until Ellen was old enough to persuade him. Until the turn of the century few trade union MPs were in fact Social-ists: Henry Broadhurst, MP, a stone mason and early Secretary to the TUC, actually held office under Mr Gladstone. Even Keir Hardie, the idealistic founder and first MP of the Independent Labour Party (ILP), temporarily aligned himself with the Liberals, whose views were then in advance of much trade union thinking.

Socialism was however evolving. The trade union movement, stirred by the realities of social injustice and influenced by Robert Blatchford's powerful writings, gathered strength. At the same time socialist principles slowly clarified, shaped by the conflicting — yet sometimes converging — philosophies of the Social Democratic Federation (SDF), the Fabian Society and the ILP. In its heyday the SDF had considerable influence on socialist thought. Formed in 1881 by Henry Hyndman and H.H. Champion it was in essence Marxist. It accepted as its guiding principles The Labour Theory of Value and the Materialist Conception of History, and continually predicted that the 'socialist revolution was around the corner'. It was superseded in 1911 by the British Socialist Party, which later became active in forming the British Communist Party.[48]

The Fabian Society, middle-class and intellectual, was important in Ellen's political development. Founded in 1883 by Hubert Bland and Frank Podmore and uncommitted to specific Labour policies, it was an educational and propaganda body which became a galvanising force, far more effective than its small membership would suggest. In the 1890s it gathered into its membership such distinguished social reformers as Sidney and Beatrice Webb, Graham Wallas, George Bernard Shaw and Lord Olivier. The Society was thoughtfully reformist, believed in the inevitability of gradualness and a policy of peaceful permeation and had no revolutionary pretensions.

Fabian Essays were published in 1889. They produced no unified analysis of society, but the essayists agreed with Keir Hardie's demands for improving the conditions of the working class. They argued for transforming capitalism into a welfare state which to ensure people a decent standard of living must take the ownership and control of the means of production into public hands. 'Fabianism became the new Benthamism and Socialism the legal consummation of a progressive policy for social reform.'[49]

Keir Hardie, whose political beliefs had so much in common with Fabian philosophy, saw no future for the working man in Parliament aligning himself with the Liberals. Like Robert Blatchford he had come to regard both Liberals and Tories as enemies of the people.[50] And so, in 1893, the Independent Labour Party was founded as a national political party, just a few months after the formation of a local branch in Manchester.

The objective of the ILP was to secure the collective and communal ownership of all the means of production, distribution and exchange and to run independent Labour candidates. The seminal Bradford Conference in 1893 adopted a programme which included the abolition of child labour under the age of fourteen, a legal eight hour working day, state provision for the aged, sick and disabled worker and for widows and orphans, the abolition of indirect taxation, taxation to extinction of all unearned incomes, work for the unemployed and 'every proposal for extending political rights and for democratising the system of government'.[51] It did not succeed in neatly uniting the disparate parties within the socialist movement, but it did make a wide appeal to both intellectuals and homely thinking working-class men and women:

It became a way of life which promised the New Jerusalem. A movement remarkable for the quality of the life it brought to its members. It was never doctrinaire and encouraged wide ranging discussion on political, social, cultural and religious topics . . . The most famous of all its journals, Blatchford's *Clarion* [also] developed field campaigning.

This exerpt from the background introductory note by her grandson to Hannah Mitchell's autobiography *The Hardway Up* is like the book itself, of special interest. For, although twenty years older, as a suffragette, member of the ILP, Manchester City Councillor and Magistrate, she knew Ellen, and on occasion worked with her in local government. Mrs Mitchell's early activities and political philosophy are a close counterpart to those of Ellen.

In the House of Commons Keir Hardie soldiered on in his lonely battle. He engendered immense hostility by opposing a vote of congratulations to Queen Victoria on the birth of a grandchild in order effectively to protest at the cavalier attitude adopted by members over the death of 250 Welsh miners in a major mining disaster.[52] But in 1900 there came a breakthrough. The Labour Representation Committee (LRC) was formed specifically to secure the election of Labour Members of Parliament. The days of the Lib — Lab alliance were numbered.

With the election in 1906 there came a shattering political change. The Conservatives were defeated after twelve years, because of Austen Chamberlain's policy of tariff reform which implied the abandonment of Free Trade, and because the trade unions were determined to have the Taff Vale judgement of 1901 reversed. This had ruled that the unions were suable in a corporate capacity. Although the Liberals were returned with an overwhelming majority there were also 29 LRC members, 14 miners' representatives and a handful of old style Lib-Labs. To one who remembered the election it was 'even more overwhelming than that of 1832, and could be compared only with the landslide of 1945.'[53] The voiceless ones were silent no longer.

Methodism

The poverty of the day and the ethos of the times were not the only factors shaping Ellen's political attitudes. Methodism also was a driving force, for 'Unlike traditional conforming sects no...... about it stood in the way of the socialist image.'[54] Indeed, Methodism was as powerful an element in the growth of the Labour Movement as the Wesleyan ethic of the Chapel in Grosvenor Street, Ardwick was in guiding the Wilkinson family.

Some would deny that the influence of Methodists benefited the labouring poor. Cobbett found them the bitterest foes for freedom in England, and in this J.L. and Barbara Hammond agreed, assessing the whole spirit of the new religion as: 'unfavourable to the democratic movement and to the growth of the trade union spirit, [calling] not for citizens but for saints . . . not for the violent redress of injustice but for the ecstatic vision'.[55] In the days of Jacobin propaganda, Methodism had provided a counter-attraction among the poor. It directed 'the first rebellion of the uncared-for millions into other channels' by 'foistering on them a self respect as citizens of another world whose franchise was not confined to the well-to-do . . . providing them with a democratic religious and educational organisation of their own'.[56] However, as time went on Methodist working men and Methodist local preachers emerged as active workers in different fields of working-class politics: 'If there were only a few Methodist Jacobins, there were more Methodist Luddites, many Methodist weavers demonstrating at Peterloo, Methodist Trade Unionists and Chartists. They were rarely . . . initiators; [but] . . . were often found as devoted speakers and organisers.'[57]

The growth of the Labour Movement was assisted by the continuous indictment of social evils expressed through Methodists who became MPs. Such men included Thomas Burt, MP for Morpeth and a contemporary of Keir Hardie, Henry Broadhurst and Joseph Arch, founder of the Agricultural Labourers' Union. Though not militant socialists they were God-fearing representatives of working-class interests and upon their Methodist trail Labour MPs followed.[58] Among the later ranks were Philip Snowden, Jack Lawson, Charles (Lord) Ammon, George Tomlinson, Ellen (the first woman Methodist to enter the House), and Arthur Henderson. 'Uncle' Arthur was not alone in finding Wesleyan Christianity a strong fountain of inspiration which lasted all his days. 'Different minds have been predisposed to socialism by many causes. In Henderson's case, as in that of thousands of lesser men who helped to build the Labour Party, the predisposing factor was Methodism.'[59]

Methodism was not the sole formative factor in Ellen's socialism, but it was important. The patience and resignation it taught were not for her — more characteristic was her cast-iron determination — but the family's beliefs and the social life around the Wesleyan Chapel gave a mighty bend to the twig of Ellen's development.[60] The Grosvenor Street Chapel was indeed a focal point in the lives of the Wilkinson family. 'Although within the home everyone seemed always to be arguing about everything non-stop in an exceedingly lively manner', the youngsters appeared to accept their parents' religion without rebellion, though each reacted differently.[61] Richard Arthur became a much-loved Methodist Minister, serving many years in the Northern Circuit and Ellen never rejected Non-conformism. She often referred to her Methodist upbringing, and practised its principles. She was 'agin drink', loathed any form of gambling, and when her secretary once allowed a neighbour to use the phone in her flat in order to place a bet, 'Ellen nearly blew my head off'.[62] She supported the Rev. Arthur, preaching in his chapel whenever opportunity, in her subsequently busy life, arose. He in turn assisted in his sister's elections, often at some professional cost. Harold, an engineer, was probably the most sceptical, although later it was Anne who claimed to be the atheist.[63]

Ellen's father, was had started to preach when he was fifteen, was long the most active Methodist of the family. Forthright in his views and a good speaker, like Ellen he had a 'gorgeous voice' although his brother-in-law, George Wood, who excelled in open-air preaching, was said to be the more outstanding.[64] There is a tale still current of how Mr Wilkinson handled a heckler with a deftness which later Ellen herself could not have bettered. A troublesome congregant kept interrupting his preaching, and when at long last he could tolerate it no longer Mr Wilkinson broke off his discourse to thunder at the hapless dissident, 'Woman! Take up thine umbrella and be gone.' Meekly she obeyed.[65]

It was probably because Ellen was never made to go to chapel in her younger days that she thoroughly enjoyed it. 'I liked the hearty singing and the cheerful services and dreamed my own thoughts through the long sermons.'[66] More than that, she tried out her skill in public speaking by making her first speech at a Sunday School foreign missionary festival. She recalls as one of her earliest memories, 'dressing up in Chinese gown and having to speak on behalf of China. I would not have one word written for me and insisted on making that speech myself.'[67] Doubtless the many preachers who visited Coral Street — 'sermons were as much current shop in our home as golf and cricket in others' — had not gone unheeded.

There is a further tale of Ellen's precocity in public speaking. A religious Granny lived next door, to whom missing chapel was a real loss. When she used to 'mind' Ellen on Sunday evenings they would hold services together. Ellen would stand on a low chair and start to preach. 'Mother was thoroughly horrified at the apparent irreverance. But we were very serious and Granny listened with flattering attention at my attempts to remember the morning sermons.' Ellen's grandmother has much to answer for, for that training in public speaking which started so early ran on into school debates. 'All of this provided a long and largely unselfconscious training for complete confidence on public platforms.'

Her sturdy non-conformist independence of mind aligned with her father's inherited forthrightness gave Ellen considerable self assurance. It did not however endow her with her father's strongly apolitical approach to life:

> His political creed was a perfectly simple one. 'I have pulled myself out of the gutter, why can't they?' was his reply to every demand for sympathy or solidarity with his own class. Generous enough in cases of individual hardship he refused as sturdily to admit that he was oppressed as that he was a miserable sinner . . . We took our religion very cheerfully. God was somehow part of the household, not an awesome Presence but friendly and understanding . . . A fellow worker in a reasonable universe.

Life was full of optimism and Ellen was daunted by no one.

From her father Ellen gained much more than Methodist morality. She was his favourite daughter, and he did everything to foster her intellectual development — respect for education was part of the Methodist tradition. He was an intelligent, somewhat lonely man, with a considerable grasp of contemporary problems. He liked attending lectures on theological subjects and often took Ellen with him. Together they heard Dr Frank Ballard on Christian Evidence, and the Free Trade Hall lectures on Darwin and Evolution:

> We went to lots of lectures on evolution, both for and against. I was barely twelve and had no background for most of it, but by the time I was 14 was reading Haeckel and Huxley and Darwin with my father. This never upset my cheerful faith in my friend

God but it produced a queer philosophical mix-up when my father added Bergson's Creative Evolution on my 16th birthday. I didn't get this fuzzy mess sorted out until I discovered Karl Marx in my early twenties.[68]

Years later speaking at the Manchester and Salford Methodist Mission she acknowledged the morality in public life her religion generated, which 'even if the individual didn't reach it, was a standard that remained. So public meetings in Manchester about the Black and Tans in Ireland or sweated labour at home used to succeed because they had a morality to appeal to.'[69] In no way over the years had Methodism obstructed Ellen's path to socialism. On the contrary, she became a living refutation of the Hammond's diagnosis. 'I am still a Methodist', she told a Left Book Club meeting in March 1939, 'you can never get . . . its special glow out of your blood. I still keep up my membership at Grosvenor Street, and when I can, attend Longsight Chapel where my brother was the Superintendent.'[70]

The ILP

Ellen says that she joined the ILP when she was sixteen as a direct consequence of the school election described earlier. Obviously she was prompted by a desire to find out more about socialism, for it is impossible that anyone of such rebellious intelligence could remain aloof from the challenge it presented. But the sequence of events leading to her membership is obscure, since Ellen refers both to Ardwick and Oswalds as 'school'. It seems likely that the mock election took place at the Teachers' Centre in 1905 (the General Election was to follow in January 1906) and she joined the ILP soon after. What is certain is that the attraction of Methodism for her was then temporarily in abeyance. 'I was', she confessed, 'utterly bored with religion and sermons . . . sick of the discussions as to what this or that text meant.'[71]

The account of her initiation into politics written some 30 years later was embroidered by hindsight. It does however convey Ellen's excited apprehension over the first branch meeting as well as the forceful impact that Mrs Bruce Glasier (Kathleen St John Conway) made upon her at the Manchester Free Trade Hall. Hannah Mitchell too was inspired by Mrs Glasier's fervour 'to carry the socialist message on to street corners and far beyond'.[72] 'The details of that first branch meeting', Ellen wrote, 'remained etched on my mind while a first love affair at the same time remains dim . . . Mere boys seemed very uninteresting creatures to the solemn High Priestess of Politics that I had presuaded myself I was.' On balance though the event proved disappointing:

> A few men strolled in. Someone read the minutes. There were a lot of incomprehensible initials . . . I did not know then that those initials represented trade unions and movements which have since become part of my own daily speech. I [left] . . . feeling that if this were politics there seemed little room for me.

At this time Ellen's political mentor was a fellow student at the Training Centre who would not let her enthusiasm become soured. He was a Jew, already a hero in her eyes because he spoke at socialist meetings on street corners, and he it was who suggested that 'I should go with him and other students to hear Kathleen Bruce Glasier, an ILP propagandist, speak the following Sunday.' But how to get to a political meeting instead of Chapel on a Sunday night? Ellen went straight to her father and told him what she wanted to do.

> He replied exactly as I knew he would — couldn't they have political meetings any other time but Sundays. I had the answer ready, all about shift workers who could not come any other night. Dad knew more about shift work than I did. But he saw how keen I was and let me go . . . It was a memorable meeting . . . I got a seat in the front row of the gallery . . . it seemed noisy to me, whose sole experience of meetings was of religious services. Rows of men . . . filled the platform . . . But my eyes were riveted on a small slim woman . . . her hair simply coiled into her neck, Mrs Bruce Glasier. [She was speaking on] 'Socialism as a Religion' and to the undersized girl in the gallery this woman, not much bigger than herself, seemed the embodiment of all her . . . secret hopes. To stand on a platform of the Free Trade Hall, to be able to sway a great crowd . . . to be able to make people work to make life better, to remove slums and underfeeding and misery just because one came and spoke to them about it — that seemed the highest destiny any woman could ever hope for.

This is a significant comment, less as a teenager's declaration of intent than as an intimation of how Ellen felt about her own tub-thumping achievements when writing in the late 1930s at the height of her success as a miraculously moving orator.

Towards the end of that landmark of an evening Ellen met Mrs Bruce Glasier who urged her to speak at ILP meetings, adding:

> We need young women for socialism, they are all going off asking for votes and forgetting the bigger things . . . We walked home excited and serious. Characteristically for those days in the ILP we were not talking of revolution but of converting great crowds to socialism through the ballot box. 'Only you fellows will be able to get into parliament and do the job, and they won't even let me vote', I said bitterly.

Ellen was not long downcast. She returned home 'so bright and full of enthusiasm' that her mother was suspicious:

> Nothing could convince her that while I had plenty of boy friends, I was more interested in politics than love affairs. But father understood. To him I poured out the whole speech, my determination to work for socialism. 'I had rather you become a missionary,' he said. 'What future can there be for a girl in politics?'[73]

What indeed!

In fact the ILP was a marvellous training ground in socialism and Ellen never forgot Mrs Bruce Glasier's encouragement. 'True she found in her warm generosity a new Joan of Arc every month', Ellen wrote years later, 'and the sophisticated may sniff, but what a difference appreciation like hers makes at 18. The old ILP was warm and homely and did not mind you making an ass of yourself, so long as you were sincere . . . while Keir Hardie just liked you for being young.'[74]

Youthful Enthusiasms

It was inevitable that the self-appointed 'High Priestess' of politics would encounter the suffrage movement. For Manchester, the quintessence of liberal thought, was a microcosm of contemporary political activities. True to the radical tradition of John Bright, pacifist, pillar of the Anti-Corn Law League, it nurtured the earliest of ILP branches and was a centre of suffrage protest long before the names of Emmeline, and her daughters, Sylvia and Christabel — 'the fighting Pankhursts' — became synonymous with the militant women's movement.

Originally the Manchester Suffrage Society wholeheartedly supported Mrs Fawcett's National Union of Suffrage Societies which sought to secure the vote for women by constitutional means; but the political parties prevaricated. Gladstone was an implacable foe of women's suffrage and his party would not commit itself, while the ILP was divided and confused. Certain Manchester suffrage workers — Miss Gore Booth, Mrs Pankhurst and Annie Kenney — rallied textile and factory hands in the North in an attempt to induce the ILP ('the new Labour Party' Mrs Pankhurst termed it) to 'accord women's suffrage a prominent place in their programme',[75] But without success. The disparate elements of the Labour Movement were hesitant. Trade unionists, if they were sympathetic at all, shared the view of Margaret Bondfield (then a young trade union secretary) among others, of supporting *adult suffrage* rather than women's enfranchisement. They genuinely believed that until the electoral register was reformed and the right to vote was dissociated from the ownership of property (even a man had to be a householder or occupier before he was eligible to be on the electoral roll), that votes for women could only enfranchise the wealthy and the middle classes; that it was in short a *class* issue. Keir Hardie, a long-standing friend of the Pankhursts, was virtually isolated from his parliamentary colleagues in his firm stand on women's rights, and 'the Cause' won low priority in the programme of the ILP.

Exasperation over this lack of a sense of urgency drove Mrs Pankhurst to breakaway action. At her Manchester home, with a small group of women, she formed in 1903 the Women's Social and Political Union.[76] They campaigned to make the ILP responsible for a new suffrage bill, and to win enfranchisement through political action. Though what that came to mean in terms of militant behaviour in the face of the Liberal Government's deceit, and in physical suffering under the heinous Cat and Mouse Act, was not then envisaged. Shadows of events to come however were cast before in the autumn of 1905 when Christabel Pankhurst and Annie Kenney were forcibly evicted from a pre-election meeting and subsequently imprisoned after unfurling a banner of protest at a meeting addressed by Sir Edward Grey. He refused even to define the Liberal Party's attitude towards the demand of votes for women, in spite of

Asquith's professed sympathy.[77] If the Liberals were devious, the Labour Party was hesitant. Not until 1913 was their policy clarified: then by an enormous majority the annual conference 'reaffirmed' support of women's suffrage and called upon the party in Parliament to oppose any franchise bill in which women were not included.[78]

The suffrage torches had long been blazing in Manchester when Ellen first ventured into the franchise battle. Surprisingly she was a constitutional suffragist rather than a suffragette.[79] Probably her parents would have disapproved of militancy; but while she was living at home, teaching, and studying for that coveted scholarship, peaceful advocacy was the more practical course. Once at university Ellen could have taken a different path, yet she remained a non-militant feminist. She always maintained that although franchise reform was essential, it was only the beginning of genuine equality between men and women. To that end she became in time a watchdog over women's rights in the House of Commons.

In her youth, therefore, Ellen ignited no letter-boxes, slashed no paintings, but with friends was active in Manchester suffrage work at a lowly level. Muriel Nichol, daughter of Dick Wallhead, MP (one time chairman of the ILP), herself an MP from 1945 to 1951, recounted how she and Ellen used to undertake together humble suffrage commitments before Ellen went to university. 'We did menial things — distributing handbills, chalking pavements and putting up posters.'[80] This was not always as simple as it sounds for as Connie Lewcock, a distinguished suffragette, recalled, 'poster parades and demonstrations often proved difficult because long skirts made us liable to fall over.'[81]

Muriel and Ellen also enjoyed music and theatre going and joined the local Clarion Clubs. They went to concerts, 'heard Paderswski play Chopin brilliantly', and were fascinated by the first violinist of the Hallé orchestra, Walter Hampson, whose technique for popularising socialism was unique. Known as 'Casey', he toured the country peppering his musical performances with ILP comment. Miss Horniman's Gaiety Theatre also delighted the girls. They savoured the plays of George Bernard Shaw and Ibsen from the gallery and treasured the deckle edged programmes which carried the proclamation that 'our sole intent is all for your delight'.[82]

The Clarion rambling and cycling clubs, whose young socialist members were known as 'Clarionettes', used to hold ILP meetings at the end of the day. North-country members, doubtless including

Ellen, would gather at weekends at Handforth Clubhouse, near Wilmslow, an old farm house converted into a residential centre which became a meeting place for socialists from miles around. Stella Davies remembered how:

> For a day's propaganda cycling, we were furnished with sandwiches, a primus stove, stacks of leaflets and *The Clarion* . . . We held open-air meetings to catch people as they came out of church or chapel . . . We scrawled slogans in chalk . . . and we sang 'England Arise' outside pubs and on village greens.[83]

The political attitude of Clarion Clubs varied. Members of East Manchester branch, to which Harry Pollitt of the Boiler Makers' Union belonged, were dyed-in-the-wool socialists and would have no truck with reform as a solution to the problems of society. They defined the distinction between evolutionary and revolutionary socialists as 'them that can wait and them as can't'[84] — a distinction which Ellen doubtless appreciated. It is likely that she took part in the activities of this branch while working for her scholarship and virtually certain that during her university years she belonged to the Central Manchester Clarion Club. It met above a restaurant in Market Street and occupied a fine suite of rooms decorated by Burne Jones's murals depicting scenes from William Morris's *News from Nowhere*. With a broad Labour membership — including *Manchester Guardian* staff, many ILP-ers and both left and right wing members of the Labour Party — it must have held great attraction for university socialists.[85]

Notes

Unless otherwise stated all interviews and related correspondence span the period October 1977 to December 1980.

1. Beatrice Webb, *Diaries 1924–1932* (M. Cole, ed.) (Longmans Green, London, 1936), pp. 132–3.
2. Connie Lewcock, interview.
3. Ambrose Appelbe, letter of 5 October 1978.
4. Leah Manning, letter of 13 November 1970.
5. M. Cole, *Makers of the Labour Movement*, (Longmans Green, London, 1948), p. 195.
6. T.A. Lockett, *Three Lives*, (University of London Press, London, 1968), p. 46.
7. In August 1980 Manchester City Council put up a blue ceramic commemorative plaque on a council maisonette in Balsam Close. It reads:

Ellen Wilkinson (1891–1947)
Stateswoman and cabinet minister
was born at 41 Coral Street on this site

8. Professor Ross Waller and Fred Johnson, correspondence and interviews.
9. Broadcast talk, 'Born and Bred', BBC North of England Home Service (27 October 1945).
10. Fred Johnson, correspondence.
11. Ross Waller, letter.
12. Broadcast talk, 'Born and Bred'.
13. Mrs Muriel Wilkinson, interview.
14. Ellen Wilkinson in Margot Oxford (ed.), *Myself When Young* (Frederick Muller, London, 1936), p. 399.
15. Ibid., p. 400.
16. Ellen Wilkinson, *Clash* (George Harrap, London, 1929), p. 183.
17. S. Davies, *North Country Born* (Routledge and Kegan Paul, London, 1963), p. 225.
18. Mrs Muriel Wilkinson, interview.
19. Broadcast talk, 'Born and Bred'.
20. Professor Ross Waller and Fred Meadowcroft, correspondence and interviews.
21. Ellen Wilkinson, letter to A.J. Saunders, 19 June 1925.
22. Ellen's father died on 27 February 1929, 'when Manchester was virtually frozen'.
23. Professor Ross Waller, letter; Mrs Muriel Wilkinson, interview.
24. Margot Oxford (ed.), *Myself When Young*, p. 407.
25. St Paul's school was closed on the opening of Mansfield Street in 1905 where Ellen taught briefly. It is now (1980) known as Medlock Primary School (Fred Johnson, interview and letters).
26. Margot Oxford (ed.), *Myself When Young*, p. 403.
27. Mrs Muriel Wilkinson, interview.
28. Dame Margaret Cole, interview.
29. Ellen definitely went to Ardwick at secondary age. Some sources (notably the DNB) wrongly refer to Stretford Road Secondary Manchester, but Fred H. Johnson, a Manchester resident who is soaked in local history, writes: 'I know of no Stretford Road Secondary School . . . it is a very long road — or was, as some has now disappeared in redevelopment — but I have never heard anyone ever talk of a secondary school in the road. In 1906, Ardwick Higher Elementary (later Ardwick Secondary) was known as Ardwick (Devonshire Street) Elementary School'. (Letter, 11 August 1979.)
Miss Helen Lord, a former scholar of Ardwick Central and member of staff there during 1941–65 remembers Ellen's visiting the school when Minister of Education and regaling them with the following anecdote: 'When Parliamentary Secretary in the Ministry of Home Security Ellen had had an appointment with a Dr. Owen, a child specialist at the Home Office: on meeting they immediately uttered "Ardwick!" Leaving for a celebratory meal they encountered a red-tabbed high-ranking army officer. All three simultaneously repeated "Ardwick!" and went off together to celebrate.' (Letter of 20 November 1978.)
30. Margot Oxford (ed.), *Myself When Young*, pp. 403–4.
31. Ibid., p. 404.
32. Helen Lord, letter of 20 November 1978.
33. Margot Oxford (ed.), *Myself When Young*, p. 408.
34. Fred Meadowcroft, interview.
35. Annie Wilkinson, letter to Dorothy Elliott, July 1951, (private papers).
36. Margot Oxford (ed.), *Myself When Young*, pp. 406–7.

37. Ibid., p. 411.

38. Ibid., p. 415.

39. Ibid., p. 416; the Jones Scholarship was of special importance because it relieved Ellen from the obligation of having to teach. She was able to evade, what to Dame Mabel Tylecote was the system of 'indentured labour for teaching'. University grants were made available to boys and girls if they promised to take a diploma in education after graduation and to teach — boys for seven and girls for five years. Since at the time married women were not permitted to be teachers this meant enforced deferment of marriage until a girl was about 27. The whole process was illegal since signatories to the 'contract' were nearly always minors: yet many women could only obtain a university education this way. Ellen escaped the dilemma. (Dame Mabel Tylecote, letter of 27 March 1979.)

40. B. Seebohm Rowntree, *Poverty* (Nelson, London, undated), pp. 351–5.

41. Ibid., footnote. Letter from Mr Booth to Mr Rowntree, pp. 355–6.

42. Ibid., p. 360.

43. R. Mudie-Smith (ed.), *The Sweated Industries Exhibition* (*Daily News*, 1906), pp. 10–11.

44. *Socialist Review*, September 1924.

45. Cole and Postgate, *The Common People, 1746–1938* (Methuen, London, 1938) p. 419.

46. Ellen Wilkinson, *The Town That Was Murdered* (Gollanz Left Book Club Edn, London, 1939), p. 112.

47. Margot Oxford (ed.), *Myself When Young*, pp. 400–2.

48. Cole and Postgate, *Common People*, pp. 404–10.

49. Ibid., p. 410; M. Cole, *History of Fabian Socialism* (Heinemann, London, 1961), Chaps. 5–7.

50. E. Hughes, *Keir Hardie* (Allen and Unwin, London, 1956) p. 66.

51. H. Mitchell, *The Hard Way Up* (Faber and Faber, London, 1968), Introduction, p. 26.

52. Cole and Postgate, *Common People*, p. 423.

53. Robin Page Arnot, interview.

54. Maurice Reckitt, interview.

55. J.L. and B. Hammond, *The Town Labourer* (Gollancz Left Book Club Edn, London, 1937) pp. 303–6.

56. G.M. Trevelyan, *History of England* (Longmans, London 1926) p. 520.

57. E.P. Thompson, *The Making of the English Working Class*, (Gollancz, London, 1963), Penguin edn, 1978, p. 430.

58. R. Wearmouth, *The Social and Political Influence of Methodism in the 20th Century* (Epworth Press, London, 1957), pp. 245–9.

59. M. Cole, *Labour Movement*, p. 249.

60. Margot Oxford (ed.), *Myself When Young*, p. 401.

61. Mrs Muriel Wilkinson, interview.

62. Beryl Hughes, interviews. Ellen had decided views about alcohol. Hugh Dalton gossips in his Diaries about an incident when she was first on the National Executive of the Labour Party in October 1927 and a member of the Programme Committee. There was a great row over the matter of drink: 'Ellen moved that there should be no reference to the drink question in the programme (I had urged her to do this) and it was carried by 7 to 2.' Henderson and Ramsay MacDonald were against. 'Uncle Arthur (Henderson) offered his resignation over this, silly old ass, and the National Executive only asked him to retract by 7 to 6!' H. Dalton, *Call Back Yesterday 1887–1931* (Muller, London, 1953), p. 172.

63. Mrs Muriel Wilkinson, interview.

64. Fred Meadowcroft and Mrs Muriel Wilkinson, interviews.

65. Professor Ross Waller, interview.

66. Margot Oxford (ed.), *Myself When Young*, p. 401.

67. *Pearsons Weekly*, 1 August 1930.
68. Margot Oxford (ed.), *Myself When Young*, pp. 402–11.
69. *Manchester Guardian*, 18 November 1941.
70. *Methodist Recorder*, 16 March 1939.
71. Margot Oxford (ed.), *Myself When Young*, p. 411.
72. Mitchell, p. 86.
73. Margot Oxford (ed.), *Myself When Young*, pp. 412–5.; for a charming pen picture of Mrs Bruce Glasier see E. Sylvia Pankhurst, *The Suffragette Movement* (Longmans Green, London, 1931) pp. 126–7.
74. *The Clarion*, 7 June 1935.
75. Ray Strachey, *The Cause* (G. Bell and Son, London, 1928) pp. 288–9.
76. E. Pankhurst, *My Own Story* (Eveleigh Nash, London, 1914), p. 38.
77. Ibid., pp. 50–1; E. Sylvia Pankhurst, *The Suffragette Movement*, p. 189–90.
78. M. Fawcett, *The Women's Victory and After* (Sidgwick and Jackson, London, 1920), p. 3 *et seq.*
79. Fred Meadowcroft, interview.
80. Muriel Nichol, interview.
81. Connie Lewcock, interview.
82. Muriel Nichol, interview.
83. S. Davies, pp. 84–5.
84. Ibid., p. 119.
85. Muriel Nichol, interview.

2   ADOLESCENCE

University Life

Ellen had every reason to be proud of entering Manchester University in 1910, for even if bias against women was less in northern universities than at Oxford or Cambridge, it was still extremely difficult to gain admission without financial backing. And this Ellen had achieved — as with many subsequent successes in her life — entirely through hard work, ability, and perhaps her charm, for she was immensely attractive. Contemporary photographs do no justice to her piled-up hair which glowed against her creamy skin, or to those large eyes which gave her so serious an air. Liveliness of mind, a determination to find things out for herself which she never lost, and great application, must have made her a good student.

She arrived at the university the epitome of eagerness. 'There I began to live life to the full . . . books unlimited, lots of friends, interesting lectures. The Honours School of History under Professor Tout and Professor George Unwin was a stimulating experience.'[1] Later she expressed reservations about the course: 'I was astonished to discover when I came into contact with the National Council of Labour Colleges (NCLC) how little real history I had been taught.'[2]

She was soon immersed in university affairs, notably the Debating and Fabian Societies, becoming secretary of the former in 1912. She reported that subjects debated included 'The Desirability of Strikes' and 'Women's Suffrage', but regretted that the 'majority of opinion is noticeably a reform one'. She also lamented the 'tendency of audiences to decline during the . . . evening, so that the principal speakers have had to deliver their crushing replies to rows of empty chairs'. With her characteristic approach of seeking a constructive solution she suggested that debates should have a time limit. Ellen's chief criticism in her annual report was that most women held non-political views — 'oh for some red-hot revolutionaries', adding, with a jaunty lack of modesty, 'Miss Wilkinson is . . . a most energetic debater who generally can be relied on.'[3]

In July 1913 Ellen gained an Upper Second in History. The class was a slight disappointment; and her professors allegedly 'bewailed the lost distinction of one of their scholarship winners'. She presumably had had high hopes 'after taking five and a half prizes out of the six the previous term', but, 'I deliberately sacrificed my First . . . to devote my spare time to helping with a strike raging in Manchester.'[4] Twelve months after graduation Ellen was awarded her Mastership. This was conferred without a thesis, though soon after the university regulations were tightened up.[5] The fact that she submitted no dissertation scotches the theory that she had been assisted in getting her MA by a fellow student, Walton Newbold — a rumour which several contemporaries recollect.[6]

Even if she did not get a First, Ellen's was no mean achievement. As she sensibly recognised, 'No one ever enquired as to the class of my degree, although the fact that I have one has often been useful.'[7] Nevertheless she was justifiably proud of it. For at a time when it was difficult for working-class girls to get to university, it was rare to have a graduate working in the Labour ranks. This probably explains why in her early political years, when acting as a candidate of any kind, serving on committees or sitting on trade boards, she always inserted 'MA' after her name. Later, the 'decoration' was enhanced by 'PC', 'MP' and 'LL.D.' — an honorary Doctorate of Laws conferred by 'the Victoria University of Manchester' Honoria Causa, on 15 May 1946. By then however she had no need to advertise her abilities to the world.

Early in her university life Ellen became an active Fabian. This was daring since the Fabian Society was then regarded as 'very progressive and one of the devils going to upset civilisation!'[8] Membership opened political doors and led to a curious twist in Ellen's personal affairs, when she was engaged to Walton Newbold. The Manchester University Fabian Society (which soon became part of the newly formed University Socialist Federation) showed 'a marked revival in its affairs generally' and by the following year 'had grown rapidly and planned a heavy programme of work for the next session'.[9] By December 1912 the joint secretaries were Lawrence Redfern and Ellen Cecily Wilkinson. Walton Newbold claimed responsibility for Ellen's appointment. He wrote with characteristic arrogance of 'devoting the academic year of 1912 to gaining my degree and to guiding the development of the Fabian Society in the university, less with a view to its probable transient importance than as one constituent in the newly formed University Federation'. He saw himself as a string-pulling puppeteer:

'We had learned so much from Kathleen Bruce Glasier that as she had a brother who was a Professor of Latin in the university we made her President in succession to Ramsay MacDonald . . . we had a sound chairman and no question but that I was to be Treasurer . . . whilst the man secretary must be popular and academically reputable . . . the key position would be that of the woman secretary.

So with Arthur Doyle, his inseparable associate, he

gave much thought to that controlled establishment . . . looked at her exam results and consulted the outgoing chairman . . . Yes, Arthur would nominate a second year student in the History School, Ellen Cecily Wilkinson . . . We found her a most excellent choice and if she was piqued that we regarded her as having utility value, strictly limited, . . . at least she knows we were the two who introduced her to the Labour Movement.[10]

Had Newbold said the 'wider' movement his phrase might be valid: the unqualified claim is typically exaggerated.

Running a local Fabian Society gives its officers rich opportunities for meeting political personalities, and this Ellen relished. During the autumn of 1912 speakers to the Manchester Society included the handsome suffragette Mrs Despard, W.C. Anderson (ILP Chairman and husband of Mary MacArthur), Mrs Sidney Webb, and Mrs Bruce Glasier. The last named made, in Ellen's words, 'a great impression on all who heard her statement on the "moral degradation and despair born of capitalism" . . . [and] "the brighter nobler age that is to be".'[11] As to Mrs Webb, initially Ellen held Beatrice in respectful awe. Already she was a giantess among researchers and with Sidney stood high in the Fabian hierarchy. Eventually Ellen grew to regard Beatrice with affection and became a not infrequent visitor to Passfield Corner, the Webb's home in Liphook, Hampshire. Years after, Ellen wrote:

She came to speak for us one afternoon in a dress of scarlet velvet and ermine . . . Rather frightened, I took the great lady to tea. 'How do you like my dress,' she asked. 'I have had it made from my aunt's coronation robes' . . . We then went on to discuss the wages of the outworker seamstresses whom I was organising into a trade union in my spare time.[12]

This throw-away remark was substantiated by Mary Quaile (Treasurer of the Manchester and Salford Trades Council and later an organiser of the Transport and General Workers' Union): 'I took Ellen round Hume where we were organising home workers in the hemming trade. This was her first experience of seeing such workers and made her determined to work for the trade union movement.'[13]

Public speaking, an inevitable concomittant of political activity, made demands which Ellen had neither wish nor reason to evade. She was listed in *Fabian News* as being available to speak on 'Socialist Theory and Women's Work, Trade Unions and Craft Guilds'. Newbold too, offered similar services, his subjects including trade union history and Labour politics.[14]

In her Finals year Ellen was co-opted on to the executive committee of the University Socialist Federation (USF). The clutch of university students active in its formation included Alfred Bacharach (Cambridge), Susie Fairhall (Manchester), Alban Gordon (Birmingham) and Robin Page Arnot (Glasgow); Clifford Allen, later Lord Allen of Hurtwood (Cambridge ILP) was Chairman. Subsequent members included Theodore Chaundy, editor of the *University Socialist*, G.D.H. Cole (Chairman in 1915 with Ellen as his vice chairman), Maurice Reckitt and Allardyce Nicoll. 'We took counsel together because we were isolated and the Federation was formed to link up university organisations, to establish them where there were none, and to maintain contact with university socialists after they had gone down,' Ellen explained.[15] Such postgraduate activities led the Fabians, with Ellen a lively participant, into fresh political pastures. The educational value of their summer schools held at Barrow House, Derwentwater, in a residential centre owned by the Fabian Society, was enriched by lecturers ranging from Margaret Bondfield and Ramsay MacDonald to Ben Tillett, Arthur Henderson and Susan Lawrence. These schools sometimes caused Beatrice Webb concern, for even though there was hot intellectual discussion, the students stayed up all hours making a great noise, playing games and breaking school regulations.[16]

USF also held its annual conferences at Barrow House. In April 1914 delegates devoted much time to excursions over the fells and to discussions round the fire. G.D.H. Cole spoke on industrial democracy — the issue of Guild Socialism was highly topical — and Fenner Brockway, editor of the *Labour Leader*, on the Rebel Movement.[17] Of this particular occasion the *Daily Herald*, pushing its tongue far into its cheek, wrote of 'all sorts of outrages on society' which the Federation had allegedly been planning and of toasts to social revolution and socialist unity. 'We are also informed that the Red Flag was sung on every possible occasion and that much beer and tobacco were consumed. The revolution may be nearer than we imagine!'[18]

If Barrow House was a centre for fun, it was also highly purposive. The young men and women attending were encouraged to recruit for serious work, and Ellen became involved not only with Guild Socialism and the Fabian Women's Group but with the Fabian Research Department (FRD) which later became the Labour Research Department (LRD). Towards the end of 1913 she was one of several of the USF recruited by Robin Page Arnot to work as volunteers for the FRD, devilling, primarily, into trade union activities. He recalled her intense concentration on whatever absorbed her and 'the eager face with which she registered approval or disapproval', a kindlier comment than that of Bernard Shaw who remembered Ellen when he was chairman of FRD 'as an amusing and interesting little red haired spitfire'.

From the FRD Ellen acquired valuable experience; (for the leading lights), William Mellor (later editor of the *Daily Herald*), G.D.H. Cole and W.N. Ewer, foreign correspondent on the *Daily Herald*, set their assistants exacting standards. Dame Margaret Cole, then Margaret Postgate, who was initiated into the Fabian Society by working for FRD, has described the 'endless statistical extracts and lists of trade union records that had then to be compiled'.[19] She also conveyed the exhilaration of working with colleagues towards a common purpose, which even the most pedestrian research could create. At this time Ellen was assimilating a fundamental precept she never forgot: that if arguments and causes are to be won they must be sustained by facts fully verified. This became a principle, reinforced later by work at LRD, which she applied rigorously throughout her public life. Speaking at the Fabian Jubilee Rally shortly before her death, paying tribute to the educational pioneering of the early Fabians, she reminded her audience how Sidney and Beatrice Webb had always set out to find facts, which so few people in the nineteenth century had troubled to do. Great myths which were looked on as facts the Webbs and the early Fabians helped to dispel. 'They sought to circulate the truth . . . and very uncomfortable it was for the great employers [of those days]'.[20]

For a time the Fabian Society was rent by internal policy disputes. A long statement, 'The Right Moment', appeared in the April issue of *Fabian News* in 1915, in an attempt to revise the Fabian Constitution. The signatories included several former University Socialist Federation members — G.D.H. Cole and Ellen amongst them — who wanted to redirect the Society solely towards research. Members were to make a vague declaration of belief in international socialism which Guild Socialists and Marxists could accept.[21] There was much more, but the statement was rejected at the annual meeting, and the constitution remained unchanged. It is perhaps significant that among the twenty signatures appended was that of Herbert Morrison.

Throughout her life Ellen gave the Fabian Society practical support. She lectured for the Women's Group, attended their annual dinners, frequently as a guest of honour, and contributed to seminars. Often she took part in summer schools — as late as 1941 she was at Dartington Hall speaking with H.D. Hughes, Herman Fraenkel and Barbara Wootton — and however busy, would readily help the Society to promote new projects. She was for example the first speaker at the early wartime Fabian luncheons, and addressed a packed gathering on 'Evacuation and Your Council' — a topic chosen because 'the Government has no policy to meet evacuation problems'.[22] With G.D.H. Cole, Harold Nicolson, Harold Laski and J.B. Priestley, she contributed — also during the war — to a series of lectures on Social Justice and to a later series on Socialism and the Future of Britain.

Curiously Ellen was not elected to the Fabian Executive until 1940 when her attendances were predictably erratic. She remained a member until January 1947, then expressed an unwillingness to continue in spite of the General Secretary, Bosworth Monck, urging her to reconsider as she would not be expected to be a regular attender.[23] Sadly, this was a hope which death defeated.

Walton Newbold — 'The Ishmael of Westminster'

Over the years Ellen had many men friends, but only once was she engaged — to Walton Newbold, during her second year at university. Though brief, the interlude led to a curiously protracted relationship and showed not for the last time in her life that Ellen could make extraordinarily bad judgements. John Turner Walton Newbold, the son of a wealthy Liberal-Irish Quaker living in Buxton, was an odd young man, whose socialism took a religious turn. On one occasion, 'he dressed as a friar and went out to convert Lancashire. He didn't get far however, because he was dumped in a pond!'[24] The engagement probably occurred during the autumn of 1912 on Ellen's twenty-first birthday and astounded both family and friends. Muriel Nichol, upon whom Newbold had already pressed his attentions, incurring her father's 'intense dislike', was 'flabbergasted'. She regarded him as 'a thoroughly detestable young man, arrogant, physically revolting and always sniffing'.[25]

The family too, thought Newbold was unsuitable. Ellen's aunt, Mrs Muriel Wilkinson, described him as 'leggy and long, like a flabby length of pump water, scruffy and singularly unattractive', a view shared by T.A. Jackson, a communist journalist and NCLC lecturer.[26] The engagement certainly was extraordinary, for the contrast between the catarrh-suffering, gangly young man of six foot and Ellen of elfin quality and Titian-haired charm, suggests total physical incompatability. Some think that Ellen was flattered by Newbold's attention; others that his intellectual vigour was the attraction.

After leaving university in 1912, Newbold concentrated on economic research, university politics and in lecturing for the ILP and NCLC. He decided to stay on in Manchester to 'direct the affairs of the University Fabian Society' so as to draw its activities to the attention of 'trade unionists, co-operators and socialists'.[27] At this stage Newbold had a considerable influence on Ellen's intellectual development. As a Quaker and an avowed pacifist he was a conscientious objector. In line with ILP policy, he saw all war as being engineered by capitalist imperialism and by international armament manufacturers against the interests of the working classes. These were views which attracted Ellen as a member of the ILP and the Women's International League for Peace and Freedom (WIL). If Newbold merely reinforced Ellen's pacifism, it is almost certain that he introduced her to Marxism. Not to the philosophical intricacies of dialectical materialism or to the Labour Theory of Value ('It is doubtful whether Ellen ever read much Marx in her life.'[28]), but to a broad understanding of the Materialist Conception of History — that the general shape of men's thinking is conditioned by the underlying economic circumstances of each historical epoch — and to the theory of the class struggle.

Newbold's ability to root out economic facts resulted in a prolific — and to Ellen an impressive — output of socialist propaganda pamphlets. They ranged from *War Trusts Exposed* (1913) to

Bankers, Bondholders and Bolsheviks (1919) and were written in a
somewhat flamboyant style. His 'exposures' were highly selective,
but capable of making tub-thumping impact. The immediacy of
their appeal, was not unlike that of Left Book Club publications two
decades later, and undoubtedly fed Ellen's bubbling curiosity.[29] Yet
Newbold was not widely esteemed. 'Both G.D.H. Cole and William
Mellor felt there was something odd about his thinking . . . he had
too simplistic a belief in the capitalist conspiracy theory',[30] although
he did valuable pioneering research work into the armaments trade.

In spite of Newbold's intellectual appeal, meretricious or not,
Ellen ended their engagement in the summer of 1913. This occurred
at a Fabian ILP summer school at Barrow House, Keswick, and
Fenner Brockway remembers:

> Ellen standing by the lake, drying her hair after a swim, very calm
> . . . Walton was in an uncontrollable state. He dashed up the
> sloping lawn in front of the House, where tea was being served
> and threw crockery around. W.C. Anderson, (who would have
> been Labour's first Prime Minister had he survived the influenza
> epidemic) put his arm round Newbold to restrain him. Newbold
> said to me: 'May I go to your digs? I must get out at once.' Ellen
> had broken off their engagement. Hence his agitation.[31]

He suffered no heartbreak however and the following year married
Marjery Neilson from Ayrshire.

The severance from Ellen appears to have been incomplete. They
served together on various committees (LRD and the Plebs League),
were founder members of the British Communist Party and
maintained contact during Ellen's early years in Parliament.
Newbold on his own evidence unashamedly used her as a means of
extracting information for research projects by 'feeding' her parliamentary questions. Yet he wrote of Ellen in the most waspish and
disparaging terms. It seems clear that Marjery — a pacifist, suffragette, and later an ardent communist — was suspicious if not
jealous of her husband's intermittent association with Ellen.
Newbold, aware of his wife's suspicions, wrote elliptically:

> As E.W. was a member of the ILP and thought herself far to the
> left, we could no longer fail to meet as completely as I had con-
> trived over the previous five years. It was not long till my wife was

discovering that she and I shared the same compromising disposition.

When Newbold became the first communist MP in 1922 he had the grace to appreciate that his victory gave his wife 'something to show for our marriage' but his conceit was undiminished. He sent a telegram to Zinoviev at the Kremlin: 'Have won Motherwell in Scotland for Communism' (the Russians had thought that Jim Gallacher was the victor), and notified the press with the calculated intent to 'draw attention away from the sensational but specious victory of John Wheatley [of the ILP] and his associates', and to enhance his own significance with the Soviets and the Comintern. Success, however, was shortlived: Newbold lost his seat in December 1923.

After a heavy parliamentary session, and illness, Newbold took some holiday breaks, apparently with Ellen. His wife, however was

> not deceived . . . by the carefully advertised Party character of two visits made by me to the South of France . . . all in good time she would see what was the mystery she sensed from the beginning in my political relations with Ellen . . . The latter had some role to fill for which my appreciation of her impulsiveness peculiarly fitted her.

This 'role', however, he never defined, but after resigning from the Communist Party and joining the Labour Party, he adopted a scornfully superior attitude towards Ellen. In a revealing outburst, he wrote that:

> [Ellen] was as lacking in sympathy with my thinking and my writing in 1924 as she had been in a similar crisis in my life in 1916. My wife knew my method of manoeuvre well enough to suspect that Ellen was again serving a purpose.

And serve a purpose she did, for when she had entered the House Newbold's investigation of iron and steel cartels took him to Aberavon, Ramsay MacDonald's constituency, and to Middlesbrough East, Ellen's seat. His entrée was facilitated by the goodwill of both Members, yet even this he failed to acknowledge. On the contrary, he contended that 'the intricacies of industrial production were completely beyond Ellen's mental comprehension . . . We gave EW a series of questions to put to the Board of Trade that must have been far without her usual range of reading.'[32] Such sustained spite can surely be explained only by the fact that deep down memories of the broken relationship years back still rankled.

After the death of his wife in 1926, Newbold withdrew from active politics, although he did not sink into obscurity, without performing some curious antics. He publicly took a stand as National Labour with Ramsay MacDonald and Philip Snowden, and acted as election agent for J.H. Thomas in 1931. 'When he discovered that MacDonald, with "extraordinary ingratitude", was to let his zeal go unrewarded he . . . denounced the National Government as a blatant imposture. This is surely a record in political tergiversation.'[33] Subsequently he met Mussolini, discovered 'a Catholic plan to extirpate Marxism in Central and Eastern Europe', and challenged the Labour Party over banking. Having rejected an alleged approach by Whitehall to cultivate M. Maisky (Soviet Ambassador to Britain) who had in 1918 translated some of Newbold's pamphlets, he turned again to historical studies.

Little is known of Newbold's later activities. 'He always had been a bit of an eccentric. Latterly he became insufferable. He seems to have reacted strongly from being a communist MP: gone to the right and disappeared from public knowledge.'[34] Almost so, but not quite. For when Ellen was a Parliamentary Secretary at the Ministry of Home Security during the Second World War, Newbold peppered her mail with scurrilous letters which implied that for a while they had lived together. These letters her Parliamentary Private Secretary, John Parker, intercepted and destroyed. 'As Ellen had had no contact with Newbold during my political association with her and had expressed her views about him very forcibly I did not trouble her with his filth.'[35]

It is less difficult to understand how such an opportunist could have had so formative an influence over Ellen, than it is to explain why she retained contact with him for so long. His aggressive toughness and intellectual arrogance seemingly had their appeal, but it was surely through loyalty rather than any lingering physical attraction that she maintained so protracted a relationship. Ellen was always faithful to friends, even if her judgement might be often awry.

Perhaps Newbold ought to be remembered in the words of a contemporary as 'the Ishmael of Westminster whose candour verged on brutality, yet who was fundamentally as sincere as he was courageous'.[36] Be that as it may, he emerges from his own scribblings as a man with little concern and less affection for anyone but himself. Yet whatever the explanation of this curiously unpersonable catalyst, he did contrive to guide Ellen along paths of political belief which she continued to tread for a very long while.

Notes

1. Margot Oxford (ed.), *Myself When Young* (Frederick Mulles, London, 1936), p. 416.

2. Ellen Wilkinson at the Annual Meeting of NCLC, 1924; Leslie Gilbert, who was one of a small group of students under the 'formidable' Professor Tout, remembers him as 'one of the leading mediaevalists', and wrote that 'our courses covered ancient, mediaeval and modern history up to, and not beyond, 1815!' (Letter of 3 February 1980).

3. Manchester University Magazine, 1912, p. 179.

4. Ellen Wilkinson 'Organising and Political Work' in M. Cole (ed.) *The Road to Success*. (Methuen, London, 1938) pp. 66–7. Leslie Gilbert, who gained a First, remembers Ellen saying to him that as he did not spend his time on trades union matters — as she did — he had time to study! (Letter of 20 February, 1980.)

5. Professor Chaloner (History Department, Manchester University) confirmed in a letter on 24 April 1979 that 'Ellen Wilkinson's MA was not by thesis, but was conferred twelve months — on 4 July 1914 — after she had graduated BA with Honours. Regulations were tightened up shortly afterwards, and consequently there was a rush to get the MA conferred before they came into force, and Ellen took advantage of this. This explains why we can find no trace of any MA thesis!'

Similarly, Walton Newbold secured his MA (in 1912), though Professor Chaloner adds that 'he actually entered the Honours school in 1905, failed to meet the University [academic] requirements and took five years to obtain an Ordinary Degree — in 1910'.

Much later Ellen made an intelligent effort to try to fill the lacunae in her knowledge. During the early days in the House 'when I was intensely lonely and the Library became my refuge, I read J.B.S. Haldane, Aldous Huxley, Whitehead and Bertrand Russell, making up for the complete lack of science in my education . . . there was much I could not understand, but conviction grew and I came to believe in truth in the science that faces facts' (*Daily Herald*, 25 November 1931).

6. Dame Mabel Tylecote and Professor Ross Waller.

7. M. Cole (ed.), *Road to Success*, p. 67.

8. Robin Page Arnot, interview.

9. *Fabian News*, December 1911 and August 1912.

10. J. Walton Newbold, personal papers, (unedited, unnumbered, undated; John Rylands University Library of Manchester).

11. *Fabian News*, March 1913.

12. *Time and Tide*, 8 May 1943.

13. *Co-operative News*, 15 February 1947.

14. *Fabian News*, July 1912.

15. University Socialist Federation Bulletin, May 1915.

16. M. Cole, *Fabian Socialism*, Appendix V, p. 352.

17. *Fabian News*, May 1914.

18. *Daily Herald*, 22 April 1914.

19. M. Cole, *Growing up Into Revolution* (Longmans Green, London, 1949) pp. 64–5.

20. *Daily Herald*, 4 November 1946.

21. *Fabian News*, April 1915.

22. *Fabian News*, October 1939.

23. Letters from Ellen Wilkinson to the General Secretary of the Fabian Society dated 17 January 1947 and from the General Secretary to Ellen Wilkinson dated 4 February 1947.

24. Fenner Brockway, interview.

25. Muriel Nichol and Mrs Muriel Wilkinson, interviews and letters.

26. T.A. Jackson also a communist, when helping Newbold defend his parliamentary seat at Motherwell during the 1923 general election, told Newbold that the only reason for his being invited there was 'to show the electorate that there is one dirtier man in the Labour movement than yourself!' (J.P. Millar, *The Labour College Movement* (NCLC Publishing Society, 1979) p. 132). Similar, if more diplomatic, views were expressed by Dame Margaret Cole, Muriel Nichol and others.

27. Walton Newbold, unpublished papers.

28. Ivor Montagu, interview.

29. Fenner Brockway, interview.

30. Robin Page Arnot, interview.

31. Fenner Brockway, interview.

32. Walton Newbold, unpublished papers.

33. L. MacNeill Weir, *The Tragedy of Ramsay MacDonald* (Secker and Warburg, London, undated) pp. 433–4.

34. Fenner Brockway, letter of 14 January 1979.

35. John Parker, MP, interview.

36. S.V. Bracher, *The Herald Book of Labour* (Labour Publications, London, 1923).

3 APPRENTICESHIPS — 'MISS ELLEN CECILY WILKINSON, MA'

Suffrage Work

Women graduates at the turn of the century were generally expected to become teachers, but if Ellen had learnt anything from her college and university experiences it was that teaching was not to be her life's work. When she confided this to her father, his comment was sympathetic and practical: 'Well, lass, dunna teach if tha dunna want to. Get another job.'[1] And she did just that, becoming full-time organiser in Manchester to Mrs Fawcett's constitutional suffragists, the National Union of Women's Suffrage Societies (NUWSS). The first suffrage meeting ever held in Britain had been organised by Lydia Becker at the City's Free Trade Hall in 1868, and soon after the Manchester City Council had 'memorialised parliament' in support of Dr Pankhurst's Suffrage Bill. Years later Mrs Pankhurst formed what became the militant arm of the suffrage movement — the Women's Social and Political Union — in her home in Nelson Street.

Feminist issues were therefore part of Ellen's Manchester heritage, and long before her formal appointment she was an active suffragist. With her sister Annie, Ellen joined the Manchester Society for Women's Suffrage, and the annual report for 1912 lists a Miss Wilkinson and Miss E.W. Wilkinson as subscribing one shilling each to the Society's Election Fighting Fund. In the same report the chairman, Miss Margaret Ashton, Manchester's first city councillor, writes of 'work done in the NE and N Manchester and the Gorton divisions . . . Mrs Robinson and Miss E. Wilkinson are organising in these constituencies where frequent demonstrations were especially necessary.' The year's activities included 'deputations, lectures for members, speakers' classes and political lobbying, all of which made a heavy drain on our resources'.[2]

Miss Ashton also reported a major change in suffrage policy. As the Labour Party was the only party that made women's suffrage a plank in its platform the NUWSS decided to support Labour candidates against the Liberals.[3] The same report mentions the campaign to amend Asquith's Reform Bill which intended only to extend the male enfranchise. To publicise this campaign the Manchester group opened two centres where Ellen and others spelt out the perfidy of the Liberals over female enfranchisement!

Voluntary participation brought its own reward and Ellen was appointed a suffrage organiser in Manchester. She was based at the Society's dingy office in John Dalton Street, but unlike her chairman relished the tough activities which achieved notoriety for the suffrage cause. Margaret Ashton hated marching in procession in the mud and dust, though she agreed that 'we must speak at street corners and in public squares and parks . . . stand in the gutter all day collecting signatures to the Voter's petition, and take an active part in all elections and all suffragist processions'.[4] To Ellen such activities were the breath of life and comprised a fair part of her work during the few carefree months she spent as an obscure suffrage organiser. How long she stayed in Manchester is not clear, but her enjoyment of it is. 'Never in my life will I again be so rich as in the first week I earned my first wage, two gold sovereigns as an organiser for the NUWSS,' she wrote.[5] For their part, the NUWSS recognised her burgeoning ability. Dame Margery Corbett Ashby remembers her as a 'first rate organiser who in addition to the necessary virtues of good organising and eloquent speaking, possessed deep convictions and enthusiasm. To her delightfully warm personality and great charm she added courage in facing hostile audiences and wit to deter hecklers.'[6]

Ellen was, however, feeling her way, aware that 'few organising jobs are life jobs. One could get so tired of working for a particular cause that an intelligent woman might find a change was the only alternative to murdering the chairman', she wrote retrospectively. Advising young women on becoming political organisers, Ellen characteristically advocated:

> Don't apply straight away to HQ . . . dig yourself into the constituencies . . . it may mean taking a job of some other kind first . . . If a young woman is alive with enthusiasm for the party of her choice and is willing to put in all her spare time at the donkey work of canvassing, addressing hole and corner meetings, running efforts to raise money, she is soon the object of grateful notice and is then on the inside of things whenever a paid post is vacant.[7]

A clear piece of autobiography!

In spite of a capacity for intense concentration on whatever job she was currently involved with, it was never Ellen's way to be exclusive in her interests. While shouldering the organisational grind of Suffrage work from the grass roots, she explored the Plebs League, maintained contact with the ILP, extended her Fabian interests and became an active supporter of the Women's International League for Peace and Freedom (WIL). With her sister Annie, as Anne was now known, she was a confirmed opponent of war, convinced (by the arguments of Walton Newbold and the ILP) that imperialism and capitalism were its root causes. Her opposition to war was as firm as her feminism, but her pacifism contained no element of cowardice. Certainly she abhorred physical force but she lacked neither moral nor physical courage. On the contrary, 'she had inherited the family trait of being absolutely fearless to the point of foolhardiness',[8] and would always support unpopular views or take up a pilloried position if she felt her stand was just.

Her maturing feminism was influenced as much by the trade union work on which she embarked early in the War, as by Fabian discussions and specialised conferences to which she contributed. For it is clear from her speeches and later writings, Ellen grew to accept that, important as winning the vote for women might be, it was merely a milestone along the way towards the long-term objective of economic justice. Her feminism came to embrace all facets of equality — social and economic as well as political — and in time she was recognised both in the House of Commons and the country as an unfailing protagonist of women's rights.

The Women's International League and Annie

Ellen's sister Annie shared her anti-war, suffrage and socialist convictions and, if less politically motivated, was just as hard working and as loyal towards chosen causes. More placid and practical than the mercurial Ellen, she had her fair share of Wilkinson ability, although as the elder sister Annie had to cherish the family after their mother died. Any chance of training for a career was therefore sacrificed, but she became active in the Manchester branch of the WIL and served as its organising secretary. In this job she evinced 'considerable skill, proved to be good with people and generally combined rectitude with tact, although . . . she could be forthright and [like Ellen] did not suffer fools gladly'.[9] The British section of the WIL formed in 1915 aimed at a negotiated and permanent peace in which the voice of women must be heard. The balance of power had only brought forth war; peace, the WIL argued, could only be promoted by international co-operation.[10]

During the First World War, to work for peace was to be branded as a traitor, pro-German and worse. Yet Annie took an active and morally courageous part in the Manchester WIL when organising was not easy. The branch was denied meeting places and, with a few exceptions (notably the *Manchester Guardian*), given unfair press reports. However there was no turning back and Annie seems to have shared Margaret Ashton's view that, 'If we go into public life we must take plenty of knocks and little praise.'[11]

Annie's activities are only sketchily recorded but it is known that she travelled for the WIL, often with Ellen, visiting Zurich, Ireland and Prague. About 1920 the sisters served on a WIL investigatory mission to assess the reprisal policy of the Black and Tans in Ireland. Extensive enquiries resulted in a report which recommended 'an immediate truce and release of Irish political prisoners, the withdrawal of armed forces and that the government be placed in the hands of locally elected bodies.'[12] The Report did not pass unheeded and later that year Ellen, with Mrs Annot Robinson, one of the founders of the WIL who had also been on the enquiry, went to the United States to give evidence before the American Commission on Ireland.[13] They were warmly received on their brief hectic visit, but 'were at . . . concert pitch all the time: the constant travelling made Ellen ill and she could not sleep', wrote Mrs Annot Robinson.[14]

The WIL developed a close relationship with the emergent League of Nations which both Annie and Ellen regarded as a symbol of hope. To them the League was the one great international agency likely to maintain world peace through collective security and for which the WIL had helped to blaze a trail. Until the early thirties Annie continued to give the WIL loyal service, then she moved south, took a flat over the London offices of Ellen's union, and was able to exercise firm, if unobtrusive, care of her unpredictable sister. Annie was undoubtedly the more reliable of the two, it was a colleague in the WIL who wrote: 'Ellen understands the noble art of self advertisement admirably . . . she is very clever but I like Annie the best. In brains she is only the reflection of Ellen, but in character more "jannock" '.[15] ('Jannock' is a Lancashire word meaning 'genuine'.)

The Trade Union Movement — 'Fight and Organise'

During the First World War women trade union officers were a rarity, and Ellen's appointment as National Woman Organiser to the Amalgamated Union of Co-operative Employees (AUCE) in 1915 was highly unusual. She won the position in open competition at a time when, as a direct result of wartime conditions, the employment of women in industry was an issue of mounting importance.

There was, however, one last stepping stone between her suffrage job and applying for that trade union appointment. At the outbreak of war she was seconded by the NUWSS to the Stockport Relief Committee 'to organise relief workrooms for women in Stockport, and to fight for better conditions on their behalf'. As secretary in Manchester to the Women's War Interests Committee — founded by Mrs Annot Robinson — she had already been involved with the struggle to secure a fixed minimum of £1 for a 48-hour week for women munition workers (when the going rate in Manchester for making shells and fuses averaged 15s), and was knowledgeable about women employed as 'emergency labour' in industry.[16] When, therefore, Ellen did apply for the AUCE vacancy she was thoroughly alive to the economic difficulties of working women and to the fact that they had been, and still were, pitilessly exploited.[17]

Since throughout her life Ellen's allegiance to trade unionism and her concern for working women were rocklike, it is relevant to outline some landmarks of the Women's trade union movement. The Women's Trade Union League (WTUL) was formed by Mrs Emma Paterson in 1874 to promote trade unionism among working women. Two years later the TUC admitted women and pledged them assistance. Women were, and long remained, suspicious of any legal restrictions on their employment, such as those which banned night work. Men, on the other hand were jealous of women allowing themselves to be used as cheap labour and so becoming a means of lowering wages. When the TUC therefore agreed in 1888 that women should receive equal pay for doing the same work as men, it was a big step forward. The Match Girls' strike of 1888 gave women's unionism a great fillip: the discipline, unity and steadiness of the girls brought success, 'startling even an indifferent middle class public into an uneasy awareness of the contrast between wages of three shillings to eight shillings a week, and dividends of 22 per cent'. *The Times*'s cry that this strike was 'the result of class war which the body of socialists have brought into action', rang hollow. In fact it won respect for the participants and gave an incentive to 'association' among unskilled workers.

Nevertheless, organising female workers was not easy. An inquiry into women's attitudes conducted by the WTUL in 1900 indicated some of the practical difficulties with which Ellen later had to contend as a trade union organiser. The basic dilemma which working women faced, then as now, was the conflicting demands of home and work. Branch secretaries found the struggle to recruit women 'disheartening', although some insisted that the fault lay with society:

> When women really grasp the aims of trade unionism they do so more firmly than men. Trade Unionism means rebellion and the orthodox teaching for women is submission. The political world preaches to women submission just . . . as it refuses them the parliamentary franchise, and therefore ignores them as human beings.

The most perceptive explanation was given by Mary MacArthur. She denied that there was any inherent feminine incapacity to 'recognise the necessity for corporate action', or that marriage was an insurmountable obstacle to trade union membership. Quite simply, the basic reason for women's unwillingness to join a union was economic: 'While women were badly paid because of their unorganised condition, they remained unorganised mainly because they were badly paid.'

To counter the exploitation of women in unorganised trades Mary MacArthur founded the National Federation of Women Workers. It worked closely with WTUL, affiliated to the TUC and advocated the legal minimum wage, since 'that seemed to get to the heart of women's economic helplessness'.[18] The Federation took a leading part in promoting the Trade Boards Act under which minimum rates of pay could be agreed for certain trades and with the operation of which Ellen was to become much involved.

Until the outbreak of war few women were organised in trade unions, but between 1914 and 1918, when the numbers working in factories and therefore eligible to join a trade union exploded, membership rose astronomically.[19] This wartime influx of women, many substituting for men, and the attendant problems prompted the AUCE to engage a woman organiser. It was not surprising that attractive, idealistic Ellen Wilkinson was appointed in open competition as the first woman organiser of the AUCE. On Sunday 18 July 1915, the Executive Committee, with Robert Bell Padley as chairman, and Joe Hallsworth as assistant secretary (so the minutes record) resolved that 'Miss Wilkinson be appointed, that she commence her duties the first week in September, and that the General Secretary should draw up a schedule of duties which the woman organiser has to perform' — the schedule to be devised after and not before the vacancy was filled! Wages were £2 5s a week, plus travelling expenses, and presumably Ellen 'gave satisfaction', for in October 1916 the Committee decided that 'her earnings should be forthwith increased to £2 17s 6d per week'.[20] Thus began an association which led to Ellen's being sponsored as a union MP, and to a life-long friendship with the President, John Jagger ('JJ') which gave weighty ballast to her political career.

The AUCE catered mainly for shop assistants and factory workers, embracing commercial employees and allied workers within its ranks in 1918. Membership was broadened by amalgamation in 1921 with the National Union of Warehousemen and General Workers, when the union emerged as the National Union of Distributive and Allied Workers (NUDAW). While negotiations were in train, Ellen vigorously opposed the new union becoming the National Union of Distributive Employees — she objected to being labelled 'NUDE'![21]

Ellen's appointment was welcomed by the rank and file of the AUCE: 'There is a large field for our new woman organiser to take up for the AUCE, and Miss Wilkinson has the whole-hearted support of the [Co-operative] Council', the *Co-operative News* reported.[22] Her major responsibilities covered recruitment of women into the union, rates of pay, conditions of employment and the union's policy on substitute labour. The Executive Committee Minutes during 1915 and 1916 abound with references to 'female labour being substituted for males in the forces.' Eventually the union adopted a broadly sympathetic policy, laying down that such women (who had to join the union) should receive the same rate of wages as the men they replaced, but they had to accept that the men would be reinstated as soon as they were able to resume work.[23] It was, however, one thing to lay down a policy, another to negotiate its implementation, and on this Ellen had many weary battles. Her hand is discernible in the 'document' distributed in 1916, about the post-war working intentions of women members. The union feared their having to face unemployment or being forced into low-paid work at a time of general distress, and was anxious to combat this by plans based on 'accurate information'.

Even before the war the AUCE had adopted an enlightened stand over rates of pay. Urged on by the Women's Co-operative Guild it had, in 1912, agreed minimum rates for men and women. This in no way guaranteed equal pay but it was an important step forward, because for the first time a standard was laid down that could be applied to all classes of women's work. Certainly by the end of the War equal pay (but not equal opportunity) existed in many districts. Ellen wrote angrily in the AUCE Journal of September 1917: 'Women with brains and initiative, with responsible and arduous posts are hampered by the strong tradition still pervading the Co-operative Movement, that a women's wages are practically settled for ever when she becomes 21, and that however important a woman's work may be she must be considered as assistant to some male manager.'

Soon after her appointment Ellen started a women's department in the union to deal with the problems of the many new women members, 'not with the intention of separating the interests of men and women in the ordinary routine of the branches, but to care for and represent women's special interests not coincident with those of men'.[24] A glutton for work, it is clear from her frequent reports in the *Co-operative Employee*, the union's journal,[25] that Ellen relished the variety of demands made upon her, though office routine held minimal appeal. Of her first weeks she wrote: 'I accompanied Mr Lumley (National Organiser) to address a dinner-hour meeting of over 500 people at Irlam (Lancashire) soap works . . . The rest of the week I spent in the office reading reports and correspondence . . . A dismissal case at Crumpsall introduced me to the managerial aspects of trade unionism.' The same month she canvassed shopworkers in Liverpool, had her first experience of a mass meeting at Sheffield, and found that the male members had not attempted to organise the women and 'bitterly resented my efforts to do so'. She attended impromptu lectures on factory law and national insurance, 'which helped to broaden my understanding of union responsibilities'.[26] The following month 'a visit to Leeds with Mr Jagger resulted in a new branch in the brush factory'; at Derby they had a 'poor meeting' but in the girls' tea room she found out that the Derby Society did not pay wages during sickness, and blank failure at Trafford Park made her determined that those girls should be recruited into the union 'though wild horses would be needed'.[27]

Hard on all this came a strike in North-eastern Lancashire. 'Here', Ellen wrote, 'we found that the women's sense of solidarity was splendid', and soon after, visiting Scotland, 'we received the warmest of welcomes and had packed meetings.'

Everywhere she found 'the question of substitute labour growing in size and difficulty' and this necessitated yet more meetings, 'for it was important for women to recognise that the issue was something more than just preventing the undercutting of men's rates'. She expressed this view strongly in the union journal of December 1915. Women were showing great interest in the battle for male rates where they were doing a man's job 'because they see that the Union is fighting their battle at the same time as protecting the men at the Front'. Ellen saw the fair wages campaign as 'breaching the wall of prejudice that ordains a woman must be paid less, irrespective of work done, . . . simply because she is a woman.' She therefore urged women to join their union, and 'to fight for the first principle of women's freedom — the recognition of equal pay with men for work well and faithfully done'.[28]

Just before this article appeared, Ellen had written to the *New Leader* rebutting an allegation that her union was hindering recruitment by their proposals on substitute labour. The union's policy, she argued, prevented co-operative societies from 'taking advantage of the extremity of the nation to cut down the standard of life of those who are fighting for it . . . and the AUCE is one of the few unions standing firm by that principle'.[29] Already Ellen's pen, as well as her voice, was becoming an asset to her union.

A suspicion arises that Ellen felt herself thrown in at the deep end. Chairing a Fabian Women's conference on women in trade unions a few years after her appointment, she emphasised the need to train women organisers and for raising both their standards and their salaries, suggesting that a woman trade unionist should spend six months in her union office before she began organising, whether coming from a university or a factory, and six months on the road under a woman colleague. It was also necessary for her 'to be familiar with the Compensation Acts, the Factory Acts and the Trade Disputes Act, and to be able to draw up terms for . . . conciliation and arbitration.'[30]

Battling against male prejudice, Ellen's appointment suited her admirably. She dashed around England organising and negotiating on behalf of working women, for whom she felt such deep sympathy. These activities directed her immense energy without wholly absorbing it, and helped to develop her distinctive skill in public speaking. Tackling serious problems such as those associated with substitute labour gave a sharp edge to a sharp mind, though the necessary patience and diplomacy were acquired only with greater maturity. Controlling her sense of urgency from boiling over into unintentional rudeness took years (if ever) to perfect. Ditherers were lashed by her tongue, for it was characteristic that Ellen always sought, an immediate response from those to whom she appealed for whatever purpose. After all, was not the motto of her union 'Fight and Organise'? The overriding reason for Ellen's impact as an organiser was that she believed wholeheartedly in the purposes underlying her union battles. To secure equal opportunity and equal pay for men and women who undertook similar work were principles which the NUDAW's President, John Jagger, upheld more doggedly than most. To Ellen they were her life's blood.

Trade Boards and the Cave Committee

AUCE, which became NUDAW in 1921, had chosen well in its woman organiser. A dynamic speaker and successful in recruitment, Ellen proved astute in negotiating and effective in helping towards strike settlements. But perhaps her most fruitful contribution to the trade union movement before she entered the House of Commons, was serving as a union nominee on trade boards.

The Trade Boards Act of 1909 was an attempt to protect unorganised low paid workers and obtain for them minimum rates of pay. The 'Revolutionary Bill' inspired by firebrand Sir Charles Dilke, 'one of the greatest and most influential anti sweaters', had wide support. Protagonists included Dr J.J. (Jimmy) Mallon, secretary of the Anti-Sweating League, later Warden of Toynbee Hall and a life-long ally of Ellen's, Clement Attlee, Professor R.H. Tawney and Fabian Ware, editor of the *Morning Post*.

The boards established under the Act were composed of equal numbers of workers and employers, plus three independent members, one of whom was chairman. They had power to fix and to alter minimum time or piece rates by negotiation, which after a period became legally enforceable. Initially only four boards were scheduled, but by 1920 there were forty-one boards in being, mainly as a result of the heavy pressure exerted by the Women's Trade Union Federation.[31] Although in the early days the boards 'proved

more cautious than government departments' — and the first board
established for the Chain Trade held 19 meetings before a rate was
arrived at — they became, in the view of R.H. Tawney, really
valuable. For apart from the wage increases secured, boards 'transferred the determination of wages from the caprice of individuals to
a representative body, and put an end to the employment of children
as apprentices in excess of trade requirements'.[32]

During 1920–1 Ellen was appointed to several boards. She served
assiduously on those for the Laundry, the Hat, Cap and Millinery
Trades and for Dressmaking and Women's Light Clothing Trades
until Parliamentary duties made her attendances intermittent.
Union colleagues, including John Jagger and Mary Welch, succeeded her. Ellen proved a stickler for protocol. In preliminary discussions on the composition of the Clothing Trade Board, for
example, she came into heated conflict with a Mr Conley of the
United Garment Workers' Union. Challenging the view that 'his
union was the only one to be considered', Ellen pertly asserted 'my
union will sit on the board by permission of the Minister and not by
permission of Mr Conley'. The poor chairman, a Mr Besso, who
wanted only to secure 'unanimous understanding' eventually
conceded Ellen's case,[33] and she won representation for her
union.

The work was not easy: negotiations were niggling and meticulous. Agreement had to be reached over the precise definition, for
example, of 'functions and processes' in all stages of 'dressmaking
and tailoring', from labelling, ticketing and tabbing, to the cutting,
making-up or finishing by hand or machine in respect of an infinite
variety of goods. The slowness of the deliberations would have
exasperated even someone of greater patience than Ellen. Dorothy
Elliott, organiser for the Federation, later chief woman officer of the
NUGMW, who was secretary of the workers' side of the Toy Trade
Board, has described just how tedious negotiations could be:

We made a claim for sevenpence [i.e. 3p] an hour for adult
women . . . the employers' side offered fourpence halfpenny; we
sat for three days; the employers coming up gradually a farthing
an hour till we eventually 'stuck' and by the vote of the independent members secured a rate of sixpence. . . We spent days discussing what is a toy — is a paper hat a carnival novelty or a toy?
. . . Details had to be settled or the inspectors could not take cases
to court with any chance of success.[34]

It was typical that at Ellen's first meeting of the Laundry Board in October 1919 she moved that 'piece work rates be increased from 8 pence to 2s. 6d. per hour'. However justified the suggestion was on grounds of humanity, it was regarded as economic nonsense by her colleagues and she was outvoted.[35] After this she made generally sober contributions or remained quiet, observing procedure and learning. This paid dividends, for she *did* learn and was eventually made chairman of the workers' side on her boards. Ellen by no means always took up outrageous positions. She patiently insisted for example that rates when agreed must be publicised — an obligation often disregarded by employers — and was firm in resisting the efforts of industrialists to reduce trade board rates.[36]

By the end of 1921 trade boards covered some 3 million workers, 70 per cent of whom were women working in sixty occupations. But the wartime boom was ending and wages were under attack. In certain trades, not controlled by trade boards, wages responded more quickly to the downward course of retail prices. This economic pattern, combined with a severe depreciation of European currencies, which adversely affected British export trade and aggravated unemployment, brought trade boards under severe criticism. On one hand repeal of the Act was demanded, and on the other the Minister of Labour was attacked for not establishing more boards. As he appeared to be acting as judge and jury, by both implementing and restricting the Trade Boards Act, he was assailed from all sides.

A Departmental committee under Humbert Wolfe, the poet, then a senior civil servant, was set up to enquire into this impasse. Sane recommendations were made which the Minister accepted, but he was so continuously harassed by employers as the depression deepened that he appointed the independent Cave Committee to enquire further into the effects of the Act. 'The tone properly set by Lord Cave was distinctly good,' wrote Wright Robinson, who as an NUDAW official attended to give evidence. 'He was a tall, commanding figure, urbane and alert under a "judicial mask".' Ellen was called on two separate occasions, substituting for John Jagger and for Joe Hallsworth, the Union's General Secretary, who were ill, and acquitted herself with honour, as Robinson described: 'She was piquant, and decided . . . the committee were probably amused that such large opinions were associated with such small stature. All the same they respected her greatly. She gave her evidence well, adopting the university manner and turning both words and sentences carefully.'[37] Later he gave a fuller account to *New Dawn*:

She stoked up an almighty hustle on herself, her colleagues and the office staff . . . compiled a case bristling with fighting facts, supported by schedules as full of statistics as a Sinn Feiner is full of fight . . . She made an immense impression by her descriptions of conditions in many drapery houses . . . and the catering trade. If any doubts lingered . . . as to low wages and bad conditions, she went far to knock them on the head . . . Asked if she did not think that wages must have regard to foreign competition and what a trade could bear, she replied that the logical essence of that argument was advocating coolie wages. But her most moving plea was for protecting women workers . . . who were too poor to organise.[38]

Concern with the organisational problems of trade boards prompted Ellen to criticise their composition. The Minister should throw his net wider. Some women on the boards had little contact with the actual conditions of either trade or industry and she regretted that so few 'of the considerable number of women expert in social conditions' had been nominated.[39]

The committee reported that hostility to trade boards had been greatly exaggerated: that they had had 'most beneficial results' and favoured their retention. Nevertheless it proposed restricting the powers of boards to fixing only minimum wages, and recommended that Parliament should decide the conditions under which future boards were to be set up. Ironically, the committee's recommendations 'greatly strengthened the policy of government interference, which was the bogey it had been intended to slay!'[40] The Report was never fully implemented, although the creation of new boards ceased for a time, and those already in being were urged to reduce their rates to meet the current trade depression.

The trade union movement adopted an ambivalent attitude towards trade boards. The TUC opposed curtailing or extending their operation; and Joe Hallsworth was not alone in asserting that they never could be 'substitutes for effective trade unionism'. Although arbitration tribunals insisted that trade boards rates were not to be considered as *standard* but only as legally enforceable *minimum* rates, the unions feared their authority in pay negotiations being undermined. At NUDAW's annual conference in 1922, Hallsworth said: 'the only use trade boards have for us is to eliminate the worst forms of super sweating. They can never do more, because they imply alliance with employers — and at the moment with government also — and workers can never be free until labour dictates the conditions.'[41] With this policy Ellen broadly agreed. People should be encouraged to join trade unions, she wrote, but 'there are still many trades in which women can only be helped through trade boards'.[42] They were 'an excellent ambulance corps' but should not be a permanent feature of industrial organisation.[43]

Arguments as to the merits of the boards rumbled on for years. Within NUDAW ranks Rhys Davies, MP, who had little regard for Ellen, remained a bitter critic. He believed that they were a factor responsible for the decline in union membership and cited laundry workers 'who were members of a trade union long before they were covered by trade boards, yet many of whom now remained outside the fold'.[44] Years later when J.C. Swanton, then the union's Northern Divisional Organiser, suggested that 'unions catering for women should be urged by the TUC to reject trade boards rates and get women into their appropriate union', Ellen retorted that the difficulty of organising women was largely caused by the conservative attitudes of men. 'I have always wanted to get women into our union on their merits, but it is necessary to convince our men that they have merits,' she wrote acidly.[45] Probably the best assessment of trade boards was made by Mrs Bamber, Ellen's fellow organiser (and mother of the late Bessie Braddock, MP): 'Bad though the organisation of women workers in industry may be, it is slightly higher where trade boards exist. They have after all rescued some 2 to 3 million workers from terrible sweated conditions,' she said.[46] And who could argue against that?

Political Growth

From the outset of her irruption into the AUCE, Ellen had had the warmest support from union colleagues, notably John Jagger. Her diminutive size, and arresting personality tended to make men feel protective towards her. Two decades later her secretary, Beryl Hughes, recalled even then 'she could charm the birds off the trees'.[47] How much more so when she was inexperienced and eager to learn the ways of the trade union world! Like 'Joan' in *Clash*, 'she were a gradely lass!'.

Ellen's union responsibilities grew as her male colleagues went to the war. 'I realise looking back that the only reason I didn't go under was the wonderful patience and kindness of the men I had to work with. They were considerably older than I, at least the leaders were, but they managed to combine treating me as a daughter and an equal . . . and my heart goes out in gratitude to the understanding comrades in work of those early days,' she wrote warmly.[48] Not all trade union colleagues had welcomed Ellen's appointment. Some resented a woman's intrusion and later the alleged influence she exerted within the union hierarchy. Though as the union had so many women members, and as Ellen was the senior woman organiser, that influence seems defensible. Perhaps the most serious criticism was that she tended to 'ride on the shoulders of other organisers'.[49] Certainly she had a flair of getting to know the right people at the right time; but with the personable warmth of a 'fiery particle' this was perhaps inevitable. No one, however, suggested that she shirked work: only that she preferred certain aspects of an organiser's routine to others: mass meetings rather than office drudgery. Harry Weate, a former union official and Manchester City Councillor, when a lively octogenarian recalled that even if Ellen did seem to know the 'right and the influential . . . she would do anything for a good cause in the interests of humanity and never gave way on the basic principles of socialism.'[50]

'To work in the trade union movement towards the end of the First World War was the finest political education anyone could wish for,' wrote Dorothy Elliott, and Ellen would have agreed. For AUCE/NUDAW work gave her wide scope. She encountered all kinds and conditions in the Labour Movement, had a rich opportunity to test out new socialist ideas, and undoubtedly began to acquire a mastery of public speaking, the electrifying quality of which colleagues still recall across the years. She cultivated her speaking skills the hard way — in the open air. As Dorothy Elliott wrote, 'These days offered wonderful training. Standing on a soap box, an organiser had to collect an audience and hold it, with traffic, children, dogs and hecklers supplying the background noise. Of course, we had never heard of a microphone.'[51]

Ellen was astute enough to want to master the techniques of her trade. Writing of Mary MacArthur, secretary of the National Federation of Women Workers, she remembered how as a 'green young undergraduate' she had heard Mary speak at a recruiting meeting:

The amiable Labour leaders talked commonsense à la Samuel Smiles and the girls were frankly bored. When, however, Miss

MacArthur demanded a wage that would provide pretty frocks and holidays the girls began to realise that there was something in trade unions . . . to the young priggish economics student it was all very shocking; but I have realised the value of her methods at many a work gate since.[52]

From her experiences of union work, Ellen assimilated the facts of practical economics in terms of strikes, and lock-outs. She saw the impact on families of irregular work, inadequate sickness provision and the looming inhumanity of the Poor Law. Keir Hardie's call for the right to work or maintenance embodied in Labour's policy statement the *New Social Order* (1918), was cardinal to her thinking.

'The lady organiser' of the AUCE soon became known as a lively-minded articulate delegate and speaker, who 'captured audiences by her obvious grasp of the fundamentals of socio-economics, her lucidity and her arresting personality',[53] and (it should be added) as an undeviating feminist. Early in her union career Ellen succesfully seconded a resolution at the Women's Co-operative Guild's conference which petitioned the Government 'to have all land and capital placed at the disposal of the state . . . every adult having the vote . . . [for] women's voices should be heard on the question of reconstruction and that ought to be before they are thirty!'[54]

Union obligations made Ellen an inveterate conference goer. Until well after she was an MP she would attend — in her capacity as a delegate or as a journalist (or both) — conferences of the TUC, the Women's Co-operative Guilds, Labour Women, the Standing Joint Committee of Women's Industrial Organisations (of which for a while she was chairman), her own union and the Labour Party. She spoke frequently, often in support of unpopular policies, and she would use her critical pen to pinpoint current controversies. In one informed article in *New Dawn*, for example, she castigated anomalies in the unemployment insurance provision under which several categories of women workers were denied benefit, urged that Labour's policy of work or maintenance 'must be made a reality and not a pious platform platitude' and lunged out at an Act which denied assistance to 'cleaners, scrubbers and laundresses . . . expecting a married woman to be kept by her husband and the single woman by her relations!'[55]

At first Ellen wrote only for her union journal. Soon she extended her range, contributing to various political papers — the *Labour Leader*, the *New Leader*, *Lansbury's Labour Weekly*, the *Sunday*

Worker. After her arrival in the House she became a feature writer
— as well as a feature subject — for national dailies and weeklies.
Her closest journalistic affinity was with Lady Rhondda's radical
liberal weekly, *Time and Tide* which throughout the thirties took a
refreshingly unstuffy, non-establishment stand and for which she
came to write regularly — but that is to anticipate events.

The union in general, and John Jagger in particular, must have
had a strong formative influence on Ellen's intellectual development. Contemporary socialist ideas and activities were examined
regularly in *New Dawn*, as the *Co-operative Employee* had been
renamed after amalgamation. NUDAW regarded capitalism as the
source of society's ills — war, unemployment and inequality. It
must therefore be changed in the interests of justice and this change
would be effected by workers' control which many believed could
only be secured through revolution, in which Russia was leading the
way. In the early twenties Ellen was not alone in thinking that the
trade unions could and should be used to break the capitalist system.
Her enthusiasm for the Russian Revolution was later modified, but
with her union she remained a firm advocate for extending trade
with the Soviet Union.

Socialist propaganda, culture and education were also discussed
in *New Dawn*. The Workers' Travel Association and the Labour
Research Department; the Fabian Society; ILP and NUDAW
summer schools; plays by Shaw and Galsworthy; books by the
Webbs, G.D.H. Cole and H.G. Wells; the work of the League of
Nations, and the International Labour Office (ILO); the Plebs
League and NCLC: all were commented upon and publicised. Out-
standingly, the implications of Italian Fascism were exposed long
before its significance had been grasped by the Labour Movement
generally. How far Ellen's attitudes were influenced by these
articles, or how far she herself shaped the policy presented through
New Dawn, is conjectural. Probably each was mutually stimulating.
Certainly she developed a strong rapport with John Jagger, with
whom she worked in a variety of socialist organisations. Her capacity for accepting new ideas — even if undigested — remained
undimmed.

From her union associations Ellen was also learning the strength a
politician absorbs from grass root support. 'Trade union members',
she wrote years later when in the House, 'are outposts in the industrial fight. When I look along the Labour Benches I see behind my
comrades, the hundreds of trade unionists who have sent us there. I

like to feel, with the other [NUDAW] members, that our work is watched by the members of the Distributive Workers' Union and that we are speaking with the voice of the men and women in the soap works or the drapers shop.'[56]

Through her union Ellen came in to the Labour College movement, for NUDAW was one of the earliest affiliated to the Marxist NCLC, and its propaganda organ, the Plebs League. The purpose of the NCLC was to educate working-class students in working-class concepts, and to this end the journal *Plebs*, edited by J.F. Horrabin and enriched by his cartoons and maps, was directed. Correspondence courses, lectures and weekend schools were held in residential Labour Colleges; subjects ranging from history, geography and economics to industrial relations, social sciences and even public speaking were taught, always with a working-class bias. 'In that teaching we [the Labour College Movement] show that all education not based on the central fact of the class struggle is false history and false economics,' wrote Raymond Postgate, chairman of the Plebs executive committee.[57] The NCLC relied on voluntary lecturers — such as G.D.H. Cole, Walter Citrine, Raymond Postgate, Ellen and even the Countess of Warwick. In addition to lecturing at summer schools, Ellen also wrote for the Council — collaborating with Postgate and Horrabin on *A Workers' History of the General Strike* and with Dr Edward Conze on a pamphlet *Why War?* and, later, on a Marxist analysis, *Why Fascism?*.

In the early twenties several prominent members of the Plebs League joined, but soon resigned from, the Communist Party of Great Britain. This caused much internal dissension, for the NCLC, though Marxist, was never a communist body. During 1924, Raymond Postgate tried to stop Walton Newbold's election to the Plebs Executive 'because of his known Communist leanings'.[58] In spite of internal disagreements, the NCLC resolutely ploughed its working class furrow, preaching and teaching class war and publishing Marxist text books. Although demand for its courses and publications contracted as unions established their own educational centres, the NCLC served the Labour Movement long and faithfully and provided basic political education, the value of which Horrabin neatly summed up by asking, 'What's the use of having a trade union ticket in your pocket if your boss has your head in his?'[59]

Ellen long retained her links with the Labour College movement, lecturing for it whenever she could. As late as 1946 she wrote to Arthur Woodburn, MP (an ex-Plebs lecturer) when Secretary of

State for Scotland, to introduce an American journalist who had come to study adult education in the United Kingdom. 'He has', she said, 'been thoroughly indoctrinated by the Workers' Educational Association who never mentioned the NCLC!'[60]

The demands upon Ellen as a national organiser absorbed but did not engulf her attention. Shuttling around the country from her Manchester-based union headquarters, dashing down to London for consultations, committee meetings and trade board sessions, she retained contact with former friends and became yet more embroiled with left-wing organisations. She was an eager 'joiner', a proclivity which did not diminish with age, as the issues of the day so often seemed to her to require instant solutions. She tended to grasp on to ideas of the moment not because she wanted to be in the progressive swim, though with friends and colleagues she usually was, but because warm, impulsive and angry with any form of injustice she frequently saw solutions implicit in new theories.

Inevitably, but briefly, Ellen became a disciple of Guild Socialism, the movement revitalised by A.R. Orage, the brilliant editor of *New Age*, and S.G. Hobson, and widely expounded by G.D.H. Cole, 'its ablest propagandist'. Guild Socialists believed that workers should have the say in the production of goods and that 'the productive life of the country should be run and organised by self-governing democratic guilds, each embracing all workers in an industry or service'. These guilds would organise industry but not own it, for the state would be the owner and provider of capital, while the guilds delivered the goods. 'Thus the fundamental objective of traditional socialism would be secured while the evils of bureaucratic collectivism would be avoided'.

These ideas made a great appeal to restless young Fabians and certain trade union leaders. Guild Socialism seemed to resolve the indignity of the worker as an anonymous cog in the productive wheel. It gave him status through responsibility for industrial organisation, although change was to come through pressure and action from the Labour Movement, not from revolution. Ellen however, was one of those Guild Socialists who did not wholly accept this. Once again a chasm over tactics yawned in the ranks: could industrial change be effected peaceably or only by revolution and the dictatorship of the proletariat? At this time Ellen firmly maintained the latter, and when in 1919 G.D.H. Cole accepted the secretaryship of the National Industrial Conference (through which he was trying to establish conditions which would lead to effective workers'

control by compromise and not collision), Ellen dubbed his association with employers as 'working with the enemy', publicly
denounced Guild Socialists 'who went a-whoring with capitalist
forces' and flounced out of membership. The Guild Socialist movement did not flourish long into the twenties. Workers were too
occupied with preserving their standards of living to bother with
schemes for industrial control.[61]

The concept of Industrial Unions (one union for each industry)
then surfaced, and Ellen became an enthusiastic protagonist. 'She
believes in it', Beatrice Webb wrote early in 1927, 'because it is the
catchword of today just as workers' control was the catchword of
yesterday. Certainly the one big union is inconsistent with workers'
control but that does not trouble her.'[62] Ellen's memories of these
shortlived flirtations were, however, evoked during a debate on the
Trades' Disputes Act in 1927:

> A group of young members of the Labour Movement were trying
> to define 'an industry', on the grounds that . . . if you could
> group together all workers in one industry . . . and have, say,
> twelve great industrial unions, you'd be in a much stronger posi-
> tion vis à vis employers. I must have spent months in discussions
> with that group which was later known as the National Guilds
> League . . . but we found . . . that so interwoven are the various
> trades and crafts that it was impossible to get any definition which
> would make it possible for us to carry out industrial unionism.[63]

Her enthusiasm had quickly waned before such practicalities.

Ellen's attitude towards her early love, the Fabian Society, was far
less volatile and although many members continued to be sympathetic to Guild Socialism, Ellen's Fabian affections remained
firm. When the USF held its annual conference in 1919, Ellen
— attending with Robin Page Arnot, Chaundy and Maurice Reckitt
among the 'veterans' — was only narrowly defeated by Reckitt for
the chairmanship. This was surely less important to her than Roden
Buxton's subsequent talk to delegates on Foreign Policy for Socialists. In this he described Bolshevism as 'the most crucial item in
foreign policy confronting socialists not only as a group of ideas but
also as a system of government which challenges the democratic con-
ventions'.[64]

In 1917 the Fabian Research Department became the Labour
Research Department (LRD), which Ellen long supported. Its com-

mittee — originally 'Guild Socialists to a man' — was a highly talented body which included William Mellor, W.N. Ewer, Robin Page Arnot and Frank Horrabin. They, together with 'JJ', Ellen and Newbold later became founder members of the British Communist Party. LRD outlived both the New Fabian Research Bureau (founded by G.D.H. Cole in 1931 'to uphold the Fabian tradition of socialist research') and its contemporary Society of Socialist Inquiry and Propaganda (SSIP) which though of brief existence enabled socialists 'to grouse loyally'.

LRD undertook extensive research work for trade unions, few of whom then had research departments of their own, and published carefully documented analyses of capitalist economics. Margaret Cole, who edited its journal from 1917 to 1925, later noted 'the steady concern of LRD at that time with industry to the exclusion of politics', and decribed how LRD effectively co-operated in the 'growling class war' by:

> showing how the conditions of life for the working class were improved against the clamour of a vocal upper class, always ready to shout against any improvement. Press and public comments upon the rates of unemployment benefit . . . had all the note of people fighting a war and go far to excuse, if they do not wholly justify, our attitude of permanent indignant hostility.[65]

This, in line with Ellen's thinking, explains why she served on the Executive Committee of LRD for twenty years with only a brief break. When she did resign it was because she had become increasingly out of sympathy with the attitudes of the LRD over the Russian invasion of Finland, and because 'I can seldom attend committee meetings I have to take responsibility for a policy with which I do not agree'.[66]

The Communist Party of Great Britain – In and Out

On major issues such as the Great War and the new Russia Ellen's feelings were clear: she was a pacifist and unequivocally sympathetic to the Revolution and opposed to war. The British Labour Movement however remained deeply divided. On the one hand the ILP, pacifists, conscientious objectors, Marxists of the British Socialist Party, leading socialists like Snowden and MacDonald, opposed the war on moral and anti-imperialist grounds. On the other hand union leaders such as Clynes and Henderson actively supported it and the government's recruiting campaigns. A feeling of unease stalked abroad, not only because of apprehension over the use of substitute labour, and dissatisfaction over wage restraints, but by reason of the appalling and ever-mounting casualty lists.

Against this background of political scepticism the Russian Revolution exploded in March 1917. Margaret Cole described her own reactions, which were surely similar to Ellen's:

> We read with incredulous eyes that the Russian people . . . had really risen and cast out the Tzar and his government . . . the arch-symbols of black oppression in the world . . . We danced round tables and sang . . . Everyone with an ounce of liberalism in his composition rejoiced that . . . tyranny had fallen. Thousands gathered at the Albert Hall and wept unashamedly . . . The news of Russia put immense heart into the left wing . . . There might be something good coming out of the war after all: for if the Russian people could overthrow their government, could not the Germans, the French or the British?[67]

By 1920 Russia seemed to be the 'hope of the world', and at a stroke to have reversed the social values of capitalism. Exploiters had been expropriated and workers of hand and brain were to be rewarded commensurately with their importance to the community. British industrial workers thought of the Russians as blazing a trail for socialism. 'It was extremely easy to believe that communism was simply advanced socialism, and that the best thing an advanced socialist could do was to become a communist and follow the guidance of Lenin and Trotsky.' The clutch of Marxists, Guild Socialists and ILP-ers, of whom Ellen was one, who formed the Communist Party of Great Britain, were activated by varying motives. There were insurrectionists; there were Marxists who believed in the class war and that Soviet interests were of paramount importance in world affairs, and as Margaret Cole saw it,

> there were also those in the Labour movement who were genuinely impatient and frustrated at the slowness of the Labour Party in initiating action. They shared the desire for a plan and a direction, of wanting to feel part of a society which was going somewhere; the need for some human authority to explain, inter-

pret and guide the individual in his or her own action.[68]

Undoubtedly Ellen's motives were as mixed as any.

Labour personalities such as Henderson, MacDonald and Herbert Morrison vehemently opposed the formation of a British Communist Party. To them the communists repudiated the 'reformist view' of changing society, and regarded parliamentary action merely as propaganda for the revolution. They believed that any communist elected to parliament would regard himself as holding a mandate only from the Party — an attitude exemplified by Walton Newbold when he became a Communist MP. This basic clash of principle led to bitter internal disagreement over communist affiliation to the Labour Party and later over the issue of the United Front. It was also an issue on which Ellen and Herbert Morrison held fiercely conflicting views; long after Ellen had become a Member of Parliament her sympathies still lay far more with the revolutionary concept than with reformism. Her faith in the unity and strength of the working-class movement was unshakeable.

If Ellen was not a prime mover in the formation of the Communist Party of Great Britain, she was certainly active during its creation. As a representative of the National Guilds League she attended the preliminary 'unity' conferences and doubtless was present at the actual inception of the Party in London in July 1920. Thereafter she became a keen advocate for the Red International of Labour Unions (RILU), formed 'to win unions from the policy of class collaboration to that of class struggle.'[69] The RILU was formally established during the summer of 1921 at a conference in Moscow, which Ellen attended with Robin Page Arnot, Tom Mann and Harry Pollitt. After the conference she and Pollitt visited Berlin to obtain information on the German situation from Phillips Price, who was studying the rise of the Communist Party in Germany and later became a Labour MP.[70] These visits were among Ellen's earliest trips abroad, though she grew addicted to travel and would eagerly rush off to any country 'at the drop of a hat', providing her visit had a cogent political purpose.[71]

As a strong supporter of the RILU, Ellen presented its case at Labour Conferences and argued, unsuccessfully, for her union's withdrawal from the 'right wing' Amsterdam International Federation of Trade Unions and for affiliation to the RILU. She saw this body at the time as 'fighting the whole policy of old trade unionism which sets a limit to the onward march of the workers.' In contrast with some union colleagues, notably Rhys Davies, MP who interpreted these divisions in the Labour Movement as between 'those who believed in industrial action and those who advocated political action'. Ellen saw 'the difference in essence as between the social democrat and the revolutionary approach.'[72]

Unemployment, and the human suffering which flowed from it, were one of Ellen's lifelong concerns. In the early days of the RILU, with members of the powerful local Manchester and Salford Trades Council, she spoke angrily and often on the issue, certain that 'as long as the unemployed keep quiet and starve nothing will be done for them'. Inevitably she came into contact with the communist-inspired National Unemployed Workers' Movement (NUWM) and Wal Hannington, its brilliant intransigent organising secretary. To the participants in this movement — formed at a time when the numbers of the registered unemployed were rising from 1.5 million early in 1921 to 2.5 million later that year — Britain was patently no land for heroes.[73] Throughout the twenties and thirties Hannington argued the case for humane treatment and adequate provision for the unemployed, who backed his protests with disciplined demonstrations and marches. Official Labour however would have none of the NUWM and pleas for its affiliation to the TUC and to the Labour Party (first pressed in 1924 by the NUDAW) were consistently rejected. Hannington's experience in the organisation of protests was not however lost upon Ellen. She remembered and consulted him in the days of the glowing Jarrow Crusade.

Soon after Ellen had joined the Communist Party, the Comintern, the central organisation of world communist parties, took action which alienated her and many colleagues. An order was said to have been issued that constituent communist parties must be 'bolshevised', i.e. reorganised on proper class war lines. Members had to accept severe discipline and to assist in the 'capture' of organisations to which they belonged. They allegedly were to form themselves into cells and to initiate action on lines laid down by their Central Committee. This implied 'accepting centrally ordained policy from outsiders for freezing out non communists and . . . manoeuvring the victims into a position of false security,'[74] and appears to have sparked off Ellen's and a train of resignations from the Communist Party. Frank Horrabin, JJ, William Mellor, Raymond Postgate and even Walton Newbold: comrades and pacifists who had been among the 'first in' were also the 'first out'.

Years later when chairman of the Labour Party, talking to Tom

Driberg, Ellen saw this very differently. 'The CP really was a band of idealists, a ginger group to the Labour Party', Driberg quotes her as saying, 'but as for any nonsense about control by Moscow, why, Moscow was much too busy to bother about controlling anybody outside: it wanted help, not control.'[75] At the time, however, she issued her own positive explanation in September 1924: 'I resigned from the CP several months ago because of the indiscriminate attacks on the Labour Government and of its exclusive and dictatorial methods which made impossible the formation of a real left wing among the progressive elements of Trade Unions and the Labour Party.' She denied that her resignation had any connection with any parliamentary candidature as 'I have been on the official Labour candidates endorsed list since last September 1923'.[76] It could be argued that Ellen had resigned because she was so very ambitious.[77] Possibly she had sensed the pending conference decision that was to exclude communists from being eligible to stand as Labour candidates.[78]

A more generous interpretation however seems as plausible. Ellen had joined the Communist Party during the time of great pro-Russian euphoria, which receded in the face of hard-line policy. She was concerned, as ever, with the best way to serve — and to achieve results — and was undoubtedly influenced by the fact that membership of the Labour Party could lead to parliamentary opportunity for getting things done — always her urgent desire.[79] When in the Communist Party, she advocated its policies, but after her resignation came to accept that problems should be settled by democratic argument. Even so, Ellen never wholly rejected the basic theory of the class war and long believed that the interests of workers and employers within a capitalist society were in perpetual conflict.

Ellen resigned honestly and without offence. She had objections to the Communist Party policies and let them be known but she never, like many a renegade, became in any sense spiteful. On this those who knew her are unanimous: 'She may have recanted but she was never a red baiter.'[80] The lack of any expressed malice towards former comrades, the sympathy and single-mindedness with which she upheld left-wing causes and chose to work with 'suspect' organisations if they furthered any purpose to which she was committed, prompted accusations of her being a 'fellow-traveller'. Too often she was ingenuous to the point of gullibility in her anxiety to right the wrong and defend the weak.

So she did what any idealistic, political person would in similar circumstances have done. Accepted on the NUDAW parliamentary panel of prospective candidates, she turned to more conventional paths, but in no way did this lessen Ellen's great compassion, or curtail her forthright independence. While she came to accept that 'the Labour Party could be a great instrument to end a system whose political superstructure is based on wage slavery and degradation', she was equally sure that 'the Party needs to get out of its Mrs Tanqueray habit of being silenced by reference to its own past'.[81]

Manchester City Councillor

Before she finally staked her political allegiance Ellen irrupted into local government, and fought her first parliamentary election. In the autumn of 1923 she was selected as Labour candidate for Gorton South Ward by the Gorton Trades and Labour Council, to stand for Manchester City Council. At the time she was still a member of the Communist Party, but this was permissible for the party had not then been proscribed. Ellen therefore could, if she wished, support constitutionally the whole programme of the Labour Party.

Her address for the council election is of interest because it bears her very personal stamp and touches upon issues on which she continuously campaigned. She diagnosed unemployment as an international problem, arising from complete breakdown of the capitalist system. 'A great corporation like Manchester could do much to find employment beyond the proposed ridiculously inadequate road making schemes.' There was a strong chauvinistic tinge in her criticism of the Corporation's placing contracts in France and Germany, 'When our own engineers are on the dole', but she was, after all, fighting a local election, and the issue of local unemployment was a persistent and haunting spectre. It was logical therefore for her to argue that 'the dole ought to be a national and not a local charge', and that it was 'wholly unjust for local rates to be used to finance unemployment benefit when need arose from national and international policies'.

She also attacked the imminent decontrol of rents and the curb on house building; reiterated the Labour Party's pledge to build more homes — for it was 'costing far more to keep workers on the dole than to set them constructing the badly needed houses', and stressed her concern for the welfare of mothers and children by demanding a clean municipal milk supply, the extension of the public health services and smaller classes in the schools.' To save money on children is like trying to save time by stopping the clock.'[82]

Gorton was a ward liable to make heavy demands on its councillors. Stella Davies, chairman and founder of the Gorton Women's Section has described the poverty that then stalked abroad:

> I shopped with women to whom the difference of a penny in price was a vital concern . . . I saw the struggle these women had to keep their children decently clad with shoes fit enough to wear to school . . . I saw them line up outside the Gorton Town Hall on Friday afternoons when parcels of groceries were distributed . . . I had seen poverty before, now I was surrounded by it.[83]

She described Ellen in that municipal election as 'an exceedingly able speaker, particularly good at open air meetings, her small figure dressed in green, with her flaming hair making a bright spot of colour in the drab Gorton Streets.' But there are also less demure recollections. Fred Meadowcraft recalls the rowdiness of Ellen's meetings, which 'appalled her family and staid neighbours . . . Ellen and her political gang were real disturbers of the peace'.[84]

When on 1 November 1923 Ellen was elected a Manchester City Councillor the *Manchester Guardian* laconically announced that overall 'there was no change'. They little knew what was coming! Neither for that matter did Councillor Wright Robinson, who was later an Alderman, a distinguished chairman of the Education Committee and Lord Mayor. Referring in his diaries to his own re-election, 'looking forward to another three years of public work', he added — in sublime ignorance — 'with Ellen elected and also Mary Welch (a younger union colleague) I feel prodigiously proud that my juniors had the fullest chances that I could give them'.[85] Ellen was on her way!

Although she never warmed to local government, Ellen came to know its working well and would tear its operations apart ruthlessly if she suspected any inhumanity or negligence. The Labour Group faced an entrenched Conservative majority, but she learnt quickly how to make effective political impact. With great panache, though with dubious success, and much to the irritation of Councillor Wright Robinson, Ellen soon after her election persuaded the Council 'to act over the plight of unemployed women'. In February 1924 she moved that a deputation should wait on the appropriate minister to emphasise the difficulties of providing suitable relief for unemployed women, and to ask the government to offer facilities for such work. Urging that women should be trained as home helps, she chided that whereas 'the unemployment of women is dismissed by the Council with a wave of the hand, if men were so treated there would be a riot'.[86]

There were undercurrents to Ellen's proposals. For the truculence with which Councillor Wright Robinson discussed them in his diary suggests that Ellen had stolen his thunder. And one can well understand his irritation as an experienced councillor at being outpaced by a stripling newcomer!

> I had to get back (from union business) for my resolution on unemployment . . . Miss Wilkinson wangled the Council to send a deputation to London to see the Minister of Labour in regard to schemes for women . . . and though she did not turn up for the [Labour] meeting held specially to give her a chance to formulate action, she was not brought to book for sheer limelighting, but ensured herself a visit to London at the Corporation's expense! The trip's the thing my lad! An advert for Ellen. Eyewash for the unemployed . . . first she proposes that unemployed women should be trained to make clothing for underclothed school children and then that additional women should be engaged as home helps . . . she was told that the first was beyond the powers of the Council, and the second was turned down because voluntary effort was already covering the ground . . . [as a sop] she and Mary Welch were added to the Works for the Unemployed Committee.[87]

He added: 'When my resolution came up . . . it went through without a grunt . . . I had heaps of facts and figures in reserve but everyone wanted to go home.' How peeved he must have been. And then the final indignity: 'The *Manchester Guardian* lumped all our Labour speeches comprising Compton, Ellen, Mary and I together'. Life in local government could be very unfair.

To this he added a human sidelight:

> Alderman Turnbull, the Committee Chairman, asked me if I would go on the deputation. Ellen buttered him up in absolving him from blame in her speech . . . 'Shall we take these two little lasses to London?' he asked, his eyes blinking with rakish merriment . . . 'although I'm 70, I'm as good as I ever were'.[88]

Nothing came of the deputation and even though Mary Welch, supported by Councillor Mrs Hannah Mitchell, continued to urge the training of home helps little progress was made.[89]

In autumn 1925 Ellen, at a now rare council attendance, again raised the unemployment issue. She stressed the difficulties facing the unemployed single woman who even though she had paid contributions was now prevented by new legislation (if she lived with her parents) from receiving benefit. There were over 8,000 unemployed women in the city, 'yet the Corporation has done virtually nothing for them.'[90]

Apart from other feminist interventions such as pleading for women Public Health Inspectors to receive the same rates of pay as men engaged on similar work, Ellen's other main council concern was with education. In March 1924 she had referred to a report which postulated the need for a full building programme to replace temporary school buildings, and urged that it be acted on swiftly with a view to absorbing some of the unemployed. The Education Committee had already 'won support on the matter in principle and the President of the Board, Sir Charles Trevelyan, awaited further details'.[91] Ellen protested against a reduction in the education budget as a 'false economy' which countenanced pupils remaining in 'little tin tabernacle-like structures all over the city'. This 'matters deeply — not to the children of Fallowfield or Withington [the wealthier areas] but to those who grow up in South Gorton, Hulme or Openshaw . . . the Finance Committee is a disgrace, concerned only about their pockets at the expense of working class children', she thundered. 'We are really manufacturing criminals of the [ill-educated] bright children who, after leaving school idle about the street because the conditions of modern industry give so few of them a chance to learn a trade.'[92]

After eighteen months Ellen's attendances at committee and council meetings became so erratic that she had to be 'struck off from membership of the Education Committee'.[93] By then she was a Member of Parliament and therefore had legitimate excuse. Yet she seems to have valued her experiences as a councillor, and commented nostalgically that 'working in Parliament ill-compared with that on a City Council such as Manchester where members get insight into the administration because they receive facts on which policy is based . . . and can make informed contributions.'[94] Was the tip of that fluent tongue tucked firmly into a defiant cheek?

There is no doubt that Ellen could have been a much more effective councillor, but with her developing political aspirations, which union colleagues fostered, the lure of local politics receded. This is not to imply that her feel for, or concern over, people diminished. Ellen was changing the framework of her political battles, but in no way redirecting her basic purpose.

Election Undercurrents

Hard on the heels of her municipal success Ellen fought her first parliamentary election at Ashton-under-Lyne in 1923. She was no stranger to electioneering and had helped R.S. Wilson, a union nominee, to win Jarrow the previous year. Then he had generously acknowledged 'Miss Wilkinson, our brave little propagandist, the heroine of the campaign, with the inimitable John Jagger who found the hearts of his hearers by his humour and pungency'.[95]

Ellen's own campaign at Ashton was not in itself important. She did not win, though she worked energetically. Wright Robinson caustically described one of her meetings:

It was a day of awful fog which invaded the hall, Ramsay MacDonald was tired, J.R. Clynes made a short Clynesian speech and Ellen was on the platform, overwhelmed by physical mass and moral fervour. When the photographs appeared in the paper she stood in the centre front like a child which must be in the picture . . . I asked her why she disliked Ramsay MacDonald . . . she said she loathed him . . . that he was like a sultan always surrounded by women and she did not want to be one of the flies in the jam.[96]

What is significant about Ellen's candidature is not the help she received from her union and the Communist Party, but the political machinations which allegedly preceded her adoption at Ashton. The undated entries in Wright Robinson's diaries are essentially subjective, but they do indicate how some union colleagues felt about Ellen's and Jagger's political sympathies at the time:

Against all the betting Ellen Wilkinson wangled her way into the Gorton South [selection conference] . . . Everybody said it would be a close vote. Councillor Davey (Gorton Trades and Labour Council) said he didn't like her as a parliamentary candidate — she was alright for a municipal election, but a communist MP was up another street — as secretary his opinion had some weight . . . She said she would get Ashton if she lost Gorton . . . I asked the reason of her assurance. She said she could buy it and that money talked in the Labour Party as anywhere else. [This referred to the financial help NUDAW, in line with other unions, gave all candidates on their parliamentary panel.] She went on to say that the man who was in the running for Ashton was more popular than she, but he had no money behind him.[97]

Stella Davies was less spiteful and more precise:

The three candidates [at Gorton South] faced about 100 delegates of which the engineers and steel smelters were the largest numbers. It was soon apparent that there was hostility to Ellen because she was a 'maverick' . . . too far to the left to be acceptable and also because she had so recently been elected to the Manchester City Council that she could not properly keep her election promises if she lived in London . . . It was evident from the size of the meeting a certain amount of rounding up had been preliminary to it. At normal trade council meetings 20 to 30 delegates was the usual attendance. . . [It was] a good example of democracy in action, with just the right amount of wire pulling to make it credible as the action of men and not angels. Ellen was defeated by an overwhelming majority.[98]

So Ellen turned to Ashton-under-Lyne and was adopted soon after her rejection at Gorton. She went to Wright Robinson:

On the verge of tears (real or assumed) saying that if our people [the NUDAW staff] did not save the situation she would lose [which in fact she did] . . . we all went along and ran the election in turns . . . she had a Gorton communist in charge of outdoor meetings, assisted by a score of comrades . . . it was impossible for them to keep off the class war jargon . . . One would be warming up to the Russian Revolution when he would be pulled up to make room for a speaker with less alarming reason for voting for a woman![99]

Although Wright Robinson had no love for the communists he took the campaign in good part, but remained apprehensive. He resented Jagger's supporting the Communist Party's application for affiliation at the Labour Party Conference, although it was in line with decisions taken by the Executive Committee of the NUDAW and recorded in the minutes. 'I think', Robinson wrote, 'that just as Jagger and Ellen Wilkinson are wangling our EC to authorise support under imperfectly understood ends, so communists in the Labour Party are trying to hustle it by guile to embark on a path alien to it.'[100]

Later his bitterness became vindictive:

> Ellen Wilkinson and Jagger in combination appear to stick at nothing that stands in their way . . . Jagger is a blind or willing accomplice . . . he always struck me as being a big man. Yet he seemed bent on dominating the union and leading the rank and file blindfold to communism.[101]

Wright Robinson went through a bad patch in his relationships with, and opinions of, union colleagues. He classed even the general secretary, Joe Hallsworth, certainly no extremist, as 'an arrogant egotist unfit for high office.' At this time he clearly disliked Ellen and Jagger very much indeed. He wrote:

> Councillor Davey asked me if, 'that big fat chap (J Jagger) who had been in constant attendance on E during her municipal fight was a bit soft'. I expressed surprise and asked for his reasons. He said that J haunted her at meetings, . . . waiting upon her like a lackey. Davey said his conduct was moonstruck and undignified.[102]

Feelings mellowed after Ellen and JJ resigned from the Communist Party, and they were reinstated in Wright Robinson's estimation. JJ again appeared to him as 'a very big man indeed', and Ellen, also back in favour, turned to nurse her second constituency, Middlesbrough East.

Notes

1. Lockett, *Three Lives*, (University of London Press, London, 1968), p. 4.
2. Manchester Society for Women's Suffrage, Report of January 1913.
3. Statement of May 1912 of NUWSS National Council, quoted in Manchester Society's Report of January 1913.

4. *The Women's Citizen*, December 1937, pp. 5–6.

5. M. Cole (ed.), *Road to Success* (Methuen, London, 1936), pp. 65–8.

6. Dame Margery Corbett Ashby, letter of 9 September 1978.

7. M. Cole (ed.), *Road to Success*, pp. 69–71.

8. Mrs Muriel Wilkinson and Mrs Kathleen Wilkinson, interviews.

9. S. Davies, *North Country Born* (Routledge and Kegan Paul, London, 1963), p. 223.

10. G. Bussey and M. Timms, *The Woman's International League for Peace and Freedom* (Allen and Unwin, London, 1965) Chapters 1–3.

11. Julia Wagner quoting Margaret Ashton in *Women's Citizen*, December 1937, p. 9.

12. Bussey and Timms, p. 40.

13. *Women's Leader*, 6 November 1925.

14. Mrs Annot Robinson's letter to her sister of 11 January 1921 (Misc. 718/116, Manchester City Library).

15. Julie Tomlinson's letter of January 11 — year unknown, probably 1926 (Misc. 718/155, Manchester City Library).

16. *Co-operative News*, August 1915; *Co-operative Employee*, September 1915; the author is deeply indebted to Barbara Drake's seminal book, *Women in Trade Unions* (Labour Research Department and Allen and Unwin, London, undated, probably *c.* 1923), Part I, 'The Women's Trade Union Movement'.

17. Board of Trade Reports of 1906 showed that about one-third of the whole body of working women earned less than twelve shillings a week, while Sidney Webb calculated from the same returns that the average net weekly earnings of an adult woman was 10s 10½d compared with 25s 9d for an adult man, and home workers, as the Sweated Labour Industries Exhibition had shown, averaged about 1d an hour (Drake, pp. 44–5).

18. Drake, pp. 26–57.

19. By June 1918 an additional 1¼ million women were working, directly or indirectly, in place of men as 'substitute labour', and the membership of women in unions rose from approximately 358,000 in 1914 to over 1 million in 1918. Similarly in 1914 women in the AUCE totalled approximately 27,000 out of 75,000 (Drake, Tables 1 and 2).

20. Executive Committee Minutes, AUCE, 15 October 1916 (USDAW Library, Manchester).

21. Dame Margaret Cole, interview.

22. *Co-operative News*, 21 August 1915.

23. *Co-operative Employee*, May 1916.

24. Drake, p. 168.

25. *Co-operative Employee* was the official journal of the AUCE from 1908 to 1917, when it became *AUCE Journal* until December 1920. After amalgamation the paper was transformed into *New Dawn*, January 1921.

26. *Co-operative Employee*, October 1915.

27. *Co-operative Employee*, November 1915.

28. *Co-operative Employee*, December 1915.

29. *New Leader*, 11 November 1915.

30. *Fabian News*, June 1918.

31. Drake, p. 100.

32. *Fabian News*, June 1914.

33. Public Record Office (PRO) — Lab/2/693, 1 August 1919.

34. Dorothy Elliott, 'Women in Search of Justice', unpublished MSS, personal papers.

35. PRO — Lab/35/169, 24 October 1919.

36. *New Dawn*, 21 January 1922.

37. Alderman Wright Robinson, unpublished papers (Wright Robinson Collec-

tion, Manchester City Archives, Manchester).

38. *New Dawn*, 7 January 1921.
39. Minutes of Evidence to the Cave Committee, 17/18 December 1920.
40. G.D.H. Cole, *A History of the Labour Party from 1914* (Routledge and Kegan Paul, London, 1948), p. 125; D. Sells, *British Wages Boards* (Brookings Institution, Washington DC, 1939), p. 262.
41. *New Dawn*, 29 April 1922.
42. *Clarion*, 12 December 1924.
43. *Newcastle Chronicle*, 2 February 1927.
44. Rhys Davies, MP, in *New Dawn*, 15 September 1928.
45. *New Dawn*, 9 April 1932.
46. *New Dawn*, 6 May 1933.
47. Beryl Hughes, interview.
48. M. Cole (ed.), *Road to Success*, p. 68.
49. Dorothy Elliott, Harold Weate, Amy Mitchell, interviews.
50. Harry Weate, Ivor Montagu, Ernest Fernyhough, Isabel Brown *et al.*, interviews.
51. D. Elliott, unpublished MSS. She was formerly organiser for the National Federation of Women Workers: 'After the amalgamation with the N.U. General Workers I became organiser for the N.U.G.M.W. and subsequently their chief woman officer in succession to Margaret Bondfield' (letter of 24 April 1979).
52. *New Dawn*, 1 March 1921.
53. *Co-operative Employee*, October 1916.
54. *Co-operative Employee*, May 1917.
55. *New Dawn*, 27 May 1922.
56. *New Dawn*, 7 July 1928.
57. M. Cole, *The Life of G.D.H. Cole* (Macmillan, London, 1971) p. 117.
58. J.P. Millar, *The Labour College Movement* (NCLC Publishing Society, 1979) p. 81.
59. Ibid., pp. 57–8.
60. Ibid., p. 132.
61. M. Cole, *G.D.H. Cole, passim*, especially pp. 52–3 and pp. 121–2.
62. B. Webb, p. 133.
63. Hansard 207, cols. 1693–5, 21 June 1927.
64. University Socialist Federation Bulletin, October 1919.
65. M. Cole, *Growing up into Revolution*, pp. 92–4.
66. Executive Committee Minutes, Labour Research Department, 6 May 1940.
67. M. Cole, *Growing Up*, p. 86.
68. Ibid., pp. 96–8.
69. James Klugman, *History of the Communist Party of Great Britain* (Lawrence and Wishart, London, 1968), vol. I, p. 109; Eddie Frow, interview.
70. John Mahon, *Harry Pollitt* (Lawrence and Wishart, London, 1976), p. 90.
71. Beryl Hughes, interviews.
72. *New Dawn*, 18 February 1922.
73. G.D.H. Cole and R. Postgate, *Common People 1746–1938* (Methuen, London, 1938), p. 547.
74. M. Cole, *Growing Up*, pp. 100–3.
75. Tom Driberg, *The Leader*, 3 March 1945.
76. *Daily Herald*, 6 September 1924; *Westminster Gazette*, 6 September 1924.
77. Klugman, vol. I, pp. 332–3.
78. In 1923 the Labour Party Conference endorsed the view of the NEC that the Communist Party and branches were ineligible for affiliation to the Labour Party both nationally and locally. It also rejected a motion from the Barrow LP that the time was opportune to secure a United Front among Labour Members in the House, and that the Whip be extended to Walton Newbold, then Communist MP for Mother-

well. This motion, overwhelmingly defeated, was sarcastically dismissed by Ramsay MacDonald, not so much for Walton Newbold's being 'away on the left' as because 'the greatest contribution he had made to Parliament was a new method of bowing to the Speaker!' Labour Party Conference Annual Report, 1923, pp. 190–2.

79. Amy Mitchell, Dorothy Elliott, Ivor Montagu, H.D. Hughes and Beryl Hughes, interviews.

80. Robin Page Arnot, Eddie Frow, Ivor Montagu, John Platts Mills, QC, interviews.

81. *Lansbury's Labour Weekly*, 23 February 1925.

82. Local Council Election Address for Gorton Ward South, 1923.

83. S. Davies, p. 222.

84. Fred Meadowcroft, interview.

85. Wright Robinson, unpublished papers, December 1923.

86. *Manchester Guardian*, 7 February 1924.

87. Wright Robinson, unpublished papers, February 1924.

88. Ibid., February, 1924 and March 1924.

89. Hannah Mitchell, 20 years Ellen's senior, was making a name for herself as a journalist, active Poor Law Guardian and ILP campaigner. She was elected the same year as Ellen to the Manchester City Council and served most conscientiously until 1935 see H. Mitchell, *The Hard Way Up* (Faber and Faber, London, 1968), pp. 203–36.

90. *Manchester Guardian*, 8 October 1925.

91. *Manchester Guardian*, 6 March 1924.

92. *Manchester Guardian*, 13 July 1925.

93. Wright Robinson, unpublished papers, undated, probably early in 1925. He wrote : 'Mrs. Taylor had to relinquish her co-opted position on the Education Committee, and as we failed to secure an additional elected representative, we dropped Ellen Wilkinson. I asked her three months ago to resign. She said she would let me have it (in writing). But no letters came, and as the year ended she wrote to the Nomination Committee asking to remain on the Education Committee. I found she had put in 22 attendances out of the possible 188 and struck her off.'

94. *New Dawn*, 20 June 1925.

95. *New Dawn*, 25 November 1922.

96. Wright Robinson, unpublished papers, November 1923.

97. Ibid., December 1923.

98. S. Davies, pp. 225–6.

99. Wright Robinson, unpublished papers, undated, but probably early December 1923.

100. Wright Robinson, unpublished papers, June 1922.

101. Ibid., May 1923.

102. Ibid., December 1923.

4 ARRIVAL — ELLEN WILKINSON, MP — 'LITTLE MISS PERKY'

Our Ellen — 'A Splendid Candidate'

You young school girls don't know anything — C.F. Masterman, to Ellen in 1923
Middlesbrough was a book of illustrations to Karl Marx — Ellen

When Ellen fought and won Middlesbrough East, women under thirty were still disenfranchised. She herself looked so young at thirty-three that a liberal candidate, C.F. Masterman, had evaded replying to her election questions 'because you young school girls don't know anything'. Subsequently he apologised, but even at her own meetings 'the Tories tried to persuade the electors that I wasn't old enough to vote'.[1]

In ten years Ellen had travelled a meteoric course from being an unknown ILP member and suffrage worker in Manchester to becoming a union-sponsored parliamentary candidate. It would have been a triumph for any aspiring socialist: for a woman it was exceptional. She had never claimed to be an intellectual, but there were few left-wing organisations of the day with which she had not been associated and which had not helped mould her political beliefs. Firmly established in her trade union, Ellen held definite views about the conflict within capitalist society and the international ramifications of that conflict. The inadequacy of provision for the unemployed and their families, and the iniquities of the Poor Law were intolerable. Society must be changed not only to tackle these problems, but also in its attitude to women. Despite her strong links with the male chauvinistic trade union world (few unions were as enlightened and progressive as NUDAW), her feminism was more strongly entrenched than ever. And her pacifism was undimmed.

The fact that so much had to be put right in society — and so urgently — explains in part why Ellen found the idea of becoming an MP attractive. It is doubtful whether she ever deliberately mapped out her career in advance — she was far too impulsive.[2] She did however recognise opportunity when it came her way. When the chance came to stand for Middlesbrough East she seized it, and NUDAW with its forces of money and manpower stood four square behind her.

'What a town to have the privilege of fighting', she wrote. 'Here capitalism reveals all its hard ugliness and the struggle for bread is bitter. Middlesbrough is a book of illustrations to Karl Marx.'[3] The constituency with its iron and steel works and shipbuilding, and its developing chemical works (which so interested Walton Newbold) had had 'a great iron master and liberal,' Penry Williams, as its MP almost uninterruptedly since 1910. With 10,000 unemployed out of a total population of 136,000, a rising incidence of death from TB and infant mortality well above the average, Middlesbrough East desperately needed a Member of Ellen's calibre.

She was selected in April 1924 for this tough male-dominated industrial area, chosen because 'the people were fair-minded and genuinely judged her on merit'.[4] In the constituency Ellen is still remembered for her energy and understanding:

> She held house and street meetings, raced around to get herself known, and was a stickler for getting things done properly. She understood the poverty of working class life . . . talked with people in their homes unravelling problems, and presented issues to them so they really understood . . . To her people were always equal . . . she was the best Member that we ever had. The unemployed in particular thought she was marvellous . . . She got her teeth into everything.'[5]

Ellen warmed to her constituency: 'Labour has a magnificent body of workers here — men write canvas cards far into the night and women are out in the streets full of hope and pep . . . They earned our success, although the victory would not have been possible without Jack Beilby the most invincible optimist on our USDAW staff . . . [and others] and our Transport Department under Harold Wilkinson [her brother] and Edgar Jagger . . . keeping us in fits of laughter . . . it was a young people's election'.[6]

Ellen was undoubtedly a popular candidate. Local feminist Alice Schofield Coates found her 'splendid . . . unsparing of herself and full of sound logic. Her meetings are always crowded and her audiences delighted. The constituency is mostly working class and the people soon claimed her as "Our Ellen".'[7]

But good organisation and a good candidate were not enough. Ellen had to present a strong policy, which she did, advocating first and foremost the expansion of trade with Russia which, she argued, could assist the North East economically and ease unemployment. On this she was vigorously supported at meetings by John Jagger and union colleagues. NUDAW had long favoured rapprochement, and in Middlesbrough, a heavily industrialised town suffering severe unemployment, the anti-Russian spectre found little credence. 'The fight was on the Russian Treaty . . . we faced the issues and I believe that was our main strength', Ellen wrote, 'we gloried in it and neutralised the effect of the bogey man'.[8]

At the declaration of the poll the market place was a living mass of humanity shouting themselves hoarse with 'Good Old Ellen.' She had indeed pulled off a remarkable coup in defeating Penry Williams,[9] reversing his sizeable Liberal majority at a time when the national tide was flowing strongly against Labour. She became one of only four women Members in the House. This was an achievement which would have thrilled someone far more phlegmatic than the 'Fiery Atom'.

Middlesbrough East was won for Labour against heavy political odds, for anti-Russian as well as anti-socialist propaganda had been rife long before the election. The minority Labour government had recognised the Soviet government and opened up trade negotiations. Russia had been promised a loan and both countries agreed to live in peace and amity.[10] But such 'pro-Russian' policies were anathema to the Conservatives. Anti-Russian — and therefore anti-Labour — sentiment had been exacerbated in the summer of 1924 by the Campbell case, which centred on the arrest of J.R. Campbell, the acting editor of the communist *'Workers' Weekly'*. He was charged with sedition under an obsolescent Act of 1797 for an article urging soldiers not to fire on their fellow workers in industrial disputes or in war. This had been written, he later explained, 'not to embarrass the Labour Government, but as part of the Communist Party's anti-militarist campaign on the tenth anniversary of the World War.'[11] The case was whipped up into a cause célèbre. Then came a bombshell: (Sir) Patrick Hastings, the Solicitor General, announced that the prosecution was to be dropped. He insisted that this had been his own decision — though he had in fact consulted the Prime Minister and the Home Secretary. MacDonald turned the issue into a vote of confidence which Conservatives and Liberals united to reject. The first Labour government was defeated.

Hostility towards Labour candidates was also fuelled by the Zinoviev 'Red' letter, published in the *Daily Mail* shortly before polling day. It purported to be from Zinoviev, President of the Communist International, and to contain detailed instructions on revolutionary schemes.[12] There had been rumours that some stunt against the Labour government was being made ready,[13] but the Prime Minister, submerged in electioneering far from London, was 'inexpressively inept and dilatory' in handling the affair. The Foreign Office made the document public before checking its authenticity, although as Professor Mowat, among many, concluded, 'it was all too pat and contained every thing the professional anti-Bolshevist could want'.[14] It has eventually been established that the letter was certainly a forgery perpetrated by 'a group of reckless Russian emigrés in Berlin and planted on the international intelligence network to reach the Foreign Office as authentic, with copies forwarded to the *Daily Mail* and the Tory Central Office to ensure the maximum impact'.[15] This it certainly did. Over 400 Tory Members were elected in October 1924 against 42 Liberals and 152 Labour — one of whom, however, was the member for Middlesbrough East.

The House of Commons

Ellen's arrival in the House was heralded by a fanfare of press trumpets. Although she held convictions highly unpopular with the Establishment, as the only woman on the Labour benches, and as the youngest and the most attractive Member, she was accorded fulsome publicity. Even more so than that given to Lady Astor (the first woman to take her seat) with whom Ellen became friendly.[16]

The suffragists were eulogistic. Ellen 'had won a notable triumph for her sex and her party, even though she represented the extreme wing of the Labour Movement'. She was a 'vigorous, uncompromising feminist and an exceedingly tenacious, forcible and hard headed politician', the *Woman's Leader* crowed triumphantly.[17] *The Times* found her eye catching, as the first woman MP to wear a brightly coloured dress and shingled hair, adding: 'the advent seems almost worthy of a commemorative mural painting in the lobby by Sir William Orphen, alongside that of Queen Elizabeth, as both have

the same attractive shade of bright red hair'.[18] Tribute came also
from the *Daily Telegraph*:

> Since the late Keir Hardie startled the House with a yellow tussore
> suit and cummerbund there has been no such sartorial effort at
> brightening up the House. The Member for Middlesbrough East
> has hair of a 'stunning' hue . . . And this shone like an aureole
> above the light Botticelli green of her dress. It was a complete
> breakaway from the sober black and white which earlier lady
> Members adopted. And why not? Is not the Labour Party the
> party for colour and vivacity?[19]

After a few weeks Ellen formulated some positive, if superficial,
impressions. Not least over the 'polite way in which men say cutting
things in the House [where] they have developed to the highest
degree the art of being thoroughly nasty with perfect politeness'.[20]
Her anger was always simmering and after the formal Opening of
Parliament she denounced the jewels worn in the House of Lords
which made

> a terrible contrast to the poverty of the masses who had elected the
> House of Commons. . . . They were out of keeping with the
> appeal in the King's Speech for 'economy' which under a Conser-
> vative government means economy in the great public services
> . . . in the face of our terrible social problems.[21]

Ellen would have been less than human not to have relished the
initial ballyhoo over her victory. Soon however the plaudits irked
and she became irritated by the innumerable references to her hair,
height, or clothes:

> Journalists seem more interested in whether I will quarrel with
> Lady Astor than with the solid hard work I have come to Parlia-
> ment to do. Yet the Labour Party's having only one woman in the
> House is not a matter of mere interest, but something for every-
> one of us to be ashamed of,

she wrote more angrily than grammatically.[22] Wisely she appreciated
the dangers of becoming a 'pet lamb' and always gave priority to 'my
important industrial constituency . . . I have women's interests to
look after, but I do not want to be regarded purely as a woman's MP

. . . men voters predominate in Middlesbrough East, thousands are unemployed and I mean to stand up to the gruelling work for all their sakes.'[23]

In Parliament Ellen started as she intended to go on: by being fiercely contentious. She made her debut soon after the King's Speech, because 'I am keen to take part in the rough and tumble of debate'. This was flying in the face of tradition — maiden speeches then were expected to be unprovocative and made after a period of time — but it was never Ellen's way to play the modest violet. She delivered a vigorous forthright speech, identified her major interests and earned wide commendation because it bore, so clearly, the hallmark of firsthand experience. Feminism took priority. As one of the 'Four Orphan's of the Storm' (a topical reference to a current popular film), she deplored the government's failure to extend the franchise to women under 30, 'because women with no vote are so neglected'.[24] She attacked the limitations on unemployment benefit which penalised women but not men; the lack of effort to find new outlets for their work, and she urged the need to extend the Trade Boards Inspectorate because 'everyone knows that there is wholesale evasion of the Act'. She also criticised new proposals affecting widows' pensions which placed heavy financial contributions on working women, and concluded that the whole tendency of society was 'to neglect the interests of those who have no vote'.[25]

Ellen passed the ordeal of a maiden speech, said Commander Kenworthy, 'with flaming colours', and even Rhys Davies condescendingly deemed it 'one of the neatest little maiden speeches I have heard from a woman in the House'. Nevertheless, there was no love lost between Ellen and Rhys Davies, a fellow NUDAW MP. On one occasion when they disagreed over a Tote Bill Ellen accused him of 'neglecting the unemployment question for totalisation'.[26] This he countered by referring to the 'self styled intelligentsia who had entered the Labour Movement recently' (quite untrue). Ellen however had the last word and denounced 'Mr Davies' ideas' of Labour Party activities 'as the clotted mixture of the cream and honey kind'.[27] He was not the only male Member resistant to Ellen's charm. On one occasion she so annoyed the Tory Member for Dulwich by her interjections at Question Time that he irritably dubbed her 'Little Miss Perky', to Ellen's intense mirth. The nickname stuck, and for a while it delighted the press.[28]

The excitement of personal triumph in no way diminished Ellen's sense of responsibility to her union. 'Much of my time must necessarily be given to political work, but whenever it would be useful to have an MP on the stomp I shall always be glad to weigh in.'[29] And she meant it. In April 1925 Wright Robinson wrote approvingly of Ellen's help in settling a great Co-operative lock-out in the North-west. Ellen was summoned to help for five strenuous days when satisfactory arbitration machinery was established, 'after which,' to quote Ellen, 'Parliament seemed like a rest cure'.[30]

In spite of her immense vitality, good health (at that time), and enthusiasm for helping any socialist cause, Ellen soon found that

> an MP's life was not all beer and skittles. Because of their large majority the Tories can work in two shifts and still vote us down. In one week we sat till four on three nights. Starting at 10am there were party meetings, committees, masses of correspondence, interviews with delegations, public meetings and seeing constituents. Physical strength will not permit one to act as general propagandist and trade union official as well . . . but fortunately there's a long recess for rest and work.[31]

She became somewhat impatient with the lack of understanding displayed by the rank and file and observed tartly that Members should have time to do some research, 'for the Parliamentary Labour Party's crying need is for better speeches with facts in them . . . The furious letters showered on MPs who refuse invitations to speak show how little the party realises what we are up against.'[32]

If she was irritated by the lack of understanding from 'outside' she became despondent at the 'paralysing difficulties' within the Parliamentary Labour Party itself. Therein she discerned a 'fundamental divergence between a large section, content to be the official opposition and never to think outside the limits and the much smaller but articulate section who think in terms of attack'.[33] This was a direct reference to the Clydesiders 'Ginger Group' which included James Maxton, George Buchanan, Emanuel Shinwell, David Kirkwood and John Wheatley. The group firmly believed that they had been sent to Parliament to challenge the old order of things at every turn, to replace it by a new society, and to demonstrate that the Labour Party was as different as possible from any other.[34] It not surprisingly was anathema to Ramsay MacDonald, concerned only to convince the electorate of Labour's political respectability.

On occasion, probably when tired, Ellen found the effect of the strangulating Tory majority really depressing. 'Nothing seems any good. Members grow indifferent, and to those who come into the House to contest the terrible poverty of the distressed areas, our impotence is heartbreaking,' she wrote early in 1926.[35]

This feeling of helplessness drove her to raise the question of parliamentary tactics. At the Labour Party conference that year, arguing that the PLP should 'put up a much harder fight' in the House, Ellen suggested, as 'older Members find it difficult to sit up all night, some kind of relay system might be devised,' although she opposed any agreements with the other side over legislative matters. On this George Buchanan strongly supported her, although he held that 'on big issues we ought not [necessarily] to fight constitutionally'. In his reply MacDonald rounded on Ellen but answered few of her accusations.[36] There was great animosity between these two. MacDonald regarded her as a 'trouble maker who asks awkward questions which should have been reserved for the more private ear of the PLP', and Ellen scorned him for his political ambiguity.

Whatever her private feelings, outwardly Ellen was active, optimistic, determined. She was an exceedingly conscientious Member, and drove herself mercilessly outside as well as in the House. It was to the benefit of her constituency that freedom from domestic ties enabled her to be so single-minded. Her political obligations were as varied as they were geographically diverse. During the early part of 1925, for example, she was up in Middlesbrough at least once a month, and enjoyed this, not only for the warm rapport she had with her constituents, but also because she could get so much reading and writing done on the journey! In February she spoke in South Shields for the Durham County Elections, in the Albert Hall at an LCC election jamboree — the year Herbert Morrison became leader of the official LCC Labour opposition — and canvassed Covent Garden porters 'in the early hours' for the same cause. In March she flew to Paris — she was an early and enthusiastic advocate of air travel — to attend a Human Rights protest meeting of French Radicals. This was followed by a regional conference of Labour Parties in Middlesbrough, an NCLC meeting in Norwich, and at the end of March a speech to the Manchester branch of the WIL. At the same time she was helping to settle the Co-operative lock-out. Towards the end of April she addressed the ILP in Derby, the Middlesbrough Unemployment Committee and the Women's Engineering Society. Before the summer recess she also took part in a 1,000-strong Labour Party procession in Gateshead and held a massive open-air meeting in

Middlesbrough.[37] This sample of typical activities was in addition to commitments in the House!

The Lighter Side

Not all Ellen's parliamentary forays were either solemn or sectarian. She had not been long in the House before she began a protest over the cramped working conditions of women MPs. At that time three of the four women Members — Ellen, Lady Astor and Mrs Philipson — shared one small room. The Duchess of Atholl, as junior minister, had an office of her own. Their room was described as a 'boudoir', though 'the only suggestion of a boudoir was a small looking glass' which Ellen could only reach by standing on a chair!

> Really rather like a tomb . . . Yet this was where much hard work had to be done and all dictating to our secretaries. We should have something larger . . . Often we are in the House from ten in the morning to midnight, with frequent all-night sittings . . . baths are provided for the men, but not for us. So until there are more women Members to justify structural alterations I'm afraid we will have to go unbathed.[38]

As a member of the Kitchen Committee she promised to press for improvements, but change came slowly. Even when there were eight women MPs, there was not even a chair apiece in the room and only one hook for all clothes. The lavatory was a circuitous walk of a quarter of a mile if a Division were on.[39] The battle for accommodation was not really resolved until 1929 when the 14 women Members were allocated a new room, but even so they had no bathroom of their own! To the responsible official, 'They come here as Members, not as women, and are supposed to share everything with other Members!'[40]

The protocol that restricted the dining arrangements for women must have been as frustrating as their inadequate working accommodation. By tradition no MP male or female might then take women guests into the Strangers' Dining Room: women could only be 'entertained' in the more expensive Harcourt Room. Ellen long fought this. But it was not until late in 1928, *after* equal franchise became law, that the Kitchen Committee removed the restriction

— a concession also extended to those who worked as secretaries to ministers and to Opposition leaders.[41] The irony of Ellen's victory was that although lady guests could be entertained to dinner they still had to wait before that right was extended to lunch.[42] There was however a pleasant postscript to Ellen's victory. Late in December 1928 'as a New Year's gift' a group of all-party MPs presented her with an automatic gas cooker 'as a mark of appreciation for her victory over traditional eating restrictions'. Four years' fight had brought a dual reward!

Small human matters, to which male Members were oblivious, often caught Ellen's attention. She questioned ministers about the hours that the police worked during all-night sittings, asked whether officers on duty in the lobbies ought not to have chairs, and challenged the conditions of catering staff, who, she was appalled to discover, were unpaid during recess, then six or seven months long. Ellen was as concerned for these men and women who had to work and live *behind* the parliamentary headlines as she was for those who actually *made* them.

As Ellen became more widely known her political commitments in the country expanded. Each year came the unavoidable call of conferences. She raced round the country, helping any friend standing in an election anywhere, explaining Parliamentary Bills she was opposing, or panaceas she was propounding. She visited Middlesbrough as often as she could and cherished her constituents. On one occasion she fell foul of Dr Dingle, Middlesbrough's Medical Officer of Health, for allegedly misrepresenting the incidence of disease in her constituency. She remained however undeterred, asserting defiantly: 'I am fighting the system that produces this suffering; it is my public duty to call attention to things as they are even if people in authority are being made uncomfortable.'

Puck-like Ellen girdled Britain, and, long after her sustained exertions during the General Strike, she drove herself unsparingly through work-crowded parliamentary sessions. Even when she broke down and was ordered 'a long rest' she recuperated in Devon and returned to the House in three weeks! Her energy was such that when during the autumn of 1928 a general election was rumoured she is reported to have visited homes of 1,000 constituents in 10 days.[43] This sounds superhuman even for Ellen but, whether this story is apocryphal or not, her sense of commitment was boundless.

Apart from her personal magnetism Ellen had a virtually priceless political weapon in her voice. She developed great speaking ability which coupled with a sense of the dramatic, she used to immense effect:

> In her voice was power and music with a tone like that of a well cast bell [eulogised fellow MP Jack Lawson], and she knew how to use it at mighty conferences, open air demonstrations, indoor meetings, or in the House . . . even though the despatch box was too high for her, and she had to stand aside from it.[44]

Ellen could work her audience into a frenzy. A neighbour described how 'she looked half asleep but could become electric; project the image she wanted and by her magical quality start an explosion.'[45]

Her skill was not always free of guile! 'She has histrionic ability of no mean quality and can turn her diminutive stature into a powerful asset for capturing sympathy', wrote a discerning critic.

> When chairing a huge demonstration she takes the platform, a frail wisp, clad in a simple gown with a demure puritan collar . . . She seats herself almost lost in a great chair, tiny feet dangling. Such a forlorn child-like figure . . . 'Ellen is over doing it' remarked a delegate. And in this there is a grain of truth but in public life today women must act a little.[46]

Ellen, nearly 40 at the time this comment was made, knew very well what she was about.

Her voice could however, in all sincerity, break down. For Ellen was a bundle of high emotionalism and would unashamedly weep in public or in the House. Dame Mabel Tylecote, the distinguished educationalist, remembers her speaking in Manchester on Spain and 'becoming so distraught over questions that she begged me to stop the meeting. This I did and Ellen burst into tears.' Like everything about her that voice was distinctive. 'It could be strident, it could be compelling. It was a tongue that scorched or dropped speech like gentle rain.'[47]

The General Strike — 'A Magnificent Generation'

The General Strike of 1926, that 'great and dramatic event', ineluctably drew Ellen into action with her fellow trade unionists and even took precedence, albeit temporarily, over her parliamentary commitments. The miners were striking to resist cuts in wages and working hours, which in the face of falling trade the owners were seeking to impose. Unlike the lock-out of 1921 when the miners looked in vain for help from their partners in the Triple Alliance (the Railway and Transport Workers' Unions), the General Strike at the outset was heralded by a remarkable display of unity within the Labour Movement.[48]

In spite of delaying tactics adopted by the Government and an amazing lack of forward planning by the TUC — it was the government who built up massive coal reserves and perfected their Organisation and Maintenance of Supplies (OMS)[49] — there was solid support for the miners from the grassroots. Hence Ernest Bevin's proud reference to 'A magnificent Generation' at the May Day meeting in London when the TUC was given an unequivocal mandate to call a General Strike. An exultant Ellen described the enthusiasm which swept the Labour ranks: for she was both participator in, and chronicler of, the Great Strike through the pages of *Clash*. In this novel she recounts the strike through the eyes of the main character Joan — 'a living red flag, the spirit of revolution' — who just happened to be a trade union organiser holding principles similar to those of the author.

Sitting in the gallery of the Memorial Hall meeting (as Ellen herself had done) at which the fateful decision to strike was made, Joan's account is evocative and clearly autobiographical:

The atmosphere was bubbling with excitement . . . the strike call would mean to some the losses of jobs held for a lifetime . . . others would jeopardise pensions . . . all would risk the livelihood of their families . . . the platform of leaders of the TUC [were] decent kindly men whose last thought was any real desire to upset the present system . . . Yet the revolutionary germ was there . . . A roll was read of all the unions. The General Secretary of each had to say 'for' or 'against' a general strike to aid the miners . . . The tension became unbearable. Eventually 3½ million 'for', barely 50,000 'against'.

Ellen continued, describing Ernie Bevin:

a great rough-hewn fellow, a transport workers' leader, who had started selling ginger beer from a cart . . . one of the ablest of the younger trade unionists . . . who in quiet tones concluded, 'We look upon your "yes" as having laid your all upon the altar for the great movement . . . History will ultimately write that it was a magnificent generation that was prepared to do it'.[50]

Of course Ellen became actively involved. Early in May, with her friend Frank Horrabin, she was sent by the TUC to tour the country, to hearten the strikers, organise meetings and assess morale. Like Joan, 'whose great value was her knowledge of the industrial North,' Ellen assumed responsibility for getting speakers and instructors conveyed north of the Humber. The major concern they found was lack of communications. Printing presses had been stilled. 'News' was disseminated only through the 'scurrilous' *British Gazette* broadsheet edited by Winston Churchill (which in its first issue so tactfully gave particulars of the latest wills!),[51] the patchily distributed *British Worker*[52], and the government controlled radio. Reliable communication between the many scattered Workers' Committees depended solely on human links and on 7 May Ellen and Horrabin had sent a report to the General Council: 'Position absolutely solid, but local movements demand news. We urge publication of local strike paper. NUDAW head office has placed private press at the disposal of the Strike Committee.'[53]

The nine extraordinary days of the 'Great Silence' made high political drama. But nothing was more remarkable than the solidarity of the workers and the latent ability revealed. Margaret Cole recorded not only the peaceable character of the whole brief struggle, but also the 'quantity of organising ability disclosed among the rank and file who manned the local Trades Councils and Strike Committees'.[54] Joan similarly commented: 'It just showed what ability was running to waste . . . Crewe, Coventry and a score of towns are being run by sheer soviets.'[55]

As the TUC had made no contingency plans the workers had much to do. 'Food and health services were not to be interfered with so they had to issue permits for the transport of food . . . to organise meetings, pickets, intelligence services and news services.'[56] Ellen had no illusions about the basic issues of the strike. 'The trade union movement', she said at Worksop, 'could not allow one section of the workers to be dragged down to a wage below starvation limit. The complete breakdown of private enterprise within the mining industry could only be resolved by nationalisation of the mines'.[57]

After nine days the TUC called the solid ranks back to work. The Labour leaders were not prepared to capitalise on the workers' successes, or to continue challenging the basis of British society. Strikers far and wide, especially in the industrial North, were stunned, angry and unbelieving. The miners however — demanding 'not a penny off the pay, not a minute off the day' — would not capitulate. Incredibly they stayed out fighting until November when they returned on the owners' terms. It had been a morally heroic but materially tragic stand.

A few months later Ellen, Frank Horrabin and Raymond Postgate produced for *Plebs* their fact-packed little book, '*A Workers' History of the Great Strike*'. Its special quality was not so much the white-hot anger in which it was written as the vivid contemporary reports of workers' committees from which the authors quoted. A publication written so close to actual events could scarcely be detached, but the conclusions expressed the assessment of the left. Significant to them was the limited outlook of most trade union leaders who

> refused to realise that the whole working class is engaged in a bitter struggle for its standards of life . . . The corpse at the inquest was not the theory of a General Strike but the nineteenth-century trade union leadership which refused to face up to the class issues of the miners' struggle.[58]

The view of official Labour was totally different, for to the TUC the strike had shown 'the limitations of industrial power' and there were recriminations against the miners. 'Superficially it weakened the Labour movement, bringing apathy, an unwillingness to strike . . . but at bottom and over the years it strengthened the working man's loyalty to . . . his own party . . . For the leaders it confirmed and strengthened all their conservative tendencies.'[59]

The Miners' Relief Fund

Although Ellen accepted a Marxist interpretation of the Strike as expounded in the *Plebs* publication, she saw the immediate struggle in terms not of theory, but of human suffering. For the miners were facing long-term victimisation with resources too small to sustain, let alone to cushion, their families against starvation: 'Only a small minority of the Mining Districts are able to pay lock-out benefit . . . The rest have entirely exhausted their resources after five years of low wages and unemployment . . . and now face sure starvation unless help is given.'[60]

As mining villages became virtually famine areas Labour women moved into action. A national appeal was launched to assist miners' families in kind. Supported by stalwarts such as Margaret Bondfield, Susan Lawrence, Margaret Llewellyn Davies and Barbara Ayrton Gould, the Women's Committee for Relief of Miners' Wives and Children came into being with Ellen as Chairman.[61] Every possible fund-raising tactic was employed, from capitalising on the Prince of Wales' donation (which had been accompanied by a note: 'HRH cannot take sides but we owe a debt to the miners'[62]), to a massive Albert Hall rally organised by *Lansbury's Labour Weekly*. The Miners' Choir raised money by touring Britain, Germany and Russia, and one-inch reproductions of miners' lamps were sold with great success,[63] all of which helped the local Women's Committees to assist needy families.

'The indefensible skinflint attitudes of local authorities towards the miners' was exposed by Susan Lawrence, MP (a friend of Ellen's) who on behalf of the Committee collated material from all over Britain. She found that relief paid to miners' families averaged 12s a week and 4s for each child, but was in many cases much lower. Although many families still had debts from the 1921 strike, poor relief was usually only given on *loan*. Official assistance in no way modified human misery. Yet the Minister of Health told the House that it was 'no duty of mine to see that the relief is adequate'.[64]

It had to come. Ellen was asked to make a fund-raising trip to the United States of America. The Miners' Federation decided to send a delegation from both the TUC and the Women's Committee in, of all months, August. The Committee felt it was not good for her as the heat was so great and she badly needed a rest, but of course she went, together with Ben Tillett and other trade unionists.[65] On their arrival they were confronted by Baldwin's widely publicised statement which denied the existence of starvation or malnutrition in Britain's mining districts. This was so blatantly false as to be risible and the American Federation of Labour, who had invited the delegation, gave it no credence.

Ellen found their American comrades warm-hearted to a degree, but the tour was exhausting. Nevertheless, her personal appeals, her tales of the 'kids at a soup kitchen in the rain who refused to return home to keep dry "because Miss, we like the smell" '[66] won widespread press coverage and extracted generous contributions. Both

Marion Phillips and Ellen considered that the effort had been 'well worth the making'.

From the fateful May to the end of January 1927 the Women's Committee raised in all the 'miraculous' sum of over £310,000 (over £3 million at 1980 prices). As A.J. Cook commented, 'The Labour women cared for humanity, whereas the Baldwin Government tried to starve our people.'[67]

'Tugging my Put'

Righteous anger, impulsiveness and a sense of the dramtic often got Ellen into trouble. During the miners' lock-out, she was much criticised for an article in *Lansbury's Labour Weekly* in which, exposing conditions in the Somerset mines, she described men 'dragging tubs with ropes round their waists and chains between their legs'. Her furious account of these conditions was vindicated during the Second Reading of the Coal Mines (Hours) Bill, when she produced in the House the contraption — the guss — to which she had referred. 'This is being worn by miners not sixty years ago, but on the 30th April this year,' she raged, and held up for all Members to see the coil of rope which went round miner's (often) bare legs, and the hook which fitted on to the tub they dragged along.[68] She also read from a miner's letter describing how 'many a time I've scraggled along on my belly with the guss on, tugging my put [barrow of coal] more than 20 yards with only nine inches between floor and roof'.[69] 'Miss Wilkinson', remarked the *Daily Chronicle*, 'has caused something of a sensation. Exhibiting the hauling rope has drama in common with Mr Burke's display of a dagger during his speech on the French Revolution, or Mr Haldane's flourishment of a cordite walking stick.'[70]

The Bill was thunderously attacked by the Labour Members. Ellen expressed their deep hostility in stating that 'If Members only realised that mining conditions were scarcely fit for beasts they would be deciding how wages could be raised, not how hours could be extended. Yet all you can say is let them work longer so that your profits can be safeguarded. It is abominable.'[71] The Bill was passed, though not before Ellen had made a final defiant thrust: 'The men who vote for this Bill ought not to sleep in their beds until they have done for their country what miners are doing for it every day of their lives.'[72]

Notes

1. Fred Meadowcroft interview; *New Dawn*, 8 November 1924.

2. Dame Margaret Cole, interviews.

3. *New Dawn*, 25 October 1924.

4. Mrs Turner, interview.

5. Jack Feeney and Mrs Godfrey, interviews.

6. *New Dawn*, 8 November 1924.

7. Mrs Schofield Coates, in *The Vote*, 7 November 1924.

8. *New Dawn*, 8 November 1924; *Clarion* 12 December 1924; Jack Beilby in *New Dawn*, 8 November, 1924.

9. Penry Williams had been MP for Middlesbrough East with one break since 1910. There was, however, a local saying that 'when Penry Williams gets in, the men and the furnaces go out'. This was quoted to the author by both Mrs Godfrey and Mrs Turner (February 1978) independently of each other, and implied his unpopularity with Labour supporters.

10. C.L. Mowat, *Britain Between the Wars* (Faber and Faber, London, 1968), p. 182.

11. J.R. Campbell, *Labour Monthly*, November 1924.

12. James Margach, *Abuse of Power* (W.H. Allen, London, 1978), Star edn, Ch. III, p. 43.

13. Mowat, *Britain*, p. 187.

14. Ibid., pp. 187–94.

15. Margach, p. 43.

16. Beryl Hughes, The Hon. David Astor, interviews; Christopher Sykes, *Nancy* (Collins, London, 1972), Panther edn, 1979, p. 280.

17. *Women's Leader*, 7 November 1924.

18. *The Times*, 12 February 1925.

19. *Daily Telegraph*, 12 February 1925.

20. *Evening Standard*, 10 December 1924.

21. *Yorkshire Evening News*, 10 December 1924.

22. *Labour Magazine*, January 1925.

23. *Yorkshire Evening News*, 10 December 1924.

24. *Yorkshire Evening News* and (London) *Evening Standard*, both 10 December 1924.

25. Hansard Vol. 179, cols. 242–5, 10 December 1924.

26. *Sheffield Telegraph*, 24 August 1928.

27. *New Leader*, 28 August 1928.

28. Hansard Vol. 199, cols. 392–3, 28 September 1926.

29. *New Dawn*, 8 November 1924.

30. Wright Robinson, unpublished papers, April 1925.

31. *New Dawn*, 20 June 1925.

32. *Lansbury's Labour Weekly*, 11 March 1925.

33. *Lansbury's Labour Weekly*, 25 February 1925.

34. Francis Williams, *A Pattern of Rulers* (Longmans, London, 1965), pp. 77–8.

35. *Plebs*, 1 January 1926.

36. Labour Party Conference Annual Report, 1926, pp. 243–5.

37. Ellen Wilkinson's books of parliamentary cuttings (Labour Party Library).

38. *Liverpool Express*, 20 April 1926.

39. *Evening Standard*, 20 March 1927.

40. *Glasgow Bulletin*, 19 June 1929.

41. *Daily News*, 16 November 1928.

42. The Speaker ruled that lady guests could in future be entertained to dinner but not to lunch in the Strangers' Dining Room. 'Do not women need luncheon, too?'

demanded Lady Astor, but the Speaker pleaded shortage of accommodation. To celebrate her victory Ellen Wilkinson entertained a party of women guests, which included Miss Rosenberg, to dinner in the Strangers' Dining Room a few evenings later. According to the Daily News of 13 December 1928 'the unwarranted sight of lady guests there caused one member, the Reverend Herbert Dunnico, to pause on the threshold exclaiming "God bless my soul". The celebration dinner was both vegetarian and non-alcoholic.' Pamela Brookes, *Women at Westminster* (Peter Davies, London, 1967), p. 64.

43. *Northern Echo*, 28 September 1928.

44. Jack Lawson, MP in *Methodist Magazine*, April 1947.

45. Fred Meadowcroft, interview.

46. *Glasgow Record*, 7 October 1929.

47. Mary Agnes Hamilton, *Spectator*, 24 August 1945.

48. Cole and Postgate, *The Common People, 1746–1938* (Methuen, London, 1938), p. 549; Mowat, p. 284, See Mowat, pp. 285–331 for a brilliant exposition of the strike.

49. Ellen Wilkinson, *Clash*, p. 59; 'The OMS . . . had all the powers of the state without any of its constitutional checks.'

50. Ibid., pp. 56–61.

51. Ibid., p. 119.

52. From Oxford Hugh Gaitskell, Margaret Cole and John Dugdale among many helped in the distribution — M. Cole, *Growing Up Into Revolution* (Longmans, Green, London, 1926), p. 123.

53. TUC Library, HD–5366.

54. M. Cole, *Growing Up*, p. 122.

55. Ellen Wilkinson, *Clash*, p. 133.

56. M. Cole, *Growing Up*, p. 122.

57. *Worksop Guardian*, 14 May 1925.

58. J.F. Horrabin, R. Postgate, and E. Wilkinson, *A Worker's History of the Great Strike* (Plebs League, London, 1927) pp. 102–3.

59. Mowat, pp. 330–1.

60. *Daily News*, 24 May 1926.

61. *Yorkshire Post*, 22 May 1926.

62. M. Phillips, pamphlet, *Women in the Miners' Lockout* (Labour Publishing Company, London, 1927 p. 21); the note continued: 'it would be an unsatisfactory end to any dispute that one side should have to give in on account of the sufferings of their dependents'.

63. Ibid., p. 40; Miniature reproductions are still obtainable at the Beamish North of England Museum, County Durham.

64. Ibid., pp. 47–9.

65. Ibid., pp. 90–1.

66. *Chicago Worker*, 27 August 1926.

67. Phillips, p. 23; A.J. Cook was the General Secretary of the Miners' Federation.

68. *Bristol Observer*, 3 July 1926.

69. Hansard, Vol. 197, cols. 1022–7, 29 June 1926.

70. *Daily Chronicle*, 3 July 1926.

71. Hansard, Vol. 197, col. 1027, 29 June 1926.

72. *Bristol Observer*, 3 July 1926; Hansard, Vol. 197, col. 1027, 29 June, 1926.

5   ATTITUDES

'The most miniature and sagacious little witch with the ornamental hair — Topsy MP' (A.P. Herbert)

Feminism and the Parliamentary Grind

Ellen was a wonderful feminist; fearless, consistent and never losing a chance to promote opportunities for women to gain equality — Mrs Hazel Hunkins Hallinan

Women have worked hard; starved in prison; given of their time and lives that we might sit in the House of Commons and take part in the legislating of this country . . . this is the closing of a great drama — Ellen, on the passing of the Representation of the People (Equal Franchise) Act, March, 1928

As a feminist Ellen never made the mistake of assuming that her arrival in Parliament was an end in itself. Though her constituents were of cardinal concern, she seized every opportunity to promote the rights of women. Her contributions to debate, the questions with which she peppered ministers, revealed a parliamentary skill, a capacity to brief herself with telling material — in which NUDAW from time to time assisted — and a doggedness in pursuing matters of principle. Above all she had an ability to translate bald facts into human situations and to expose administrative incompetence. One such occasion arose at the committee stage of the Board of Guardians (Default) Bill. Ellen cited the case of a women who had had to go to the work house without her 'box' which contained all her earthly possessions, because her landlady had retained it as security for the rent, for which the Guardians would not pay. In recounting this one vivid incident she exposed administrative harshness and all its insensitive inflexibility.[1]

Ellen made sustained contributions in committees and in debate, notably on the Widows' and Orphans' Pensions and the Unemployment Insurance Bills. The Widows' Bill was full of anomalies and in many respects patently prejudiced. With her colleagues Ellen fought long and hard to modify its injustices. She argued for the widow whose husband had 'paid in' for years, but who received nothing unless her children were under 14 years old, for the two million unmarried women mostly wage earners, who had contributed all their lives yet only received their old age pension at 65 if they remained at work until that age, and for adequate provision for mothers with young children.

Interlaced with amendments and endless debate on this Bill were controversies over the Unemployment Insurance Bill, and in particular the means test which made such bitter impact in breaking up families, driving the young from home and undermining a man's self respect. The needs of Middlesbrough were never far from her mind. In a censure motion castigating the government for its failure to act over the unprecedented gravity of the industrial depression, Ellen argued yet again that trade with Russia could offer real hope for alleviating unemployment. She urged the extension of credit facilities which would be used by the Soviet Union to purchase heavy capital equipment.

Ellen had never laid claim to being an expert on education. She was, however, alert to any deficiency which especially affected women and children. Her challenge to the President of the Board of Education over 'the existence of classes of 60 in many schools when there are empty rooms and unemployed teachers', was as opportune as her prodding over a Departmental circular substantially reducing expenditure on nursery education. She pleaded for taking children 'out of the grime, horror and ugliness of our big industrial cities and giving them bright nursery conditions on which to lay the foundation of those social habits which make good citizens'. She ended her tirade peacefully, welcoming the appointment of the Duchess of Atholl, her future ally during the Spanish Civil War, as Parliamentary Secretary to the Board of Education. Speaking with uncanny foresight, Ellen concluded 'Many of us feel that of all the services where a woman can be of use it is in the sphere of education.'[2]

On feminist matters Ellen never missed a trick. She challenged the Minister of Health to exclude women from oakum picking under the Casual Poor (Relief) Order as it had been 'condemned long ago for its soul deadening effects',[3] and battled hard to get more women police appointed, having elicited that there were only 85 such officers in the whole country. Backed by the National Union of Societies for Equal Citizenship (representing some 30 women's organisations), she tried to amend the Municipal Corporation Act so that all authorities would have to employ women in their police forces. She was backed from all sides of the House.[4] The Home Secretary, Sir William Joynson Hicks, was not unsympathetic but retreated behind the argument of respecting the autonomy of local authorities. He conceded that there was value in women police handling offences against women and children, but an economy axe decimated even the few numbers of women who were then employed[5] and Ellen's Bill made little progress. When much later three women were appointed to the permanent staff of the CID there was jubilation among the feminists, as this opened doors to a new career for women.[6] The question of women police recruitment emanated from an attempt, partly orchestrated by Ellen when still on the council, to enrol more women in the Manchester force. This was rejected because, she alleged, 'of the prejudice of the Chief Constable and older members of the Watch Committee'.[7]

Nothing affecting women was too insignificant for Ellen's attention. She exposed the iniquitous decision refusing pensions to nursing staff who had suffered mental breakdowns from war service; derided the illogicality of women being barred from the diplomatic corps on grounds of their alleged inability to keep a secret as a 'relic of masculine prejudice'[8]; conducted a protracted, ultimately triumphant, campaign to enable British women who married aliens to retain their British citizenship; [9] chided the government for not appointing a working-class woman to serve on the Food Commission[10]; and attacked Winston Churchill, when Chancellor of the Exchequer, for taxing cheap artificial silk 'on which working class girls so greatly relied for their clothing'. In a rare instance of parading her learning Ellen then accused Churchill of 'harking back to the fifteenth century when under Sumptuary Laws of Edward VIth silk was taxed because the wives of the burgesses were adopting the manners of the Court!'[11] She trounced Neville Chamberlain for failing to include a woman referee on a Pensions Appeal Tribunal, and when a rather bewildered minister explained that a court of referees was a legal panel of barristers she flashed back 'there are plenty of women barristers now'. That settled Mr Chamberlain: he agreed to give the matter further consideration.[12]

In those early years Ellen must have electrified the House, but in no sense was she a suffrage battleaxe. She was as sensitive to the small unvoiced disadvantages facing women as to their major handicaps. She was not only incensed by the *Daily Express* campaign against the appointment for her friend Mary Agnes Hamilton to the

Board of the BBC conducted on the grounds that as a socialist (and woman) she could not be impartial[13], but also caused a furore by suggesting that the current domestic position of women was tantamount to slavery. 'A man never learns the cash value of a good wife until she falls ill and then he has to pay a housekeeper!'[14] Patient self sacrifice was the great vice of working women. 'What women want of politics and of industry', she told a conference of Labour Women, 'is to be considered as human beings. The clinging ivy theory is out of date.'[15] These views were applauded by Vera Brittain, 'for expressing a remarkable change in standards . . . it is to be hoped that Miss Wilkinson will continue both in and out of Parliament her campaign against the moral slavishness of women.'[16]

Once the illogical injustice of women's disenfranchisement had been resolved, Ellen fought on, demanding economic equality. This she saw as a matter to be resolved, 'not by a scrap between men and women, but by organising women in trade unions'.[17] But more than that she sought to extend women's horizons and their opportunities. As a trade union organiser she urged the Minister of Labour to provide adequate training facilities for women. The prevailing assumption that unemployed women, whatever their trade, could always enter domestic service incensed her, particularly as that work was not covered by insurance benefit.[18]

One of her sustained targets was the inequality in pay and status within the Civil Service. Time and again Ellen pleaded for modification of the Treasury rule that female staff must resign on marriage. She appreciated that 'if a woman's work was merely mechanical any change such as marriage could well be for the better', but for highly trained women the problem was different. 'It made a woman look at a man critically when he became not a refuge from the wretched typewriter' but represented 'just a small home in place of an interesting job'.[19] Ellen scored a clever tactical success in the campaign for Equal Pay. In 1936 she introduced a motion to give the same scales to women as to men in the 'common classes' of the Civil Service. The House of Commons paid men and women the same; Jennie Lee, a recently re-elected Member, she said, received the same basic salary as Lloyd George who had been there forty years. John Jagger (seconding the motion) reminded Members that the House had passed a resolution in 1920 encouraging equality in the Civil Service, surely the time had come to give it effect![20] Ellen's motion was carried narrowly, but after much procedural manoeuvring the Prime Minister turned the issue into a vote of confidence and the decision was reversed. Nevertheless it was a minor victory — the only time that the government had been defeated on Supply since 1931.[21] Treasury attitudes softened during and after the Second World War: the marriage bar was lifted and equality of pay gradually introduced. It was, however, a long haul for qualified women to be employed in the senior posts. 'That silent, invincible masonry of men', as Ellen termed it, writing in *John Bull*, took many moons to conquer. Perhaps one of the biggest nonsenses, she noted in the same article, was Dame Rachel Crowdy's being 'squeezed out from a position in the League of Nations Secretariat to be replaced by two men and a woman!'[22]

The principle of 'equality before the law' was also important to feminists. It certainly affected Ellen's attitude over the abdication saga when she opposed proposals for a morganatic marriage between Edward VIII and Mrs Simpson. To her such a suggestion 'implied that although Mrs Simpson was fit to be a wife she was unfit to be a Queen'.[23] 'The King is asking Parliament to take from the woman he is going to marry the rights that are hers by law and to deprive her and her children of their inheritance before they are born.'[24] This was an impossible proposal for any committed feminist to sanction.

An endless range of organisations sought and received Ellen's backing. One body which she often assisted, first as President of their Manchester branch, and later as National Vice President, was the Electrical Association for Women. She fully appreciated then that educating women to accept the newly available electrical appliances was a positive step towards easing domestic pressures.[25] Years later she said, 'I want to see better planned kitchens and firmly believe that an ancient frying pan over an open fire is vastly inferior to . . . an electric oven that a woman knows how to use. I speak from experience having tried both.'[26]

Ellen was anxious for women to be less housebound so that they could be active in the community and thus learn to use their votes intelligently. She insisted moreover that one woman was totally inadequate to represent all women's viewpoints: 'Much as I admire the Duchess of Atholl, she does not represent anything I stand for and she could say the same even more strongly about me!' She pressed therefore for more women MPs and for many more women to be appointed to responsible public positions. She urged their value to Royal Commissions, on the Bench and as Jurors, and demanded that women barristers should be considered for positions of

Recorders.[27] She often lamented the absence of young married women in public life. 'My friend Muriel Nichol . . . a magnificent speaker, would certainly have been in Parliament if there had not been a definite feeling against selecting women with young children as candidates', she wrote.[28]

'Mere' domestic matters were often Ellen's concern. She loved children and was profoundly shocked by the nation's infant mortality rates which in 1929 had been the highest since 1905. 'Marriage', she suggested, 'should be scheduled as a dangerous trade, since there are more deaths from childbirth than from dangerous diseases'.[29] She sought the extension of maternity and child welfare centres, arguing that their provision ought to be mandatory on local authorities, and supported campaigns for free milk for school children promoted by the Children's Minimum Nutrition Council.[30] She was of course an eager sponsor of 'The Boots for Bairns' — the Children (Provision of Footwear) Bill. An all-party group of women MPs, led by Margaret Bondfield, wanted local authorities in certain areas to provide, with Treasury backing, footwear for 'necessitous' children. Some charitable bodies did distribute boots, but supplies were hopelessly inadequate.[31] Ellen went further and wanted grants for children's clothing generally. Many children, she said in debate, were underfed and underclothed, went to school in 'cotton chemises' and were ravaged by rheumatism.[32] She was extremely angry over the lack of sympathy for the Bill, which fell when Winston Churchill refused financial assistance.[33] Kingsley Martin was right, Ellen never willingly let the individual be forgotten in the statistics.[34]

It seems extraordinary that Ellen was not active in the controversy over birth control, a ticklish, recurrent theme at the Annual Conferences of Labour Women. In 1926 the NEC had decided that, because of deeply held convictions, advice on birth control should not be made a party political issue and were clearly anxious to avoid a schism. Ellen's aloofness seems inexplicable other than in terms of respect for Roman Catholic opinion in her constituency. It is highly improbable that she would have trimmed her sails had she appreciated the need for disseminating information, but in the thirties the link between poverty and over-population was obscure.

The introduction of Family Allowances was however a policy on which she did speak out. At her union conference in 1929 she argued that it would help increase the purchasing power of working-class families depressed by unemployment and low wages.[35] It was an unpopular theme; Mrs Bamber, a fellow official, accused its supporters of believing it easier than fighting for Trade Union rights and Rhys Davies spitefully observed, 'Miss Wilkinson imagines that if we adopt the principle of Family Allowances we could settle the problem of incomes of the working class.' A joint Committee of the TUC favoured the general principle, but opposition continued from those who saw Family Allowances as an 'absolute lever for attacks on wages'.[36]

On matters of personal liberty Ellen often goaded authority into action. She raised a national storm in the press over the case of a mother of four young children, who had been sentenced to three months imprisonment for attempting suicide. Her husband was unemployed, they were beset with debts, and Ellen found the judicial ruling preposterous. 'Attempted suicide', she declared, 'should be taken off the list of crimes. This woman needs sympathetic kindly help not jail.' Diverse appeals to the Home Secretary eventually resulted in the mother's release.[37]

Ellen, who advocated compassionate treatment of families by the courts, was equally outraged when a mother who stole was sent to prison with her baby,[38] and even intervened over the dress of female prisoners, the form of which, she claimed, perpetuated the ideas of sixty years ago.[39]

If Ellen introduced no overtly feminist legislation (although her Hire Purchase Act was a real achievement in extending protection for women as consumers), she did possess a quality of rare worth to the women's movement; the ability to inspire self confidence in others through her capacity for personal sympathy. Margaret Simey, politician and reformer, when a young, overworked and underpaid organising youth club secretary, remembers Ellen's visiting Manchester (in 1929) to address the AGM of the Manchester and Salford Union of Girls' Clubs. On that occasion Ellen stressed that girls as well as boys should be trained to earn a living,[40] but it was not for the speech that Mrs Simey most vividly recalls Ellen across the years. 'It was because she took me aside, urged me to keep up the good work, and made me feel that it was all worthwhile . . . I still feel the warmth of her personality, the sense of passion of this glowing little creature from another world.'[41] Clearly Ellen could give to the younger generation something of that burning encouragement that a decade back Mrs Bruce Glasier had transmitted to her.

After the vote had been extended to women of 21, the women's movement tended to fragment into different bodies ranging from the

Married Women's Association to the Six Point Group. Each had specific aims: equal pay, legal rights, matrimonial justice. To these ends Ellen, with her sympathy for those who had to face the monotonous family chores of existence, gave continuous constructive help. She was certainly one of the several women MPs who 'transformed the stuff of politics'. 'The purpose and nature of legislation, are profoundly different from pre war years,' Ray Strachey wrote in 1936, 'Health, housing, pensions, education, maternal mortality and living conditions have leapt into the forefront of national affairs.'[42] Another contemporary, Mrs Hazel Hunkins Hallinan, reinforced this view. 'Ellen, fearless and consistent, never lost a chance to promote opportunities for women to gain equality.'[43] She was indeed one of the many who, undeterred, kept up the attack on male chauvinism. Even so it took a Second World War to regenerate a strong new women's movement, as intelligent as it was abrasive.

Labour Regains Office

The Baldwin government soldiered on amid mounting unpopularity. Great bitterness was engendered in the Labour Movement by the Trade Disputes and Trade Unions Act (1927) — the government's revenge for the General Strike. Major strikes and lock-outs were made illegal, fresh restrictions were imposed on picketing and trade unionists had to *contract in* to pay their political levy to the Labour Party. In international affairs the Conservatives had steadily undermined Labour's achievements. They had killed the Anglo-Russian treaties, and rejected the Geneva Protocol for the peaceful settlement of international disputes, which Arthur Henderson had so patiently negotiated. Russia and the security of Eastern Europe were ignored and Germany was welcomed into the League, although she was forced to repay her war reparitions by heavy borrowing from abroad. Against this background of insecurity and tension the tide of Fascism was rising.[44]

On the home front as Ellen saw it, 'the Tory leaders, step by step, pursued a financial policy to the maximum advantage of the rich'. Housing subsidies had been cut and Neville Chamberlain's local government and rating reforms 'favoured the wealthy rather than the poorer areas'.[45] It was however upon the government's attitude to unemployment that her scorn centred. The meagre benefits had again been curtailed, the unemployed had to turn from 'insurance' entitlement to the grudging 'charity' of local Poor Law Guardians ♦ and no provision had been introduced either for training the workless or making jobs available. In terms of ideas for tackling unemployment the government, as Ellen and many colleagues saw it, was bankrupt.

When the general election broke in May 1929, Labour had much to attack. Yet the Party's manifesto was a broad inconclusive statement of objectives which 'committed a Labour Government to nothing precise'.[46] It presented a programme of social reform in which socialism found no mention, but did propose solutions to unemployment such as capital works programmes, development of the home market by increasing purchasing power and assistance to industry by export credits. Nationalisation of the mines would only be implemented 'if Labour received a clear majority'. The general moderation of the programme, a further stage in a move to the right which ♦ MacDonald had been steadily engineering, was highly displeasing to the ILP and the left wing.[47]

Ellen entered the election with her flag high, for it was a unique occasion. Some 5 million women over 21, enfranchised by the Representation of the People (Equal Franchise) Act 1928, were voting for the first time. The ghost of Mrs Pankhurst must have smiled. 'It was the quietest election I have known', Ellen wrote, 'I made raids into other constituencies, but Middlesbrough East seemed to have made up its mind to vote for me.' For the first time in an election wireless was widely used and of this she approved: 'It did a great educative service for electors.'[48]

Labour won that sunny May election but it was a pyrrhic victory. They had no overall majority and the government, headed by MacDonald, Arthur Henderson and Philip Snowden, had to rely on the Liberals for working support. Yet the team had one distinction, for the first time in British history a woman, Margaret Bondfield, ♦ was made a minister (of Labour) and sat in the cabinet. This was a fitting fanfare to the Franchise Act, and a tacit tribute to the composition of the new House in which there were fourteen women Members, nine of whom were socialists. Among this talented group were Mary Agnes Hamilton, Dr Marion Phillips and Jennie Lee, none of whom survived the 1931 débâcle, and Megan Lloyd George and Eleanor Rathbone, who did. Jennie Lee, now Baroness Lee of Asheridge, a friend of Ellen's, was at 24 the youngest Member of the 1929 Parliament.

In this ill-fated government Ellen held her first official, if lowly, appointment. Susan Lawrence, redoubtable LCC member, former Stepney councillor and first woman chairman of the Labour Party, who was made Parliamentary Secretary to the Minister of Health, chose Ellen as her Private Parliamentary Secretary (PPS) — 'the least of God's creatures'. Ellen had a warm admiration for Susan, some 20 years her senior, who, she once said 'drank in statistics from blue books as some MPs imbibe whisky'.[49] In the House Susan had proved herself to be a pulverising opponent in debate particularly in exposing the 'ramp' of Neville Chamberlain's De-Rating Bill. Both she and Ellen loathed cruelty exercised towards the weak and both were gluttons for work. Determined to understand Departmental responsibilities at first hand they once evoked horrified comment from their officials by deciding to visit refuse dumps around London — on of all times — a Saturday morning! Susan, also emotional and left-wing, was the more controlled of the two. Beatrice Webb saw her as a 'would-be revolutionary socialist, had she not got a too carefully trained intellect to ignore facts'.[50] She was a disciplined democrat, essentially loyal to conference, and once a major decision had been reached would endure, as Ellen did, any amount of mis-representation rather than appear to question party policy in public.[51]

Both women had much in common and Susan taught Ellen a great deal. She, like Ellen, was indignant at what she regarded as the over-cautious policies of the government. Neither made any secret of their sense of frustration with MacDonald's leadership, but Ellen as a 'minor minion' was less officially committed than her friend. The position of PPS, though widely regarded as a 'stooge' job, can be the first rung up the parliamentary ladder and offers opportunity for learning about government administration from the inside. On this Ellen seized. She weighed up the workings and the limitations of parliamentary democracy, saw something of the burdens of office which ministers have to carry, and Cassandra-like recognised even then that, with power so heavily concentrated in the cabinet, ministers were frequently loaded with work 'beyond human endur-ance'.[52] Ellen had few illusions about her role. She was as shrewdly aware that 'a PPS who can turn the wrath of back benchers into safe channels when they are out for a scoop is a treasure',[53] as she was of the implications of parliamentary cajolery: 'The flattery of being taken into ministerial confidence is the subtlest of all methods of dealing with the really dangerous back bencher.'[54]

Ellen came to assess the influence of the Civil Service as the most continuously powerful element in government. The theory that it is loyal to whatever government is in office she dismissed as risible: 'During the brief tenure of the Labour Government, it was amusing to notice how the higher Civil Service so obviously regarded itself as the caretaker for the real owners during the temporary occupation of the poor relations', she wrote. 'Any Minister foolish enough to quarrel with his own entourage, therefore, could soon be brought to heel . . . The wise Minister learns.'[55] It was doubtless due at least in part to the understanding acquired while working for Susan that Ellen, when minister herself, managed her senior staff so well. While however in the private office she patently distrusted the civil service, certain that no satisfactory social reforms could be effected by a government which ignored its relationship with the administration.[56]

The Donoughmore Report

Knowledge of the working of government was deepened for Ellen by her appointment in 1929 to the Donoughmore Committee on . ministers' powers. Chaired by Lord Donoughmore, with Sir John Anderson, the Duchess of Atholl and Professor Harold Laski among the members, it had a singularly modern remit: to examine the alleged encroachment by Ministers of the Crown upon the sovereignty of Parliament, or, as Harold Laski later described it, 'To investigate the phantom army of bureaucrats lusting for power'.[57] There had long been a wholesome suspicion in Britain of the powers given by Parliament to ministers and their civil servants, to implement by detailed regulations the principles laid down in Acts of Parliament. This suspicion was aggravated by the general growth of collectivism which necessitated the use of delegated legislation and by the onslaught of Lord Chief Justice Hewart in his provocative book *The New Despotism* (published in 1929) which attacked rules issued by government departments under their statutory powers.

Because state intervention by Parliament affecting the lives of individuals and the organisation of industry had burgeoned, the use of delegated powers was inevitable. The National Insurance Act, 1911, for example, could not have operated without delegated legislation to make it effective. Neither Ellen nor Harold Laski were unsympathetic to state intervention. Both, however, were highly suspicious of the secrecy which shrouded much enabling legislation: 'The giving of decisions arbitrarily without explaining on what they are based is about as good a definition of autocracy as you can give', Laski said in his Note appended to the Final Report.[58]

Although Ellen did not noticeably enrich the deliberations of the Committee, her contributions are interesting for indicating facets of her parliamentary experience. She was, for example, concerned about the right of an individual to write to his MP or minister. Was it not the case, she asked Sir Charles Hipwood (Board of Trade), that departments took the attitude that anyone writing to their minister was a crank, and ipso facto a nuisance? Moreover, so far as Parliamentary Questions went, was it not the job of skilled draftsmen to produce a reply that would soothe the House of Commons and give the impression the questioner was rather a fool? 'From my experience of sitting through many hours of Questions that is the conclusion I come to.'[59]

The question of an MP's access to information also troubled Ellen. In theory, according to the Treasury Solicitor Sir Maurice Gwyer, most departments favoured 'prior consultation with interested parties'. In practice, Ellen countered, MPs could not adequately criticise regulations when only ministers had access to departmental information:

Gwyer: Every Minister has a PPS who knows a good deal about what is going on.
EW: Is it not a fact that a PPS would be murdered if he dared give any information?
Gwyer: I am not suggesting that a PPS should give away secrets, but there is access to the Minister — a great deal of access by private [i.e. back bench] MPs. They certainly write a good many letters.
EW: And receive extraordinarily guarded answers.[60]

Ellen argued that, as the average Member was expected to have expert knowledge on everything from 'Charing Cross to potatoes', parliamentary criticism was a farce. 'It is utterly impossible for Members to have informed views on one-tenth of the work before them', she declared.

The Donoughmore Report published in April 1932 exonerated the Executive from encroaching upon Parliament's powers and accepted that unless Parliament delegated some law making powers it could not pass the requisite legislation. Significantly, so far as Ellen was concerned, it also grasped the nettle of secrecy. 'We do not doubt that justice is, as a general rule, done. But it should always be remembered that justice is not enough. What people want is security for justice and the only security for justice is law publicly administered.' The Committee made numerous recommendations, but its proposals were ignored for more than a decade. Its influence was, however, seen in the subsequent changes made in the drafting of Bills and in the establishment in 1944 of a Select Committee to scrutinise delegated legislation.[61]

Both Laski and Ellen appended Notes to the Report. Laski expressed distrust of the Establishment, arguing that the Committee had underestimated the innate prejudice of judges and their tendency to misinterpret the intention of Parliament as incorporated in legislation.[62] In her more fiery, less legalistic Note, Ellen proposed that Parliament's delegatory legislative powers ought to be widely extended and new ways found to effect this. The current cumbersome method whereby the whole House examined each piece of legislation meant that much time was wasted by Members. Parliament could deal with general principles of proposed legislation, the details should be left to the experts. 'Nothing is so dangerous in a democracy as a safeguard which appears to be adequate but is really a facade.'[63]

The Donoughmore Report made little public impact, but to Ellen the experience acquired was valuable. A deeper understanding of the legislative process served her well both when she came to pilot her own Hire Purchase Bill through the House and later as a minister. She also gained a bonus from her working contact with Professor Harold Laski, whose exceptional understanding of the British Constitution taught her much. It is highly likely that Laski's own warm admiration for Ellen dated from that time.[64]

As Ellen's estimation of Parliament mellowed she came to see its *raison d'être* as protecting the ordinary man, and she proudly related how when the House was packed to hear the historic announcement of the Abdication, Parliamentary Question Time could still take precedence, 'so that the problem of a Glasgow widow whose pension was short of five shillings could be dealt with'. To her the House really did stand for a man's right to freedom of speech and action. 'As the traditional guardian of our liberties, Parliament is not doing its job too badly; but perhaps I am prejudiced.'[65] She had indeed become an 'excellent Parliamentarian'.

If however her experience as a Member of Parliament strengthened Ellen's respect for the Commons it did nothing to enhance her opinion of the Lords. Quite the contrary, for time and again their

Lordships obstructed legislation which the Labour government had been anxious to get onto the Statute book. 'While the House forgot that there was a second Chamber during the five years of Tory Government because it went to sleep, the Labour Government is finding what an effective weapon the Lords can be for the Tories when out of office,' she wrote angrily. 'In a country that calls itself a democracy it is scandalous that an unelected revising Chamber can be tolerated in which the Conservative Party has such a permanent and overwhelming majority.'[66]

The Lords snuffed out or mutilated into impotence legislation as diverse as the Coal Mines Bill (1930) which sought to reduce the miners' working hours, and the Education Bill which in line with TUC and Labour Party Conference decisions, sought to raise the school leaving age to 15. The failure of the Education Bill sparked off the resignation of the minister, Sir Charles Trevelyan, who cared deeply about his Bill and as an able left winger was strongly out of sympathy with MacDonald's 'wavering socialism'. Further, a compromise solution to the issues of proportional representation — the 'Liberals' darling' — incorporated in the Representation of the People Bill (1931) was totally ruined by the Lords. Since MacDonald relied upon Liberal support, provision in the Bill for the alternative vote was an important sop to Liberal opinion. Compromise had been reached in Committee, but the Lords restored plural voting and limited the alternative vote to London and the larger boroughs; the Bill got no further.[67]

If Ellen was less active on the floor of the House as a PPS than she was as an 'uncommitted' back-bencher, she remained alert, often seeing the impact of national trends in parochial perspective. During 1931 among many interventions in Parliament she challenged the impact of the iron and steel industry's monopoly which intensified unemployment in Middlesbrough; questioned the slow start of the Tee Bridge project in view of its job potential; intervened over the Access to Mountains Bill because of 'the great interest in hiking amongst young people'; and opposed a Domestic Services Commission because 'domestic servants should have a minimum wage agreed through Trade Boards.'[68]

It had been an article of faith with Ellen since her university days that international co-operation was the path to peace along which the League of Nations and its technical agencies could lead. When therefore she accompanied Susan Lawrence, who was an official delegate to the League Assembly, to Geneva during September 1930 she was delighted at 'being let behind the scenes', and in seeing Henderson 'get down to brass tacks,' as a resolute pacifist to whom the League was the 'hope of the world'. His great strength, she wrote after his death, lay in his disinterested devotion to duty, and in his support for the League Covenant. 'To him democracy was a work- ing creed like his Methodism. A Conference-agreed policy statement of representative men and women was a working directive, not an irrelevence to be ignored when it suited him.'[69]

During its short tenure of office the Labour government's main success was in international affairs. Henderson with Briand and Stresemann worked for peace and disarmament: the government recognised the League as an instrument for resolving international disputes at the Hague, and also took the initiative over India. The First Round Table Conference to discuss the issue of India's future was set in train, although the government's continued repressive policy in the face of civil disobedience was detested by its left wing.[70]

When, the year after losing her parliamentary seat, Ellen was invited by the India League to lead a small delegation including Krishna Menon and Monica Whatley to India the opportunity was irresistible. During the autumn of 1932 the party travelled some 12,000 miles in three months. They visited village communities, studied rural poverty, investigated jails. Ellen visited Gandhi in prison — 'where he was spinning and full of energy' — and returned home eager to plead for his unconditional release, con- vinced that the mass of Indian people regarded him as their only saviour. 'While Gandhi lives there can be no peace in India without his cooperation.'[71] 'To keep him locked up and to slam the door of negotiations in the face of the most moderate of men is invincible stupidity,' she told a meeting in Manchester of the India League, at which John Jagger presided. 'Had Britain', she asked, 'learned nothing from the lessons of Ireland?'[72] Ellen submitted a full report on the conditions and the repressive measures taken against Congress supporters which her delegation had observed. It was a report 'written in fire and sorrow', and in Kingsley Martin's view belied any suggestion that at that time she 'had lost either her anger or her faith'.[73]

In home affairs, the King's Speech of 1929 had indicated that only mild measures of social reform could be expected. Arthur Greenwood's Housing Act, for example, allocated state subsidies for tackling slum clearance but did not make such clearance com- pulsory, and Herbert Morrison's Transport Bill, which created a single public corporation for operating London's transport services, was still incomplete when the government fell. All in all many Labour MPs were not happy. The socialist adage of 'Work or Maintenance' had not been implemented: public works schemes had been side-stepped in the face of capital cut-backs, and the government had no real plans for radically tackling unemployment.

Not surprisingly to some of Ellen's friends there was a moment during the course of the 1929–31 Parliament when it looked as though 'partly out of rage with the futility of the Government, she might lose her direction. For the first year she worked very hard as a PPS . . . then she seemed to lose interest, became erratic in her attendance . . . went mildly social and [seemed] overcome by the impatience which is the penalty of a mind as quick as hers . . . but the danger, if it was ever real, soon passed,' Mary Agnes Hamilton recalled in retrospect.[74]

If however the government was criticised by the left for its omissions and timidity, in all fairness it was faced by overwhelming economic forces. The collapse of Wall Street in October 1929 only a few months after the election spiralled into an unprecedented world slump and unemployment in Britain rose from 1.6 million in December 1929 to 2.5 million the following year. Ministers were overwhelmed, and the government lacked any overall economic plan. Later, Lord Francis-Williams, former editor of the *Daily Herald* and astute inside observer, commented: 'What strikes one is how little Members of the Cabinet . . . concerned themselves with the economic and financial situation until the very last.'[75] In the face of all this, Snowden as Chancellor stood doggedly by his beliefs in free trade and in maintaining the gold standard. A prisoner of orthodox finance, he depended entirely on the guidance of the Bank of England through its Governor, Montagu Norman, but Snowden played a male Trilby to Norman's Svengali. The Governor in his turn was under the influence of the American bankers demanding stringent economies before granting further loans to impoverished Britain.

The Mosley Memorandum and the May Committee

During this agonising period the only overall plan for tackling unemployment came from Oswald Mosley, then a new recruit to the Labour Party, whom briefly Ellen admired, although when he became the leader of the British Union of Fascists she saw him as a pariah. Mosley, one of the three 'advisers' to J.H. Thomas, the minister responsible for employment, drew up his own plan. In this he made proposals for enlarging consumer purchasing power, protecting the home market, developing British Agriculture, rationalising industry and controlling the banks. To eager young left wingers the memorandum made good sense; to Snowden its retreat from free trade and from orthodox banking policies was reprehensible, and when submitted to Cabinet the document was rejected. Mosley resigned and MacDonald 'with the Tories baying for protectionism' took over responsibility from Thomas for employment policy.[76]

That, however, was not the end of the matter. Mosley took his case to the 1930 Labour Party Conference where the Government came under heavy fire, from Maxton and Ellen among others, for its timidity in refusing to apply socialist remedies to the current crisis. A resolution calling for a full report on the Mosley memorandum was narrowly defeated and Mosley was elected to the NEC.[77] Mosley continued to campaign within the Labour Party, seeing himself as the potential leader of the left. Among his propaganda publications the Mosley manifesto of December 1930 demanded action on the lines of his memorandum which A.J. Cook, and seventeen MPs, including, John Strachey, Nye Bevan, and Ellen backed. Soon after this Mosley, failing to win further support, formed the New Party, was expelled from the Labour Party and retreated into his Fascist wilderness.

The government dithered. Harassed from within, and unsure of the precarious support from the Liberals without, they set up a Royal Commission on Unemployment Insurance. From this emerged the Unemployment Insurance (No. 3) Bill, which incensed many besides Labour's left wing. The 'Anomalies Bill' as it became known, purported to deal with 'abuses of the dole', but in addition to increasing contributions it generally reduced benefits and deprived certain classes of the unemployed (mainly married women) of benefit. Ellen, Susan, Jennie Lee and Charles Trevelyan among many, fought the Bill clause by clause. In particular, Ellen and Jennie Lee argued that if a married woman had dependents, or if her husband was incapacitated or unemployed, she should not be excluded from benefit on the grounds that she was not genuinely seeking work. They won some grudging concessions, but not before Ellen had angrily stated that under the Bill 'perfectly respectable milliners and dressmakers are to be offered the workhouse . . . it is intolerable . . . I cannot and will not vote for it'.[78] Together with Eleanor Rathbone, MP she won another small success when the minister (Margaret Bondfield) agreed that two women instead of one should be appointed to the Advisory Committee dealing with abuses under the Bill. Not for the first time Ellen wondered why it was presumed so often that one woman could represent all women in her own bright self, 'yet nobody ever says that one man can represent all men'.[79] This bitterly contested Bill was finally passed in July, but some thirty left wing members voted against it.[80] On the Third Reading Ellen appears to have abstained, an act of defiance for a PPS which confounded press opinion that 'she was becoming respectable and shedding her extreme views like leaves in autumn'.

During the last six months of the government Ellen was uncharacteristically quiet in the House, but this seems more likely to have been due to her being thoroughly disillusioned with MacDonald's policies than with having become a tamed tigress. The suggestion that she had more brains and drive than half a dozen males put together, and that had the Labour government stayed in office 'she would have been considered for early promotion',[81] was highly conjectural. Brains, yes; willingness to co-operate with MacDonald, no. But the option did not arise: the days of the government were numbered.

Snowden, anxious only for a balanced budget and broadly in sympathy with economy calls, had set up early in 1931 the infamous May Committee to investigate further methods for effecting retrenchment. Chaired by Sir George May of the Prudential Insurance Company, the Committee was heavily anti-Labour in membership and in July after Parliament had risen produced an intentionally sensational report, described by J.M. Keynes as 'the most foolish document I have ever had the misfortune to read'.[82] It breathed panic, depicted Britain on the verge of bankruptcy and recommended swingeing economies. The budget should be balanced partly by increased taxation, but mainly by a 20 per cent cut in unemployment relief.[83]

Snowden had not anticipated the political impact on his own party. The cabinet split over how the Report ought to be implemented. A minority found any cut in unemployment benefit unacceptable, so harmony was irreparably shattered. Resignations followed and after much vacillating MacDonald, having been 'implored' to do so by the King,[84] agreed to form a temporary coalition government 'to defend the pound', with Stanley Baldwin and Sir Herbert Samuel, for Lloyd George was ill. The tempers and tensions of that fateful August have often been related. Whatever the interpretation it is certain that MacDonald's action took most of his cabinet colleagues by surprise and disgusted the PLP who promptly • expelled him with his supporters and elected Henderson as Leader.

The PLP went into opposition, determined as Ernie Bevin and the TUC urged, to fight the May Committee's cuts in unemployment rates.[85] Bevin, advised by Keynes and G.D.H. Cole (who, with Citrine of the TUC, had produced alternative policies for dealing with the crisis) regarded retention of the gold standard as totally wrong in the economic situation.[86] A few weeks later in mid-September the coalition Government, advised by the Bank of England, did in fact abandon the gold standard and so jettisoned the basic principle which it had been created to defend. Clearly it was time for MacDonald to go to the country.

Electoral Disaster

The general election of October 1931 was fought against a background of confusion and panic. Confusion over the causes of the crisis and panic over the 'Post Office Savings Scare', deliberately created by the Liberal Walter Runciman, MP (and to which Snowden to his lasting shame gave credence) that a Labour victory would mean gross inflation and the confiscation of people's savings to pay for the dole.[87] A really good scare, as Ellen remarked bitterly, proved better than any argument.[88]

In a tough sometimes unpleasant campaign (at one stage she was physically attacked) Ellen opposed tariffs because they would cause high food prices — and argued that the only hope for British industry lay in reorganisation 'on national lines'. But even though handbell ringers heralded with a homely clatter her many impromptu meetings, 'it was a thoroughly gloomy election'. The results, she wrote, in a personal election post-mortem, 'could not have been worse yet the fight in Middlesbrough East was the best I have known'. She came within 100 of her previous vote — the highest ever recorded there for Labour — partly because:

Alfred McVie, my agent, couldn't have been bettered and the NUDAW organisers fought like tigers in a bitter atmosphere of national hostility . . . The press, the BBC, the Church and the cinema, every employer, every social worker who was not actually a socialist, set to work on creating a great 'wind up'. Fear hung over every meeting and invaded every home through the wireless where Labour had only three speakers to the twelve of the other side.

The Conservatives won 470 seats and Labour representation fell heavily. Yet even so the party polled nearly seven million votes. Among those who 'went down' with Ellen were Margaret Bondfield, Nye Bevan, Hugh Dalton, Susan Lawrence, Manny Shinwell and Herbert Morrison. George Lansbury became Chairman of the crippled PLP, and Clement Attlee was chosen as his deputy.

Ellen never doubted MacDonald's and Snowden's personal responsibility for the failure of the Labour government. She regarded their having retained minority office in 1929 and trying to 'put patches on the social fabric' as 'tragically wrong', because 'it forced the Party to take responsibility for events quite outside their control'. Moreover, the class struggle to Ellen had in no way abated, but the workers should have been certain of what they were fighting for. 'It is no use building Jerusalem in perorations; the average voter wants to see the blue print of the city.' In short the Labour Party should have produced and followed a strong positive policy for socialism.[89]

Notes

1. Hansard, Vol. 197, col. 2350, 8 July 1926.
2. Hansard, Vol. 189, cols. 1759–60, 17 December 1925.
3. *Bolton Journal*, 3 July 1925.
4. *North Eastern Daily Gazette*, 20 November 1925, *Time and Tide*, 18 December 1925.
5. Hansard, Vol. 189, col. 263, 8 December 1925.
6. *Daily Mirror*, 18 March 1933.
7. *Manchester Evening News*, 20 November 1925. An amusing example of male chauvinism arose in 1931 when a deputation including Miss Picton Turberville, MP, Megan Lloyd George, MP, and Ellen, together with representatives from the National Council of Women waited on J.M. Clynes, Home Secretary, to discuss extending the number of women police. At the meeting Lord Byng, Head of the Metropolitan Police, argued the administrative difficulties of obtaining quarters for women police. It was, he said, impossible to get suitable premises to accommodate 70 women police 'and lodgings were administratively inadvisable' (*Manchester Guardian*, 29 April 1931).
8. *Daily Express*, 24 March 1928.

9. Hansard, Vol. 388, cols. 980–1, 12 March 1929.
10. *Newcastle Chronicle*, 5 March 1925.
11. Hansard, Vol. 188, cols. 433–7, 30 April 1925.
12. *Newcastle Chronicle*, 16 July 1925.
13. *Time and Tide*, 1 April 1935.
14. *News Chronicle*, 31 October 1927.
15. *Oxford Mail*, 4 June 1930.
16. *Manchester Guardian*, 17 June 1930.
17. *Fabian News*, 7 January 1920.
18. *The Times*, 10 March, 1925.
19. *Daily Herald*, 11 October 1929.
20. Hansard, Vol. 310, cols. 2017–23, 1 April 1936.
21. *The Times*, 26 October 1936.
22. *John Bull*, 23 March 1932.
23. *Time and Tide*, 12 December 1936.
24. *Daily Herald*, 9 December 1936.
25. *Yorkshire Post*, 25 October 1937.
26. *Electrical Age*, December 1946.
27. Hansard, Vol. 344, cols. 1474, 3 March 1939.
28. *John Bull*, 24 November 1934.
29. *Birmingham Post*, 21 October 1929.
30. Marjorie Soper, letter of 31 March 1978; *Daily Mirror*, 15 April 1935.
31. Hansard Vol. 223, cols. 1029–32, 4 December 1928. In Mountain Ash, Glamorgan, for example, ninety% of able-bodied men were unemployed, 11,000 children were on the school registers, but only about 2,800 pairs of boots had been distributed.
32. Hansard, Vol. 223, cols. 1351–62, 5 December 1928.
33. Ibid., cols. 2817, 18 December 1928.
34. Kingsley Martin, *New Statesman*, 15 February 1947.
35. *New Dawn*, 27 April 1929.
36. *New Dawn*, 9 May 1931.
37. *Daily Herald*, 2 September 1931; *Sunday Referee*, 6 September, 1931.
38. *Pearsons Weekly*, 7 January 1933.
39. Hansard, Vol. 318, col. 2170. 10 December 1936.
40. *Lancashire Post*, 8 October 1929.
41. Mrs Margaret Simey, letters of 16 September 1979 and 1 August 1980.
42. R. Strachey, *Fortnightly Review*, 1936, Vol. 146, pp. 337–48.
43. Mrs Hazel Hunkins Hallinan, 1 October 1978, interview.
44. C.L. Mowat, *Britain Between the Wars* (Methuen, London, 1955), pp. 335–46.
45. *New Dawn*, 16 March 1929.
46. G.D.H. Cole, *A History of the Labour Party* (Routledge and Kegan Paul, London, 1948), p. 279.
47. Ibid., pp. 212–14.
48. *New Dawn*, 15 May 1929.
49. *Labour Magazine*, November 1929.
50. Webb, *'Diaries'*, pp. 23–4.; David Martin on 'Susan Lawrence' in J. Saville (ed.), *Dictionary of Labour Biography* (Macmillan Press, London 1976), vol. 3.
51. *Labour Magazine*, November 1929.
52. *Time and Tide*, 2 April 1932.
53. Ellen Wilkinson, *The Division Bell Mystery* (Harrap, London, 1932), p. 121.
54. Ibid., pp. 140–1.
55. *Time and Tide*, 26 June 1937.
56. *Time and Tide*, 30 April 1932.
57. H.J. Laski, *Reflections on the Constitution* (Manchester University Press,

Manchester, 1951), pp. 42−3.
58. Report of the Committee on Ministerial Powers (Cmd. 4060, HMSO, April 1932), Appendix 5.
59. Committee on Ministerial Powers Minutes of Evidence, Vol. 2, paras. 3509−11, p. 259, 19 February 1930.
60. Ibid., paras. 130−6, pp. 11−12.
61. E.C. Wade and G. Phillips, *Constitutional Law* (Longmans, London, 1970, 8th ed.) p. 594.
62. Committee on Ministerial Powers, Report (Cmd. 4060) p. 135.
63. Ibid. pp. 137−8.
64. Frida Laski, in letter to Greville Eastwood (letter to author).
65. *Cheshire Daily Echo*, 10 March 1938.
66. *New Dawn*, 20 August 1930.
67. Mowat, pp. 365−6.
68. Hansard, Vol. 248, cols. 2121, 25 February, 1931; Vol. 251, cols. 686−9, 20 April 1931; Vol. 252, cols. 1357−8, 14 May 1931; Vol. 253, cols. 820−2, 9 June 1931.
69. *Time and Tide*, 14 April 1938.
70. G.D.H. Cole and R. Postgate, *The Common People* (Methuen, London, 1938,) p. 578.
71. *Daily Herald*, 7 December 1932.
72. *Manchester Guardian*, 12 December 1932; *Birmingham Post*, 13 February 1933.
73. *New Statesman*, 15 February 1947.
74. Mary Agnes Hamilton in *The Spectator*, 24 August 1945.
75. F. Williams, *A Pattern of Rulers* (Longmans, London, 1965), p. 108.
76. Mowat, p. 359−60.
77. G.D.H. Cole, *History of the Labour Party*, pp. 239−42.
78. *North Eastern Daily Gazette*, 22 July 1931.
79. *Evening Standard*, 16 July 1931; Hansard, Vol. 255, cols. 1861−2, 21 July 1931.
80. Ellen's name does not appear among those opposing the Bill in the final vote. Those who voted against the government included Oliver Baldwin, Fenner Brockway, J.F. Horrabin, Jennie Lee, Charles Trevelyan and Frank Wise.
81. *People*, 23 November 1930.
82. Humphrey Berkeley, *The Myth that will not Die* (Croom Helm, London, 1978) p. 32.
83. G.D.H. Cole, *History of the Labour Party*, pp. 249−58, and Berkeley, pp. 31−9.
84. Berkeley, p. 88.
85. Berkeley, p. 111.
86. In their pamphlet *The Crisis* (New Statesman, London, 1931) G.D.H. Cole and Ernest Bevin wrote: 'Labour has decisively rejected the policy of wage cutting, unemployed baiting, and putting back economic and social progress that is advocated by the self-styled 'National' Government and the financial interests behind it. But it cannot successfully defeat that policy unless it is prepared to advance at once to the determined enforcement of a constructive Socialist policy of its own.' (Quoted in G.D.H. Cole, *History of the Labour Party*, p. 258.)
87. G.D.H. Cole, *History of the Labour Party*, p. 255; C.L. Mowat, *Britain Between the Wars*, p. 411.
88. *New Dawn*, 7 November 1931.
89. *New Dawn*, 7 November 1931.

6 PERSONAL INTERLUDE

Ellen was always so anxious to put the world to right that
love affairs had to wait — Amy Mitchell

Ellen's Character and Enthusiasms

Life was not, however, all work. Ellen was a highly sociable creature
— with her looks how could she not be? Like most politicians she
enjoyed meeting anyone who was anyone, although she never forgot
that 'the poorest he that is in England hath a life to live as the greatest
he'. Many opportunities to enjoy life came her way. Parties at Lady
Rhondda's and at Kingsley Martin's, dining out, making speeches
with H.G. Wells or Bertrand Russell, junketting at the Durham
Miners' Gala one week, visiting Clivedon the next (Lady Astor and
Ellen were temperamentally very close),[1] celebrating the first
anniversary of Morley College with Lilian Bayliss or dancing late
into the night 'in golden slippers and green frock' — life indeed
could be fun.

She also loved silly games and was adept at charades, particularly
those with a political nuance. Maurice Reckitt recalled her playing a
Soviet Commissar at Scotland Yard with great *élan*, and Kingsley
Martin related a similar occasion when 'a cautious old gentleman
named Mr Bottle overcome by Ellen's eloquence, swore to join her at
the barricades'.[2] She entertained all sorts and conditions of people,
welcoming numerous friends from overseas. The family well remember Gandhi sitting cross-legged on the floor of her flat and treasure a
little flag with spinning wheel on it which he gave them.

In the inter-war years Ellen dressed with arresting distinction. She
could look really 'breath-taking' in black velvet with a deep white
lace collar, enhanced by a Greek mask-like golden brooch. Latterly
with failing health and overwork her clothes sense deteriorated, yet
she always cared about her physical appearance and did not disregard the beauty parlour. 'The great thing for a politician is to stay
alive' she often said, and in later life found Elizabeth Arden a
lifeline.[3]

Summer schools and seminars, social and serious, were an integral part of her life. These Ellen enjoyed, particularly at Easton

Lodge, Lady Warwick's 'great lump of a building' standing in a huge untidy park with H.G. Wells's home Easton Glebe nearby.[4] Maud Bickford, a trade union organiser, recalls visiting there, 'when Ellen and Uncle Arthur used the opportunity for considerable private discussion . . . we also spent much time on the tennis courts. She and H.G. Wells opposed me and Alister MacDonald [Ramsay's son]. They won.'[5]

Ellen was equally at home at Bloomsbury parties, socialist conferences or at Cliveden weekends. She could admire people outside her own political circle — Sir John Anderson, Lord Beaverbrook, Winston Churchill and Lady Astor — profoundly disagree with them, yet mingle gaily with them socially. Although Ellen never forgot her working-class origin, she could make friendly contacts with those whose privileges she attacked. Like Nye Bevan, she could fraternise with people in spite of their politics.[6]

Lord Boothby, recounting a personal experience, underlines this. In 1940 when he got into political difficulties over an alleged failure to disclose a personal interest when advocating the repayment of Czech assets in Britain to their owners, she wrote him:

> The feeling everywhere is "why on earth couldn't this be settled by a private wigging . . . we can't afford to lose a man like that from the Ministry of Food", [for a time Lord Boothby was Parliamentary Secretary]. . . . I suppose these remarks are *lèse majesté* or contempt of court, but this is just what all the people I meet are saying. Good luck.

This, Lord Boothby wrote, was entirely characteristic.[7]

She was generous in thought and deed. The late Arthur Blenkinshop remembered Ellen as 'one of the few politicians prepared to give young people her concentrated attention and encouragement', a view shared by Dr Rene Saran. Such grateful memories are capped by Jennie Lee (who first met Ellen at an NCLC weekend school with Winifred and Frank Horrabin): 'when I arrived in the House as a younger woman she was kindness itself'.[8]

To family and friends Ellen was affectionately generous: 'She loved and understood children, gave wonderful presents and was great fun.' On occasion she even lent her car to her secretary, no mean gesture in pre-war days![9] Susan Lawrence was not alone in finding Ellen 'the kindest and most generous friend that anyone ever had the good fortune to possess'.[10]

Pomposity and solemnity were alien to Ellen's nature: eagerness to get things done would bubble into informality. She is remembered as minister addressing an audience of youngsters in the East End of London: 'She broke off in the middle of a prepared speech, lent forward grinning conspiratorially, and confided "this isn't what I was told to tell you!" '[11] An inability to refuse help to worthwhile causes led to Ellen's overworking and over-committing herself. This tendency her secretaries endeavoured to control, for she would not infrequently arrive late at meetings or forget to turn up. It was almost impossible to organise Ellen. Rush, hurry, unpunctuality, muddled papers, were as endemic as her difficulties in meeting journalistic deadlines, although through the care of her staff, she usually got there. If she failed, her charm in apology was fathomless.

In no way was Ellen all sweetness and light. She could be waspish, sharp and hurtful, albeit unintentionally so. In Parliament her impetuosity got her into trouble from which the loyal JJ often pulled her. Her misjudgement of people and situations could amount to gullibility — as Dame Margaret Cole often said, 'Ellen could be a goose.' Her tendency 'to make rapid judgements and to take snap decisions' was confirmed by many, although in Lord Redcliffe-Maud's experience she ruthlessly disciplined her quick temper: 'especially when she suspected she had a prejudice, she would insist on hearing and discussing all that her advisers had to say'.[12]

Ellen, never too old or too weary to learn, was ever prompted by a desire to find out for herself. Not long before she died she asked a friend to recommend an artist who would give her lessons in painting 'because I must know what it feels like to be taught how it's done'.[13] Her love of foreign travel was fed by the opportunities which came with success, both as a politician and as a journalist and her trips had to be planned well ahead. Her own holidays were often spontaneous. Climbing in England or hiking on the Continent when young, sunbathing in the South of France and skiing in Switzerland offered brief breaks for enjoyment.

She once listed her hobbies as horse-riding and golf, but there is little evidence she was even remotely proficient at either. More accurately, she might have specified 'reading, the theatre and films — when time permits'. She was immensely well read as her journalism reveals. If a love of the Arts was not pre-eminent, she was always quick to appreciate books, plays and films with contemporary political merit. From the early thirties she had been interested in the People's Theatre in Newcastle (now fused into the North East Arts Centre) which emerged from the old Clarion Movement. 'It was very political (like Unity Theatre in London), was linked with Wallington and the Trevelyans, and had Sir Charles as its President,' Arthur Blenkinsop recalled.[14]

Her appreciation of the theatre therefore was based more on a play's content than on its artistry, but her judgement was good. She once saw Maurice Browne in *The Unknown Warrior*, a play about nuclear fission — a concept then totally unknown — which so fired her enthusiasm that she introduced him to Dorothy and Leonard Elmhirst. These liberal-minded millionaires, founders of Dartington Hall in Devon, promised Browne financial backing when he found a play 'he had to do'. This he did: it was R.C. Sherriff's *Journey's End*. The play, of trench life in the Great War, had first been given a Sunday showing by the Stage Society with a new actor, Lawrence Olivier. When produced commercially by Browne in 1929 it was an international triumph. Little wonder that Ellen attended a party to celebrate the play's 500th performance![15]

The lobby for a National Theatre was gathering momentum. At a luncheon given in Browne's honour, Ellen expressed the hope that a National Theatre would become a reality, encouraging music and the other arts, and assured her audience of 'growing support for such a concept in the House.'[16] She joined Sunday Theatre Clubs, and avant-garde film societies; she served on the Council of the London Film Society, and was quick to appreciate the didactic and propaganda potential of the cinema. Films she envisaged as an educational force to serve as a night-school for the working classes. They offered a new means of teaching 'not by telling but by showing'.[17]

Censorship of films was much discussed and Ellen became joint secretary to an all-party committee, which included Fenner Brockway and George Strauss, to reform existing anomalies. For the inconsistency with which local authorities exercised their powers of censorship made patent nonsense. Whereas the LCC could approve a showing of Gorki's *The Mother* by the London Film Society whose membership fee was 'high' (25s = £1.25), the same authority could and did deny a showing of the same film to working people by the Stage and Film Society whose subscription was a humble shilling.[18] The committee also criticised restrictions upon Sunday showings and the reliance of local authorities upon the examination of films by the Board of Film Censors, largely controlled by the trade. Ellen and her colleagues argued that, since the biggest exhibitors were American, most films from the USA were approved, while excellent Russian, Swedish and German films, often of scientific character, were rejected.[19]

The fight was carried into the House. J.F. Horrabin, Ellen and others urged J.R. Clynes, the Home Secretary (1929-31), to consider establishing a National Board of Film Censorship as distinct from the unofficial trade-controlled body. Clynes rejected any change, but failed to refute Horrabin's allegation that the 'LCC held strong views as to the utter futility of local authorities being put into the position of censors'.[20]

The Family and Matters Domestic

As her political life expanded, Ellen came to rely heavily on sister Annie to manage her domestic front. Annie was 'someone to be reckoned with' and 'Her strongly marked features, mass of grey hair and elegance made her . . . attractive and stimulating in her own right.'[21] Loyal and dependable, Annie hovered in the background, a practical, unobtrusive and invaluable back-up. In the early thirties when both sisters were living in London, albeit in separate flats, she kept an alert eye on Ellen's domestic needs.[22] Ellen needed Annie. The hectic life she led, the erratic hours, the strenuous travelling engagements, encouraged neither a regular routine nor care for her health. Both sisters had inherited the family weaknesses of bronchitis and asthma, and although in early life Annie was the more acute sufferer, Ellen's physique, with age and overwork, deteriorated more rapidly. Yet she would never give in, to the point of foolhardiness, unless events so forced her.

Ellen, a car addict, was accident prone. She had a small Austin Seven — daring in the mid twenties — and drove with great panache to the House from her flat (next door to Jennie Lee and Nye Bevan), but carelessness involved her in frequent minor accidents. Once she ran into a horse and cart: 'She didn't hurt the horse, it just lay across the bonnet! but there was great family mirth!'[23] Accidents usually arose from Ellen's lack of concentration as she rushed around so full of ideas that road sense eluded her. Mercifully the Austin rather than Ellen suffered. After a crash in Middlesbrough, a pile-up in Sussex and an argument with a van in Covent Garden she escaped unscathed, but she was badly shaken in a collision near Banbury.[24] Not all accidents were of Ellen's making, and during the 1931 election campaign she suffered an unprovoked attack from a group of liberals who 'damaged her car deliberately and gave her such a hustling that she had a badly bruised shoulder'.[25]

With age, Ellen became increasingly liable to accidents. In part this was due to her cramming so much into a day, but over the years she incurred more than her share of physical mishaps which aggravated her bronchitis and asthma. She faced illness, as she faced danger, with stoic fearlessness.[26] Vernon Bartlett, an international journalist, whose main impression of Ellen was 'of a person with unusual courage', recalled an incident at Geneva in the thirties, which was typical:

> During the League of Nations Assemblies, we used to bathe in the Lake near the hotel where the British delegation used to stay. Most of us were pretty good swimmers, but Ellen could barely swim at all. Some of us began swimming out to a raft, and I well remember the doggedness with which Ellen tried to follow. We shouted to her to go back, but she persisted puffing and swallowing a lot of water. In the end we had to help her back or she would undoubtedly have drowned. This is certainly no tribute to her common sense, but it was most certainly one to her courage.[27]

Ellen's political life necessitated her having a base in London. Her tiny divan furnished flat in Bloomsbury with Lenin's portrait hanging over her bed, of which she used to say 'I look at it every morning and get cracking',[28] was as welcoming a place for committee meetings or parties as it was a haven for anti-fascist refugees. A mutual need to evade London's grime for health reasons, however, coupled with Ellen's eagerness to grasp some privacy away from parliamentary pressures, prompted the sisters to find a home in the country. In 1936 they acquired Twixtlands in Penn, Buckinghamshire, a 'small T shaped highwayman's cottage with a pleasant garden'. For a while lighting and cooking were paraffin fuelled, but the large brick fireplace was always warmly welcoming and later a delightful portrait of Ellen painted by one of her Civil Defence firemen hung above it. The family recall her and Herbert Morrison sitting on either side of the fireplace grappling with Cabinet and other official papers.[29]

Often 'tight up with worry and anxiety' Ellen would snatch a precious weekend at Twixtlands, for she found the country 'balm to her taut nerves'.[30] In a rare personal revelation she once wrote of:

the calm that came from a pre breakfast walk at Penn in early
March . . . after a relaxing sleep of utter silence . . . with the sun
washing down on light brown trees I became conscious of a light
veil, almost a breath, of green over leafless bushes. The sky was so
blue that I seemed to be moving in a medium of blue green light.
Thinking stopped. The worries weren't there. I had become part
of something bigger.[31]

Progressively, and especially during the war, Annie made Twixtlands a comfortable retreat for Ellen and their friends. She really
became 'Ellen's walking stick'.[32]

If Ellen was dependent on Annie, she had a deep rapport with her
elder brother Richard Arthur, a man of character. He had worked as
a joiner to enable Ellen and Harold to go to university, and then
studied at a Methodist theological college in Richmond, Surrey. As a
minister he spent twenty-seven years in his native Lancashire.[33] The
'Rev. Arthur', a good preacher, was proud of Ellen's political flair.
'My sister is one of the best-known women today', he said during an
election campaign. 'She stands for peace, is in the forefront of social
reform and has the welfare of people at heart.'[34]

Brother and sister were mutually supportive. Every year each gave
the other at least a weekend of practical help. Ellen would occasionally preach for her brother and officiate at his parish functions. He
would work in her elections — 'Once at Jarrow Arthur arrived to
find Ellen being carried out feet first and feared the worst. She was,
however, only suffering from having had a tooth out. So that weekend he took seventeen meetings for her!'[35] In his own way the Rev.
Arthur was a remarkable personality. After retirement he and his
wife went to live near Dunstable, where he continued to preach and
visit until his death. The chief strength and delight of his Ministry
was his love for people. 'I have had a happy life', he said only a week
before he died at ninety-three, 'Methodism has been good for me.'[36]

Harold, the youngest of the family, was not political. He was an
engineer and worked for Metro Vickers for whom 'he tested large
electric dynamos to destruction'. This he undertook with such
fearlessness in the face of danger (a family characteristic) that he
became known as the 'mad mechanic'. Later, with the BBC in
London, he was injured in the Blitz and had a nervous breakdown.
He too survived his biblical span of years.[37]

Affairs of the Heart

Ellen could be outrageously impulsive both in what she did and in what she said. When young she tended to think that every new idea or organisation of the Left offered the ultimate panacea. She was a compulsive 'joiner', often before she had examined basic implications.[38] Yet once she had given her allegiance she only retracted it when new circumstances convinced her that different action was necessary.

In her personal relationships Ellen was similarly impulsive and equally loyal. It is highly improbable that she ever took a calculated decision not to marry.[39] Yet because she cared so much about putting the world to rights and enjoyed rushing around trying to do this inevitably domestic ties seemed as shackles, and love affairs had to wait.[40] Ellen's whole pattern of life led logically to her remaining single. Walton Newbold had been rejected — and rightly so — on grounds of incompatibility. Ellen, like Joan in *Clash*, though highly emotional, had no desire to surrender her independence, but opted for 'the thrill of leadership, of being in the battle with the workers and of doing things that matter'.

Clash has a strong autobiographical flavour. Joan, the heroine, accepted that, if a woman of brains and power chose a career as the most important thing in life, 'she must make it a whole-time job if she is to compete on equal terms with men of her calibre . . . She might have love affairs, even marry, but if she means to do big things, then work is in the front of the picture.' Like Sarah Burton, the headmistress in Winifred Holtby's panoramic novel, *South Riding*, Joan's career counted above personal commitment. And this fact is not irrelevant, because Vera Brittain, the writer and a close friend of Winifred Holtby, confirmed that the character of Sarah Burton drew at least in part on Ellen Wilkinson.[41]

Opinion is divided as to the depths of Ellen's political ambition. Some argue that she never missed a trick and deliberately cultivated the 'right people'. Trade union colleagues had no illusions and some implied, though wholly without malice, that Ellen did tend to 'use' people.[42] Most friends believed that she cared about getting on only to help right the wrong and could not fail to meet prominent figures by virtue of her political obligations. What does seem certain is that by 1931, having tasted the crumbs of office, Ellen was aware of her political potential, and of the advantages in being free from domestic commitments. Fighting for the underdog and for socialism took precedence in her life. 'She poured into the Socialist Movement the creative energy which other women have given to husband and children', Ellen wrote later of Marion Phillips, in an unconscious epitaph of herself.[43] Even so, many men wove their way through Ellen's life, 'for she could do anything with them',[44] but each had to have the same interests as she. It was people's minds and their politics that initially interested her, impulsive affaires were far more in character than long-term entanglements.[45]

During the thirties Ellen's socialist and anti-fascist activities brought her into contact with distinguished foreign journalists — H.R. Knickerbocker, Louis Fischer, Fred Voigt of the *Manchester Guardian*, among many others. Their freedom to get about the world and their international contacts she greatly envied.[46] One such was Otto Katz (later known as André Simone) a talented propagandist and intriguer'.[47] Born in Prague, he worked in the Berlin entourage of Willi Muenzenberg and after the rise of Hitler fled to Paris from where, as André Simone, he helped produce the famous *Brown Book of the Hitler Terror*. He met Ellen over the Commission of Enquiry into the Reichstag Fire Trial. Lilian Hellman, the American writer, recalls Simone, when he was Director of the Spanish News Agency, as a 'slight, weary looking interesting man who had moved in many circles'.[48] To Arthur Koestler he was an unscrupulous opportunist. Dark and handsome with a somewhat seedy charm, 'He was attractive to women, . . . and used them adroitly to smooth his path. Paradoxically he was a very likeable human being, with the generosity of the adventurer.' Koestler recalls Simone 'directing his earnest charm at Miss Ellen Wilkinson and Mlle Genevieve Tabois, then the columnist-oracle of the *Oeuvre* . . . but', he added, 'these relationships were purely functional'.[49] Katz appears to have been an unprincipled womaniser. Ivor Montagu put it more gently: 'He had' he said, 'a most persuasive way with the ladies.'[50]

It is nonsense to assume that because Ellen had a range of male friends that she was promiscuous. She never wholly rejected the morality of her Methodist upbringing, though she was no Mrs Grundy and would never condemn anyone for enjoying sex. One friend who remembers her lending the Guilford Street flat 'for someone to have a bit of sin in', added 'I do think that Ellen was far too single minded about politics to have become too involved with anyone. And she was always very discreet.'[51] Nevertheless, there were three men identifiable in Ellen's life — John Jagger (JJ), Frank

Horrabin and Herbert Morrison — with whom she had long and loyal relationships.

'JJ', Yorkshireman, NUDAW President, was tolerant and supportive towards Ellen from her earliest days in the union, and remained so until his death. He provided as stable an anchorage to her political life as Annie did domestically. Those who knew Ellen well regarded JJ as a father figure who pulled her out of scrapes and gave her a secure base. Certainly he always materialised if she was in a politically tight corner. 'JJ was always careful of his reputation — he was married — but Ellen appreciated his qualities and especially his good brain.'[52] It is significant that in *Clash* Ellen describes William Royd — the key trade union figure in Joan's union — as 'Joan's refuge . . . as well as her chief . . . a tall, strongly built Lancashire man with a reserve of power hidden under a vague air of general geniality'.[53]

'JJ', as he was always known, was born at Saddleworth in 1872 and joined the AUCE when it was founded, the year of Ellen's birth. He worked in Oldham, went to Rangoon, travelled in the East, returned to employment in the York Co-operative Society and resumed an active role in union affairs. He was appointed full-time District Officer for Yorkshire the year after Ellen became the National Woman Organiser, and worked for the amalgamation of the AUCE and the Warehouse Workers' Union 'with great tact and diplomacy'.[54] He was unanimously elected President of the newly created NUDAW, and in 1935 he became MP for Clayton in Lancashire. An admiring pen portrait was drawn by Wright Robinson soon after amalgamation:

> This burly humorous and drawling President of ours, with an occasional irrational and uncalculable mistake emerges head and shoulders above any man . . . in our union. He is fair to colleagues, . . . and will say the best word for anybody accused. He is trusted by everybody and he deserves it.[55]

A strong sense of humour characterised JJ. He once listed his hobbies as 'walking when I cannot ride, sleeping when I cannot talk, and telling the truth in such a manner that people do not believe it', adding, 'for the other side of the story apply to Mrs Jagger'.[56] Ellen applauded this trait of irreverence: 'The ways of D.N. Pritt the lawyer and John Jagger the Trade Union leader have shown that no authority can discipline anyone with a sense of humour.'[57]

During the war JJ was PPS to Herbert Morrison both at the Ministry of Supply and the Ministry of Home Security. Tragically he was killed in an accident on his motorcycle in July 1942 during the blackout when travelling from Twixtlands to Beaconsfield Station back to the House. He had refused to use official cars because he would not waste petrol.[58] A much respected man, JJ was remembered as 'a President who knew all his members, made no discrimination between the highest and the lowest, and who always stood by what he believed in'.[59] A view reinforced by Ernest Fernyhough, former MP for Jarrow:

> JJ was the best Chairman I have ever encountered. When tempers were frayed at a difficult conference he was outstanding, and in his calm quiet way could let out steam from those people who thought that bawling was the only means to get attention.[60]

Perhaps Jagger's greatest contribution to his union was as a negotiator. He once said that 'if one cannot convince, it is policy to weary . . . especially if one can gain one's point by so doing!'[61] Above all he had the faculty for getting the best out of people, a quality Ellen learned to emulate.

It has often been suggested that Ellen and JJ were more than 'just good friends'. Muriel Nichol was not alone in thinking they may have lived together[62] and Wright Robinson expressed great scepticism during the twenties about their 'strange undefined' relationship, though he also expressed similar doubts about several other members of his staff![63]

There is however no firm evidence that Ellen and JJ had more than a close companionable working partnership. They shared common political objectives — both were left wing and strongly pro-Russian — and their union commitments converged. But the near twenty year age gap between the tiny Ellen and the burly avuncular JJ raises real doubts, which his granddaughter, who remembers them both, shares: 'I had always taken JJ and Ellen's association as genuinely platonic. If he had a meaningful relationship I would have said that it was with Anne, but this is purely guesswork.' A guess with which others concurred.[64]

There is little doubt that JJ exercised a wise and steadying influence upon Ellen. He encouraged her along a far more constructive political route than that cut out by Walton Newbold; tried to keep her enthusiasms within practical bounds; and was almost certainly instrumental in getting her name on to the union's Parliamentary panel. He was universally trusted, widely regarded as a 'very nice man indeed'[65] and remained a quiet, deep thinking, left-wing socialist with a full measure of shrewd Yorkshire commonsense. Ellen owed him a great deal.

Frank Horrabin, the inimitable cartoonist and cartographer, sometime editor of *Plebs*, who briefly became Labour MP for Peterborough (1929–31), was also a close colleague. He has been engagingly described by Dame Margaret Cole as 'looking when dressed for the part, exactly like the Mad Hatter — though he was neither mad nor bad, but sweet all through'.[66] Ellen and Frank had been campaigners and propagandists together in the Labour Movement long before she became an MP. After Frank 'the kindest of men' was elected to Parliament he is reputed to have carried her into the House when she was ill. They shared the same secretary, spent intermittent holidays abroad together and were generally thought by parliamentary colleagues to have been very close indeed. When later Horrabin was editor of the *Socialist Leaguer*, Ellen described him as 'quiet, intellectual and caring for the things of the spirit'.[67] Leah Manning, former MP for Epping considered that:

> early in the thirties when the long friendship with Horrabin was ended by his marriage, its close cut her deeply. It had been a warm, romantic attachment and Ellen went to India to try to forget . . . When she came back she was subtly changed.

The fires were still there, but more under control.[68] This may well have been true. For in the summer of 1932, before she went to India, Ellen had cryptically referred to 'a sudden and overwhelming bereavement which knocked me flat'. Whatever the reality, they long remained friends.[69]

Her relationship with Herbert Morrison was far more complex. Ellen had known him since her early Fabian days; sat with him on the NEC and had often spoken with and for him in the LCC elections. She clashed furiously with him at party conferences and, as a left-winger, disagreed heatedly with him over various basic political issues for Morrison — brilliant organiser and leader of the LCC — was a life long red hater, if not baiter. Nevertheless as Morrison became a prominent personality within the Labour hierarchy, time and again she acknowledged his abilities. For she not only admired achievers, but also must have been susceptible to his cockney ebullience, irrepressible optimism and lively charm.[70] Morrison was also a sympathetic feminist which undoubtedly pleased Ellen. He appointed able women to positions of public responsibility in hitherto male dominated preserves, such as chairmanships of LCC committees and membership of the Metropolitan Water Board, he made Dr Charity Taylor the first woman prison governor and generally had 'boundless faith in the capacity of women in the professions.'[71]

In her political commentaries Ellen often compared Morrison to Attlee. In the latter she divined 'springs of hidden power whose strength comes from a sense of deep devotion to a cause coupled with real personal disinterestedness'; in Morrison — the irreverent realist — she saw the essential proletarian.[72] 'Attlee', she added later:

has two fatal handicaps, honesty and modesty, but he is a subtle strategist, understands people and plays with his team . . . Herbert Morrison is an able administrator and a bit of a brute — the rudest man I know — he will invite you to his table and then read a detective novel . . . but . . . he is giving London almost exclusively gifts needed by the nation.[73]

From the mid-thirties Ellen doggedly sought to promote Morrison's candidature for leadership of the Labour Party, which is difficult to reconcile with their conflicting attitudes over basic principles. This suggests that her leadership machinations were prompted by something other than a purely political purpose. They were close friends, although 'Herbert certainly could get cross when Ellen did not do what he wanted politically',[74] and on occasion they adopted very emotional attitudes towards each other. They are remembered dancing at one particular Labour Party Conference in a manner which had strong sexual overtones. Physically they seemed well suited.[75]

Herbert certainly needed female companionship. Since politics were his life's blood, he rarely relaxed and his personal life was coldly prosaic. His first marriage, as distinct from his happy second 'round', was bleak. Mrs Morrison after a bad pregnancy (they had one daughter, Mary Joyce) 'suffered a nervous collapse and decided that there was to be no more sex . . . only their closest friends knew of the deep unhappiness of both.'[76] The aridity of this relationship was symbolised by Mrs Morrison's denying Herbert the pleasure even of coal fires which he loved, because of the dust they created.[77]

It was therefore to be expected that Morrison would have women friends — and he did. But there is an absence of documentary corroborative evidence — as distinct from gossip and hearsay — about his relationship with Ellen and indeed with others, except Lady Allen of Hurtwood, to whom he proposed marriage.[78] He was highly discreet inhibited by a fear over any exposure that might damage his career.[79] Nevertheless it is almost certain that towards the end of the thirties the relationship between Ellen and Herbert became more than platonic. They were lovers later rather than earlier in their lives and even if this was not a prolonged episode they remained close. Throughout much of the war they worked in ministerial harness. Often Herbert would visit Twixtlands at weekends — as he did the homes of several women friends, to seek calm from the burdens of office — to enjoy the welcoming hospitality that Annie dispensed.

Morrison's attitude towards Ellen when she was Minister of Education raises another query. It has been suggested[80] that Ellen was deeply hurt by his not supporting her in cabinet over raising the school leaving age. His opposition is difficult to explain. Perhaps it was formulated by his antipathy to Ernest Bevin who had long advocated the policy for which Ellen pressed. Moreover, in spite of certain LCC members having firm views on education he rarely expressed any interest.[81]

There are few records extant of Ellens' inner feelings on marriage, apart from opinions in *Clash*. Probably the most significantly revealing are those written in 1936 in a book review of *South Riding*:

> If the ambition of a modern girl is to be a doctor or a politician she inevitably kicks her colt feet around till well into her thirties, suffering and learning from her mistakes . . . a man may enjoy working with and talking to women in their forties, but it is only the exceptional man who can be in love with her . . . What usually happens to the woman who becomes absorbed in a career is that when her appetite for work is satisfied, her sex instinct is roused by a man who by his experience of life may be her real mate, but who has contracted obligations much earlier. That he may be through with these emotionally, only adds to the complications.[82]

The autobiographical implications are patent. It does seem highly likely that she was alluding to Herbert, even though both JJ and Frank Horrabin had also 'contracted obligations'.

Morrison believed that men in public life, ambitious to reach the top, must be like Caesar's wife.[83] Presumably it was to sustain this principle that he made so curious an omission in his autobiography, published in 1960, and dedicated to his second wife, Dimple (Lady Morrison). No references whatsoever are made to Ellen throughout, even though she promoted his bids for leadership, worked herself to exhaustion as one of his wartime Parliamentary Secretaries, and was the only woman in the 1945 Labour Cabinet. These are extraordinary omissions. For even if there never had been a close personal relationship between them, Ellen, one of the most colourful Labour women of two decades, had tripped in and out of Morrison's life. One can only conclude that the gap was intentional, because he felt there were matters to conceal. Perhaps in view of the dedication of his book, Morrison saw his silence as both golden and judicious. The great contentment that stemmed from his second marriage took absolute precedence. Faithfulness to the memory of his long comradeship with Ellen belonged wholly to things past.

Notes

1. Rt Hon. David Astor, Beryl Hughes and Maurice Reckitt, interviews.
2. 'In 1921 Ellen led the left flank of the National Guilds League . . . we had a famous Guilds Week at the Fabian Summer School that year. Margaret and Douglas Cole were at the top of their form; but the outstanding speech came from Ellen. So effective was her revolutionary eloquence that an exceedingly cautious old gentleman, Mr. Bottle, leapt from his seat to say he would draw his sword and join her at the barricades. The week ended with a grand 'revue' in which a guillotine . . . ended the lives of most of the actors . . . Ellen with flaming hair down to her waist and a vast red bow over her chest stood on a monstrous pile of corpses, exalting that ''at last we have got rid of all the people with middle class ideas''. She alone was left; the rest were butchered to make a Fabian holiday.' (Kingsley Martin, *New Statesman*, 15 February 1947.)
3. Beryl Hughes, Billy Hughes, and Lord Redcliffe-Maud, interviews.
4. M. Cole, *Growing Up Into Revolution* (Longmans, Green, London, 1926), pp. 145, 146.
5. Maud Bickford, letter of 6 December 1977.
6. Beryl Hughes, interviews; Rt. Hon. David Astor, interview; Kingsley Martin, *Picture Post*, 22 June 1940; Thelma Cazalet Keir in the *Sunday Times*, 9 February 1947; Lady Rhondda in *Time and Tide*, 15 February 1947; Betty Archdale, letter of 7 May 1978.
7. Lord Boothby, letter of 29 March 1978.
8. Dr Rene Saran, interview; Arthur Blenkinsop, interview; Jenny Lee, *My Life with Nye*, (Cape, London, 1980), p. 39 ('Ellen and Horrabin were impressive lecturers and good company'); Jenny Lee, letter of 25 November 1977.
9. Mrs Kathleen Wilkinson and Beryl Hughes, interviews.
10. Susan Lawrence in *Fabian Quarterly*, March 1947.

11. Professor H.J. Dent, letter of 20 April 1978.

12. Sir John Maud, *The Times*, 8 February 1947.

13. Lady Rhondda, *Time and Tide*, 15 February 1947.

14. Arthur Blenkinsop, interview.

15. M. Browne, *Too Late to Lament* (Gollanz, London, 1955), p. 305; *North Eastern Daily Gazette*, 25 March 1930.

16. *Daily Telegraph*, 23 November 1929; *Daily Herald*, 26 November 1929.

17. *Daily Herald*, 5 January 1925.

18. *Daily Film Renter*, 25 February 1930.

19. *Today's Cinema*, 5 July 1930.

20. *The Stage*, 19 March 1930.

21. S. Davies, *North Country Born* (Routledge and Kegan Paul, London, 1963), p. 223.

22. Mrs Muriel Wilkinson, Ivor Montagu, Fred Meadowcroft and others, interviews.

23. Mrs Muriel Wilkinson, interview.

24. *North Eastern Daily Gazette*, 11 April 1931.

25. *North Eastern Daily Gazette*, 24 October 1931; *News Chronicle*, 30 November 1937.

26. Beryl Hughes, interview.

27. Vernon Bartlett, letter of 15 May 1978.

28. Margaret Stewart, interview.

29. Mrs Muriel Wilkinson and Mrs Kathleen Wilkinson, interviews.

30. For an arcadian description of Penn village around 1939 see Cathleen Nesbitt, *A Little Love and Good Company* (Faber and Faber, London, 1975), pp. 188–90.

31. *Time and Tide*, 6 March 1937.

32. Harry Weate, Amy Mitchell, Ivor Montagu, Beryl Hughes, interviews.

33. Mrs Muriel Wilkinson, interview.

34. *South Shields Daily Gazette*, 12 November 1935.

35. Mrs Muriel Wilkinson, interview.

36. Extracts from an obituary notice via the Reverend W.N. Charles Woldbridge and the Reverend R.D. Moore.

37. Fred Meadowcroft, interview.

38. Dame Margaret Cole, interview.

39. Dame Margaret Cole, interview.

40. Amy Mitchell, interview.

41. Shirley Williams, letter of 5 December 1977. Vera Brittain, mother of Shirley Williams (former MP and Minister of Education) was a close friend of Winifred Holtby. Both were authors and regular contributors to *Time and Tide*.

42. Harold Weate, Dorothy Elliott and Amy Mitchell, interviews (all were trade union colleagues).

43. *Labour Magazine*, February 1932.

44. Mrs Muriel Wilkinson, interview.

45. H.D. (Billy) Hughes, Ivor and Helen Montagu, Heinrich Fraenkel, interviews.

46. *Time and Tide*, 21 December 1935.

47. Claud Cockburn, *I Claud* (Penguin, London, 1967), pp. 187–9.

48. Lillian Hellman, *An Unfinished Woman* (Little, Brown and Co., Boston, Mass., 1967), Bantam edn, 1970, p. 68.

49. Arthur Koestler, *The Invisible Writing* (Hutchinson, London, Danube edn, 1954), pp. 237–59.

50. Ivor Montagu, interview.

51. Betty Archdale, qualified barrister and headmistress now retired, acted as private secretary to Ellen during the 1930s when studying for the law. She was known as 'the office' because of her efficiency, particularly in election campaigns (Betty

Archdale, *Indiscretions of a Headmistress* (Angus and Robertson, London, 1972), p. 150–5.
52. Sir George Bishop, Mrs Muriel Wilkinson, interviews.
53. Ellen Wilkinson, *Clash* (Harrap, London, 1929), p. 8.
54. *New Dawn*, 1 January 1921.
55. Wright Robinson, unpublished papers, December 1921.
56. *New Dawn*, 1 January 1921.
57. *Time and Tide*, 8 May 1937.
58. Arthur Logan Petch, Myra Hutchings, interviews.
59. Harold Weate, interview.
60. Ernest Ferneyhough, MP, interview.
61. *New Dawn*, 20 August 1921.
62. Muriel Nichol, interview.
63. Wright Robinson, unpublished papers, May 1923.
64. Myra Hutchings, Beryl Hughes, Lord George Strauss, interviews.
65. Dame Margaret Cole, interview.
66. M. Cole, *Growing Up*, p. 69.
67. *Clarion*, 23 June 1934.
68. Leah Manning, letter of 13 November 1970.
69. Dame Margaret Cole, interview.
70. Sir George Bishop, Arthur Blenkinsop, Dame Margaret Cole, Beryl Hughes, John Parker and others, interviews.
71. Lady Morrison, *Memoirs of a Marriage* (Muller, London, 1977), p. 46.
72. *Time and Tide*, 28 December 1935.
73. *Sunday Referee*, 18 October 1936.
74. Ivor Montagu, interview.
75. Dame Margaret Cole, interview.
76. Lady Morrison, pp. 41–2.
77. B. Donoughue and G.W. Jones, *Herbert Morrison* (Weidenfeld and Nicolson, London, 1973), p. 472.
78. Polly Allen, interview; Lady Allen, *Memoirs of an Uneducated Lady* (Thames and Hudson, London, 1975), p. 236.
79. Donoughue and Jones, p. 473.
80. Michael Foot, interview.
81. Dame Evelyn Denington: 'He was just not interested in education'; interview.
82. *Time and Tide*, 7 March 1936.
83. Donoughue and Jones, p. 392.

7   ATTAINMENTS — 'RED ELLEN'

Journalism

Her writing was as vivid as her personality — Lady Rhondda

There was no doubt about it. As Michael Foot, MP said, "Ellen was a brilliant journalist."[1] So in the face of uncertainty over her parliamentary future she was fortunate in having an alternative source to the House through which to earn a living. After the disastrous election of 1931, the NUDAW re-established Ellen on their payroll as well as their list of parliamentary candidates. She was therefore again available for union work, but also able to pursue her second love — journalism. In this profession 'she had so great a flair and wrote with such force, wit and pith that at one time it had seemed a real possibility that her skill might deflect her from a political career', the *Manchester Guardian* wrote.[2] This in fact never happened — though 'letters or journalism lost a craftswoman to politics' — and Ellen did contribute on many subjects to a great variety of publications until she became a junior minister. Her articles, mainly for the popular press, were never without bite, for 'She cared about what she wrote more than the money she received and people and causes took precedence over her financial needs . . . Ellen [as Lady Rhondda said] possessed great generosity of mind.'[3]

For a while she had aspired to be a novelist and *Clash*, her first published book, had received mildly encouraging notices. Political novels were then unusual and those by a woman exceptional. Ellen explained that she wrote it:

> in snatched minutes in the House of Commons library and during train journeys up to Middlesbrough — those six gorgeous hours when one's conscience couldn't even begin to bully, . . . [so] even when the critics did their worst those two months of creative happiness could not be taken away.[4]

The novel, which was serialised in the *Daily Express*, was generally regarded as the forerunner of better things, yet even so it was not unsuccessful and had a print of about 3,000, which Ellen's agent regarded as 'quite good'.[5] The novel was also published in braille[6] which suggests that the author had popular appeal. She was 'A minx who carried through a hundred battles with her dashing courage, her quick temper and her glowing idealism [and] possessed the quality of good news value', as one reviewer commented[7].

Her second novel, *The Division Bell Mystery*, a detective story centred on the House, appeared in 1932 when her recollections of the private office were still fresh. It is amusing for its exposure of parliamentary quiddities and for voicing her thinly disguised personal reactions, for example, the back-bencher running upstairs to vote, 'who hadn't the least idea what it was all about . . . but that was the joy of the House. It gave everyone such a comfortable feeling that something had been done.' The book is still reprinted in America and a handful of copies is sold each year.[8] Ellen never wrote the definitive novel she allegedly intended — one in which the working classes were to take the centre of the stage.[9] Her best and wittiest book (published in 1931) was a collection of pen pictures, *Peeps at Politicians*. Ellen, who had once described the House of Commons as being 'full of future ex prime ministers',[10] fully justified in this book Winifred Holtby's assessment of her as 'a first rate journalist . . . writing with verve and wit, who had an eye for idiosyncracies'.[11]

The personalities she sketched included Sir William Jowitt, 'one of the few lawyers in the House who . . . talked as if he regarded you as a particularly dim juryman'; Jimmy Maxton, 'so handsome that he could make a reputation as a revolutionary on his looks alone'; and Winston Churchill 'to whom facts were the last thing of any concern . . . who loved ideas for their own sake, but who is cheerfully indifferent as to whether any new ones he acquires match the collection he already possesses'. Others of whom she wrote were Jennie Lee, 'beside whose colossal self-assurance Lady Astor appears like a fluttering girl', and Major Clement Attlee, in whom Ellen found 'a consciousness of laughter repressed, which makes it difficult to forget this quiet little man who was ironically amused at the queerness of humanity, too fastidious for intrigue, and too modest for over-ambition'. The sketches, shrewd and unmalicious, were widely chuckled over and showed little evidence of the vitriol into which Ellen allegedly had dipped her pen.

Throughout the thirties she wrote prolifically for newspapers and magazines ranging from the *Daily Herald* to *Pearson's Weekly*.

Even when back in the House she was able to continue journalism by getting up at six and working till nine before dealing with her post and parliamentary matters. In topical pungent articles, Ellen attacked any and every kind of injustice, from homosexuals being prone to blackmail, to the BBC's Director General 'becoming the judge of what we ought to want on the radio'.[12] Of course politics had high priority. Beaverbrook gave her an enviably free hand in the *Daily Express* and she also kept astute tabs on Labour personalities for the *Clarion*.

Visits to India, America and Germany widened international contacts. John Gunther of the *New York Times*, G.E.R. (Eric) Gedye, author of the powerful *Fallen Bastions*, Norman Ebbutt of *The Times* and Edgar Mowrer, author of *Germany Puts the Clock Back*, were among the sophisticated well-informed and mainly left-wing journalists with whom Ellen delighted to associate. Even so, on one occasion after she had been smuggled into a press conference in Berlin, she did decide that 'newspapermen were the world's Cassandras, and if ever I were a minister I would *listen* and let the pressmen talk to *me*!'[13] 'The life of a trusted foreign correspondent, with freedom to get about the world is an enviable one', she wrote in 1935, adding:

> Varied 'missions' have taken me to nearly every country in the world . . . The introductions I value when heading for trouble are not those to the bigwigs, but to the British and American correspondents . . . Their talk, if they trust you, pulls up the blinds of a country's politics.[14]

If Ellen produced lively political commentary, she also proved a good newshound for her paper, the *Sunday Referee*. When in Germany during March 1936 she was one of the first correspondents to get through a report about Hitler's troops marching into the Rhineland. This she did by phoning London 'with my head under the bedclothes so as not to be heard in the next room'.[15]

Possibly the most unusual experience she reported occurred on a lecture tour when she visited car workers on strike in Detroit:

> I was hauled through a window at midnight into a large plant which had been seized by the workers. The first striker I saw was a lad exhausted by picket duty, fast asleep on a car seat, hugging a cowboy story book . . . It was weird addressing the crowd in

those silent works. Afterwards I answered a fire of questions . . .
from a seat of a half-finished car.[16]

Ellen's chief loyalty was to Lady Rhondda's *Time and Tide*. Her
first signed review, of Low's cartoons, appeared in December 1930,
and from then on she contributed features, criticisms and leaders,
writing under her own name, the pseudonym East Wind, and in the
symposium of 'Four Winds'. From 1935 until the War there was
scarcely an issue which did not contain something signed or unsigned
by her. These columns fully reflected Ellen's major interests, but she
also wrote with rare appreciation of little things. She described the
'ultimate luxury' of buying a book the day it came out, or her delight
in semantic invention such as the word 'Muggeridging' which to her
meant 'denying the value of anybody's efforts to improve the evils
one sees and do nothing particular about it oneself!'[17]

Although a good journalist who could write lightly of light issues,
her political objectives were essentially serious and Ellen would ruthlessly dissect the implications of fascism and unemployment. She
detested both as threats to human dignity. Writing early in the Nazi
era, she warned against 'treating Hitler as a bad smell, a temporary
nastiness to be disinfected by boycott, or perfumed by legality.'[18]
Not surprisingly she was violently attacked in Hitler's own paper
which referred to her with singular inaccuracy as 'the Jew of Jews'.[19]

Ellen could also personalise issues with an inimitable twist. She
wrote of meeting in her local Bloomsbury bookshop a man who had
been for months in a Nazi concentration camp: 'his talk was of the
little day-to-day things, the camp routine, the mean little nastiness
too trivial to put into books . . . its petty surburban tyrannies'.[20]

She also described her affinity with the unemployed; of joining

a night march of Tynesiders tramping for seven miles in a bitter
wind in a demonstration against the meanness of the Means Test
. . . anyone who thinks that the class war is a myth invented by
James Maxton should talk to groups . . . in the grim little towns
of Durham county.[21]

Later came evocative articles about Spain in the Civil War; of how
miles from Madrid she met a clutch of men from Durham and South
Wales. Against a background of improvised torches on sticks, shedding a weird light on the ranks of khaki figures in Spanish cloaks,
'softly we sang the Internationale in memory of those who had

greeted me last May and who were now lying deep in Aragon. They had died for freedom and the right to one's own soul.'[22] Though generally Ellen's style was tough, sharp and witty, sentiment could creep in to reveal an acute sensitivity. Referring for example to Mavis Tate, MP, who died after a horrifying visit to German concentration camps, Ellen commented, 'her beauty was like a touch of frost and moonlight'.[23]

Scathing indignation unfailingly stamped her political assessments, particularly of Chamberlain's foreign policy. She was disgusted at 'Hitler's London Group of Britain's upper crust', whom von Ribbentrop, the German Ambassador in London, had so infiltrated that 'the Fascists were encouraged to think they could drive a wedge between Britain and her democratic allies'.[24] She expressed despair over Mussolini's invasion of Abyssinia and at Hitler's dismemberment of Czechoslovakia:

> In these days of shame . . . the present negotiations between Britain, Germany and Czechoslovakia are aimed at making Hitler's path easy for him . . . [They] read like a chapter in a new Gibbon, The Decline and Fall of the British Moral Empire.[25]

Lady Rhondda relied heavily on Ellen for ideas and for advice at the editorial board meetings which met weekly at the Ivy Restaurant in London.[26] She gave all her contributors great latitude, which doubtless strengthened Ellen's appreciation of her as owner/editor. Through the years, 'we would have royal rows, almost always about politics, but the deepening shadows of the coming war with Germany had much to do with our comradeship', wrote Lady Rhondda after Ellen's death. 'For on that we saw eye to eye. We neither of us pretended to believe in anything we did not hold to be true.' Ellen could be shaky over deadlines, though her copy was worth the press day scramble she often caused. Lady Rhondda certainly thought so. 'Her writing, for which any paper would have paid anything she asked, was as vivid as her personality. But Ellen wrote chiefly for causes and rarely ever worried about money.'[27]

Political understanding, Ellen believed, must be founded on facts, hence the publication of *Why Fascism?* in 1934, written in collaboration with Dr Edward Conze, a European refugee with a first-hand knowledge of Italian Fascism.[28] Their book analysed the economic roots of Fascism in Europe and of Mosley's projected policies for Britain. The basic causes of economic instability on which Fascism thrived were under-consumption and over-production. These, Ellen and Conze argued, could only be eliminated by the establishment of socialism. But to build socialism propaganda must be based on the factory, workshop and field, where wealth was created. 'Socialism cannot be presented as a gift from the PLP. It must come from the active participation and eagerness and understanding from the masses of the people.'[29] Their semi-Marxist analysis was not definitive and the book is somewhat turgid: but it is interesting for the light it sheds on Ellen's political beliefs at a time when she was in the parliamentary wilderness.

The Town That Was Murdered, 'a picture of capitalism at work', is undoubtedly Ellen's most lasting book. Published by the Left Book Club in 1939, it presented the history of Jarrow's economic growth, its total dependence on one shipbuilding firm, Palmers, and detailed the human misery to which that dependency gave rise. Again, it is a book written with some assistance, this time from George Bishop, then a brilliant research student, now a distinguished and knighted industrialist. His views on the economic development of Jarrow and the growth of the paternalistic Palmer's shipyard are readily identifiable from Ellen's sharp and angry accounts of the shocking conditions in Jarrow. The book is a powerful indictment, and prompts the thought that even if financial help for the unemployed today is more generous, and its administration arguably more humane than in the thirties, the feelings of rejection, and frustrated helplessness which unemployment generates still stalk abroad. Ellen's was a potent pen.

Jarrow — a New Constituency

Anyone who has been a parliamentary candidate knows that almost no one in the constituency believes that any candidate does any act of ordinary kindness without an eye on votes — Ellen

To us Ellen seemed a real Socialist, not merely a formal Labour Party member — Councillor Paddy Scullion

As a result of the Jarrow Crusade, Ellen gave to the Labour Movement and to the political world the concept that unemployment is intolerable — Rev. Lord Donald Soper

It would have been wholly understandable had Ellen grown dis-
enchanted with politics after the defection of the party leadership
and her own lost seat. She remained unbowed however and without
self pity, certain that 'no Labour Government should ever take
office again in a minority', and that, 'we must think and plan and
know what we will actually *do* when we get back into office'.[30] She
faced defeat defiantly. 'Although for a week I felt as if the whole
framework of life had crumbled, being torn up by the roots after
seven years could be rejuvenating'. With a candour MPs rarely
adopt she confessed:

> Parliament had been the centre of my life and suddenly I was not
> there . . . but it does an MP good to see that what he regarded as
> the centre of Britain's whole life is to most folk a curious assembly
> with incomprehensible ways.[31]

Hints were soon being dropped that Ellen would not stand again at
Middlesbrough East. It was no longer a safe seat and her union
regarded her as too valuable to lose. When therefore R.J. Wilson,
the NUDAW nominee and former Member for Jarrow decided that
'five elections and nine years was enough for any man in his mid
sixties' Ellen seemed the obvious successor. After parting on warm
terms with her Middlesbrough East constituents (they gave her a
silver teapot and a travelling case in appreciation of her 'seven years
dedicated service'[32]), Ellen was adopted as prospective Labour
candidate for Jarrow.

Jarrow at that time was a town of heartbreak — a workhouse
without walls. It was a constituency epitomising the human misery
of unemployment, which Ellen was to bring before the nation as the
town that capitalism murdered. Inevitably her selection caused some
dissension within the local party and the agent resigned in protest.[33]
Several members wanted a man — 'because politics are mainly concerned with economics and finance, a man should be found to tackle
them.' Although Ellen had a great advantage in being a NUDAW
nominee and in Jarrow being recognised as a union seat, no evidence
has surfaced to suggest any pre-adoption shenanigans. She would
not have been chosen had her fluency and informed mind failed to
convince the hard-headed delegates that she really was a person of
ability. For a woman to be selected by a safe constituency in the heart
of a male dominated shipbuilding area was highly unusual, and Ellen
was under no illusion about prevailing male chauvinism. At the

Labour Woman's Conference soon after her selection, she regretted that women 'do not get fair shares in the allocation of good constituencies'.[34]

Over the years Jarrow, which she won in 1935, received Ellen's caring attention. And the constituents took her to their hearts. Paddy Scullion, a former Councillor, Mayor and Alderman, still remembered her — 40 years later — 'full of fire in a short fur coat as old as her Grannie, which she always said she kept for Jarrow to make her equal to the Jarrow folk and they to her . . . she visited us as often as possible, would come into our homes and was soon known, as she had been in Middlesbrough, as "Our Ellen".' She spoke at Sunday night propaganda meetings in the Labour Party's small wooden hut, or to gatherings of a thousand and tears often came into her eyes when she attacked the living conditions of her Jarrow folk. Ellen was immensely well served by Harry Stoddart, her agent, who 'pushed her name everywhere and held the fort marvellously'. He ran surgeries, fed her with local problems, and is remembered as 'a man who would not hurt a fly'.[35]

Ellen was no stranger to the misery and human wastage created by unemployment. She had already pleaded in the House for the iron and steel industries to get together under a nationalised board to fight continental competition, and had urged their total reorganisation with workers' participation. 'If we establish a real partnership we shall get the whole atmosphere changed with a willingness to look at trade union rules.'[36] If Ellen fought hard for the people of Middlesbrough, she fought even harder for the people of Jarrow, leading deputations to Westminster before she had been elected, pleading for the unemployed, and advocating the replanning of the Tees-Tyneside area as a *whole*. 'The Government should regard it — with its coal, chemicals, steel and shipping — as one big experimental area . . . dovetailing the various industrial interests', she wrote.[37] Jarrow too should be planned, 'but that cannot be done while land remains at prohibitive prices. I am sick of hearing about the sacred rights of private property. I want to hear about the sacred rights of human life.'[38]

Ellen steeped herself in Jarrow's complex industrial problems. As virtually a single industry town, its life blood of employment flowed from Palmer's shipyards.[39] Since the First World War, owing to contracting demand, one-third of all British shipyards were closed and sold, including in 1934 Palmers, 'the only shipbuilding concern to handle within its own walls the whole process from iron-quarrying and steel making to the launching of ships'.[40] As demand fluctuated, murmurs of nationalisation were countered by talk of rationalisation, and in 1930 National Shipbuilders' Security Limited (NSS) had been set up to make shipbuilding profitable by eliminating inefficient competition and scrapping redundant sites.[41] The final ignominy which Palmers suffered after closure was the proviso imposed upon the purchasers that the site must not be used for shipbuilding within a period of forty years.

As if all this were not enough, plans to revive the steel industry were scotched by the government. Jarrow had been selected in the investigatory Brassert Report, as a centre for a vast new integrated steel plant, where good quality Bessemer steel could be produced cheaply, but such an innovation would be a price challenge which rival firms distrusted. So even though demand for steel was rising because of rearmament, the Iron and Steel Federation killed the scheme by denying access to the markets it controlled. All overtures to the government on behalf of Jarrow proved fruitless. Ellen understood these economic manoeuvres only too well, and they are fully spelt out in her book, *The Town That Was Murdered*. To her the essence of unemployment, which she firmly believed only sound socialist planning could rectify, was the family misery and accelerated poverty which stemmed from it. In Jarrow some skilled craftsmen had been idle for 15 years, and in December 1932 nearly 80 per cent of the insured population was out of work,[42] a level which did not fall substantially until the War brought full employment in its wake.

In the 1930s living conditions in Jarrow were appalling. The death rates both of adults and of children were among the highest in the country and the incidence of deaths from tuberculosis was double the national average. A 'leprous blight' had indeed afflicted the town 'wherein men of 26 had never had a job and the boys and girls leaving school faced only a desolate future'.[43] Ellen, angrily challenging the Minister of Health's statement that there was no real starvation or malnutrition in her constituency, quoted the case of three young male workers who had died in swift succession from malnutrition, and whom the local vicar had described as 'looking like egg shells — all right outside but when faced with an infection in winter they had cracked'.[44] All over Britain, as Harold Laski echoed, while wealth accumulated men decayed.[45]

During the period when Ellen first joined battle with authority over the agonies of Jarrow she had a curious encounter with

MacDonald, related in her book with a surprising tolerance. Early in 1934 she led a mass deputation to lobby the former Labour leader, now Premier of a Conservative Government, at his Seaham constituency. He received representatives, listened to the woes of women bringing up families on the dole, promised them consideration and then made an outrageous gaffe. 'Why', he asked Ellen, 'don't you go out and preach socialism which is the only remedy for all this?' 'What a priceless remark from him', she commented.[46]

The Jarrow Crusade — 'A Great Folk Movement'

During the run-up to the 1935 election the Conservatives had made repeated pledges about their obligations to the distressed areas. Yet, the election won, all overtures on behalf of Tyneside in general and Jarrow in particular by MPs, the Jarrow Council and local businessmen for the regeneration of local industry were ignored. In the House Ellen demanded action: but in vain. 'Their attitude is damnable', she said, 'We cannot have a shipyard; we cannot have steelworks. What do they propose to do?'[47] The government's attitude — its lack of sensitivity and unwillingness to act — was epitomised by the heartless remark of Walter Runciman — President of the Board of Trade: 'Jarrow,' he said, 'must work out its own salvation.'[48]

This was the final straw. Since suggestions and deputations had proved fruitless, the people of Jarrow made a decision 'that may well have averted revolution'.[49] They themselves would tell their plight to the nation. A special Jarrow Borough Council meeting unanimously resolved to prepare a petition praying the government 'actively to assist Jarrow's resuscitation of industry', and resolved that 'a march be organised to present it'. The council drew attention to incensed public opinion which the situation had engendered, and requested the government, 'not to persist in asking forbearance of the people whose patience and resistance, tried to breaking point, are almost beyond knowing which way to turn for relief of the distress which they have for years experienced'.[50] A week later the council made a further decision. All physically fit townspeople were to be permitted to take part in the march, but — ironic chauvinism — 'Women were not to be encouraged'!

Ellen was well experienced in protest with and for the unemployed. As an old supporter of Wal Hannington's National Unemployed Workers' Movement, she had unofficial discussions with him prior to the Jarrow Crusade because, she told him, 'you're an expert in organising hunger marches'. Hannington suggested that the Jarrow contingent should join with the march he was currently organising. This Ellen recommended to the Jarrow Council, but the proposal was rejected, because the NUWM was a proscribed organisation.[51]

The Crusade, as it became known, had all-party support from the council, and was organised with military efficiency by Councillor David Riley. Ellen described him — a hefty Irishman who throughout the operation was never seen without his bowler hat — as a man 'with a will of iron and a way with him'. They had several stand-up fights in the early days, 'but on the march I succumbed willingly to his leadership as did everyone else'.[52] Riley was greatly heartened by the hospitality received from both Labour and Tory councils along the route, 'I never thought that there was so much generosity and good nature in the world' he said.[53]

On 5 October 1936, the Jarrow contingent of 200 men, each medically checked and equipped with a kitbag, were given an official send-off. A group of journalists saw them depart, but Lord Ritchie Calder, then a reporter on the *Daily Herald*, was one of the few who walked all the way. The Crusade was blessed by the Bishop of Jarrow, although he subsequently retracted, explaining that he had only taken supportive action 'because the Chief Magistrate had asked him'.[54]

Ellen did not, as folklore relates, walk *all* the way from Jarrow to London, though she did cover much of the journey on foot, and spoke nightly at public meetings organised en route. Her participation had its disadvantages because of her short stature — Ritchie Calder recalls her taking 'three steps to every one of ours which upset the rhythm of the marchers'. Nevertheless her courageous toughness was a great incentive; all too often she was seen walking 'almost unconscious on her feet'.[55] One of Ellen's secretaries, Betty Archdale, her chauffeur during several election campaigns and on the Crusade, tried to prevent Ellen's overdoing things: 'I drove slowly and deliberately and wasted time when we were trying to catch up with the marchers, but she spotted what I was doing and told me to get a move on.'[56]

Half way through the march Ellen rushed up to Edinburgh for the Labour Party Conference, determined to win official support for the Crusade. She made one of the most outstanding speeches in her career, in which she opposed the conference's suggestion for yet another report on the Special (i.e. distressed) Areas and castigated the NEC and the National Council of Labour for their purely negative policies. The NEC, she said, disapproved of the Crusade because some of those protesting might be Communists,

> yet you cannot expect men trapped in the distressed areas to stay there and starve because it is not convenient having them come to London . . . I only hope that when Sir Walter Citrine [Secretary of the TUC and a bitter anti-Communist] gets to the pearly gates, Saint Peter will be able to convince him that there is no Communist inside. I tell the Executive that they are missing the most marvellous opportunity of a generation. The March of Jarrow is a great folk movement. What propaganda speech is equal to that vast object lesson of the town that was murdered in the interests of the Stock Exchange and rationalisation? . . . The Party must put itself at the head of a great movement of moral indignation . . . If we cannot do this, what use is our Labour Movement? . . . Unemployment is bigger than a political party. It is a national danger and a national scandal.[57]

Histrionic or not, it was a speech of impassioned sincerity made through tears, and had immense appeal; but not enough. For the conference, under a leadership that was fumbling, incompetent and without any sense of direction (in Harold Laski's view), decided to remain aloof, merely agreeing to set up — under Hugh Dalton's chairmanship — a Committee of Enquiry into the Distressed Areas to produce a policy for rehabilitation.

Ellen was heartbroken at this seemingly negative response. In fact the committee's report — *Labour and the Distressed Areas*—published early in 1937, was practical and constructive, even though Dalton admitted the same year to the Labour Party Conference that glib talk of rapid economic recovery in the distressed areas 'was a cruel mockery'. Ellen then paid tribute to the excellence of the report, made in her own words an *amende honourable*, and recognised the importance of the regional industrial planning it proposed.[58]

After her Edinburgh intervention and two meetings in Manchester, Ellen rejoined the marchers, though she had to defend herself against spurious allegations that she merely 'dropped in on them intermittently'.[59] In fact, as she wittily observed, 'so many motorists along the route raised their hats to us that we began to feel like monuments!'[60] Certainly the men were generously treated. Sammy Rowan, seconded from the council to handle cash matters, remembers 'two hundred pairs of underpants and grey flannels being given us, and cobblers of the Leicester Co-operative Society working through the night to repair our shoes'. Councillor Riley noted that 'the men's health at the end of the Crusade was much better than when we started'. This he attributed to 'plenty of good food, assured accommodation, exercise and the moral effect of a positive goal after years of idleness through unemployment'.[61]

Pouring rain had succeeded the golden autumn weather when the men reached London on the last day of October. Yet they were undeterred even though (in Ellen's words) 'we all looked so ramshackle and weary that the waiting press men dubbed us the picture of a walking distressed area'.[62] Ramshackle or not, the contingent made a lasting impression on many observers, not least on Eleanor Goodrich, a life-long socialist, who could recall even at the age of ninety, the marchers' arrival in London. 'I remember seeing Ellen at their head and the sight of that procession moved me so deeply that when I reached home I cried desperately.'[63]

Officialdom was coldly unsympathetic. The government thoroughly disapproved of the Crusade, declined to meet the marchers and rejected Attlee's plea that the men had every right to approach Parliament 'as the Great Assize for redeeming grievances'. The Bishop of Durham in a letter to *The Times* declared such marches to be revolutionary, 'because they substituted organised mob pressure for the provisions of the constitution',[64] although the Bishop of Sheffield, who earlier had blessed the men en route, had affirmed that they were doing 'a most English and constitutional thing'.[65]

In line with time-honoured protocol the petitions were presented at the Bar of the House. The one from Jarrow, with its 11,000 signatures, bound in a blue leather hand-tooled book, was deposited by Ellen, reportedly in tears. The second from other Tyneside towns had 68,500 signatures and was handed in by the Conservative, Sir Nicholas Gratton-Doyle, as the longest-serving MP in the Newcastle area.[66] The courteously worded Jarrow petition anxiously prayed 'that HM Government realise the urgent need for providing work for the town without further delay, actively assist resuscitation of industry, and render such other actions as may be meet.'[67] Ellen briefly, but emotionally, reinforced this dignified plea and reminded the House that whereas 'formerly 8,000 mainly skilled workers were employed in Jarrow, now only 100 men are at work, and those on temporary schemes'.[68]

After the presentation, marchers and Jarrow notables addressed a crowded meeting in the House of Commons. Members of all parties saw the Mayor, Alderman J. Thompson, hold out his chain of office, point to its gold anchors, 'symbols of the thousand ships we built at Jarrow', and heard his warning that Members of Parliament would regret letting a great national asset be scrapped in the interests of private profit'.[69]

The Crusaders returned home by train and among those who saw them off was (Sir) Malcolm Stewart, Commissioner for the Special Areas who had yearned to help in the face of his severely restricted powers. 'Your march,' he told the men, 'will remind the country of the courage and the patience with which you have endured unemployment'.[70] The Borough Council formally praised all participants in the Crusade, which had been 'a credit to the town, and in a forceful though peaceful way had brought the position of Jarrow before the world'. They applauded Councillor Riley for refusing ever to admit defeat from the inception of the whole idea and warmly thanked Ellen, 'for her courage and example . . . marching at the head of the men for the greater part of the journey.'[71]

The Crusade had an interesting spin-off, related to constitutional rights. The government had refused the men of Jarrow audience on the grounds that grievances should properly be aired through Members of Parliament. This decision was passively accepted by the crusaders, although, as the *Manchester Guardian* remarked, 'if any marchers ought to have been received by a minister, it was they'. The Labour opposition were less amenable, urging the government to reconsider their policy and to receive representatives from Wal Hannington's NUWM who had marched the same week from Scotland and the North with their MPs. Ellen accused the government of making 'a fetish of precedent', while Chuter Ede declared with anger equal to Ellen's, 'I am not in the House to preserve precedents that deny the rights of humanity.'[72] The Government stood firm and then, to everyone's amazement, turned turtle. The Minister of Labour, Ernest Brown, received a deputation from the NUWM. It may well have been that the men of Jarrow did not make themselves 'nuisance enough';[73] unlike Hannington's contingent they did not parade up and down Whitehall, nor did their leaders try to obtain an interview with the Prime Minister.

The negative attitude of officialdom contrasted with the sympathetic initiative which came from the South of England. Sir John Jarvis, an industrialist who was High Sheriff of Surrey, with Chuter Ede, inaugurated a practical 'relief scheme' whereby Surrey 'adopted' Jarrow, and promoted projects for the unemployed. This idea, generous-minded but superficial, enabled a new park to be laid out in Monkton Dene, Jarrow, and, with help from the Commissioner for Special Areas, created a new sports arena where men could work voluntarily without losing unemployment benefit.[74] Sir John also announced, shortly before the crusaders presented their petition, his intention to start a tube mill and allied industries in Jarrow. This was resented, because it created the impression that such action would resolve all Jarrow's problems, whereas it offered nothing more radical than 'patchwork assistance'.[75] Yet Sir John's efforts deserve acknowledgement. In Ellen's view he injected a sense of urgency into attracting industry to Jarrow[76] and after long negotiations with the Consett Iron Company, in which Ellen was directly involved, the town did get its new steel works, though not the big integrated plant of the Brassert Scheme. Nevertheless, the plant, on part of Palmer's old site, was warmly welcomed 'even though the workers had no share whatsoever in the control of the new rolling mills'.[77]

What then did the Crusade — which according to the Rev. Dick Sheppard so disturbed the nation that things began to happen — really achieve? It threw a national spotlight on the plight of the unemployed; it directed attention to the economic implications of the distressed areas; and it stimulated interest in factory trading estates. Such schemes were promulgated by a Middlesbrough accountant, (Sir) John Sadler Forster[78] who pursued his vision for assisting the jobless by creating government-sponsored industrial estates.[79] Ironically, and tragically, it was not peaceful crusading but the impetus of rearmament which brought industrial activity back to Jarrow.[80] The north-eastern shipyards were only fully invigorated by the demands created by war. The fundamental problems of the distressed areas, however, were only seriously tackled when hostilities ceased.[81]

The Crusade however did have intangible results. Quite simply, as Paddy Scullion said, 'It enabled us to keep our self respect.' And, too, it disturbed the middle classes. Many, becoming guiltily aware of the madness of want amid plenty, began to ask questions and for the first time veered towards socialism. 'If we had even a remote sense of social justice Jarrow — and Ellen — made us think about reform,' one observer remembers.[82] Opinion was even stirred overseas; the *African Post* wrote sagaciously: 'unless a person proves his condition is desperate, no one will ever be concerned'.[83] For her part Ellen had always seen the Crusade as a protest and not as a panacea. 'It struck,' she wrote, 'the imagination of the people of Jarrow',[84] but for once she made an understatement. It moved the conscience of a nation.

History has identified Ellen with the Crusade, even though hers was but one of many voices in that massive folk cry. Yet her vivacious tenacity and foot-slogging determination, reinforced by a poignant, pugnacious pen, stamped Ellen's contribution as special and one which the people of Jarrow did not forget. During a grim period of the Second World War — on 25 July 1941 — the council conferred upon their Member of Parliament the highest civic accolade, the Freedom of Jarrow. 'For distinguished and eminent service . . . To you the Borough has been an object of special care', read the citation. This acclamation by her own people was Ellen's real moment of glory.[85]

The Hire Purchase Act, 1938

> The Act was one of the few important measures of social reform of the decade — Branson and Heinemann, *Britain in the Nineteen Thirties*, p. 261.

For a while after Jarrow Ellen remained in the limelight. A prophet however is not without honour and several local Labour Party members severely censured their MP. This aroused considerable comment out of which, characteristically, Ellen made political capital for the benefit of her constituents. She reminded the world in a letter to the *Manchester Guardian*:

> The lack of work . . . brings inevitably a tendency to magnify small disputes out of all proportion. The transition from the fully lived enthusiastic days of The Crusade means that the unemployed Jarrow men need to make more adjustments than those with comfortable lives can realise.[86]

She continued to receive criticism for allegedly neglecting her constituency, and for dealing with matters beyond the town's immediate interests. 'Jarrow has a globe trotting MP, Miss Wilkinson is work-ing for too many causes to do justice to Jarrow', a local newspaper complained.[87] In fact, whatever required Ellen's attention in West-minster and beyond, she never neglected Jarrow. On the contrary in January 1938 when a steel rod making works was opened there local industrialists warmly acknowledged her help over negotiations and 'had nothing but admiration for the way she had Jarrow interests at heart', the formerly hostile local paper eulogised somewhat shame-facedly.[88]

It was in fact concern for her constituents over hire purchase abuse that had first prompted Ellen to initiate action which resulted ulti-mately in a memorable parliamentary triumph. A Middlesbrough solicitor had drawn her attention to the impact on family finances which hire purchase could effect. He cited the case of a constituent who, having paid off three quarters of the HP instalments on his furniture, became unemployed and fell into arrears. He lost all his goods, had to pay court costs when sued by the vendor, and this was all entirely legal. Such was the account Ellen gave to the House when, under the Ten Minutes Rule, she asked leave to introduce her Hire Purchase Bill in December 1930.[89] This drew no opposition, was formally accepted, but lapsed when Parliament was dissolved. So not until 1937, having won a place in the Private Members' Ballot, could she proceed with a reform widely thought to be very necessary.[90]

During the gloomy thirties few working-class families were able to resist the lure of hire purchase agreements. Buying on the 'never-never' held a magnetic appeal. To many of the eight million families in England who lived with little or nothing between them and destitu-tion but their weekly wages, unemployment relief or old age pen-sions (and two million of these people had no margin whatsoever for savings)[91], hire purchase was unavoidable. To obtain the family bed, chairs, radio or even clothes, people would agree to pay small weekly sums and signed contracts to that effect, but the implications few understood and even fewer could afford. A housewife had imme-diate possession, but it was rarely explained that until the full sum had been paid for the goods she had no *legal* ownership and they were on hire. Commercial interests valued HP for stimulating demand and by the late thirties probably two-thirds of all mass-produced goods from clothing to cars were sold on that basis. Yet the cash price of the items and the high rates of interest charged were rarely disclosed.

Probably the nastiest aspect of this flawed legislation, termed by Ellen 'the cancer of the whole system', was the 'snatch-back'. As she had instanced in the House, if a hire purchaser defaulted for whatever reason firms could legally take back goods — even on the penultimate instalment — without having to refund down-payments. On average some 600 cases of seizure without compensation occurred daily, J.R. Leslie told Members, and many goods, particularly radios and furniture, were profitably resold. One trader admitted taking back a wireless set seven times and selling it at the original price on the eighth.[92] Often when goods were 'retrieved' by 'bruisers' additional possessions were seized arbitrarily to cover court costs. Consumers, too easily cajoled into signing agreements, were caught in legal nets from which the judiciary could not free them. As Judge Frankland of Leeds said: 'Week after week I listen to the accounts of minor tragedies affecting the welfare of working people and in the vast majority of cases I am utterly powerless to avert them.'[93]

Clearly there were many aspects of hire purchase provision which merited Ellen's serious attention. In this she was greatly assisted by Dr (Jimmy) Mallon, her old ally from trade board battles. He set up a working party of social workers, practising lawyers and county court judges to collate information about HP abuse. Their authoritative evidence enabled Ernest Watkins, solicitor and member of the Haldane Society — a society of socialist lawyers — to draft the first outline of the Bill which Ellen eventually presented. Watkins was an interesting man. With Ambrose Appelbe and other Haldane Society colleagues, he had helped to pioneer a Poor Man's Lawyer Centre at Toynbee Hall, one of the first in Britain. Ellen had sat in at the Centre on several occasions, once at least with HRH the Prince of Wales. She dined often at Toynbee and spoke to the Enquirers Club there, of which Professor Tawney, Beveridge and Lord Woolton were members. 'She was', Appelbe recalls, 'a flame of inspiration.'[94] For several years the Toynbee Group worked to get agreement between hire purchase firms and social workers all over the country, and although the Bill was steered through the House by Ellen its success was grounded in the hard spade work of Jimmy Mallon and Ernest Watkins.

Ellen's handling of the Bill was exemplary. From the outset, unexpectedly temperate and tactful, she stressed that 'no honourable or reputable interest has anything to fear', and that she was hostile only to 'those firms unscrupulously using loopholes in the law'. She assured MPs that her Bill was 'merely a small *social* reform over which a common measure of agreement had been sought'.[95] A brief propaganda film in the famous March of Time series helped to popularise the Bill — the brain child of George Woods, a credit checker and bitter critic of the Hire Purchase system, it exposed the racketeering methods employed. Personalities associated with the Bill, Sir Harold Bellman, Lord Amulree, John Jagger, Dr Mallon, E.S. Watkins and of course Ellen were among those who participated in the film, which provided some telling publicity.[96]

Broadly the Bill covered both credit sales and hire purchase agreements. It required traders to display on the goods the actual cash price plus the sum added for interest, and protected hirers who had paid at least one third of the sum contracted. If people genuinely could not afford to pay their full weekly commitments, the Courts were given powers to vary the payments but not the other conditions of the hire purchase agreement. Ellen regarded all this 'a pretty big concession to the HP firms. But I was assured that the British Constitution might drop from its foundations if judges were given the power of variation.'[97] Her major speech explaining the Bill on its Second Reading was remarkable both for its humility, humour and grasp of detail, and for the fact that she had only, within hours, returned on a frighteningly turbulent flight from Republican Spain.

Throughout the subsequent niggling negotiations with all interested parties, Ellen displayed exceptional restraint and consummate skill. When the Bill was finally piloted through in May 1938 she received widespread praise and was acclaimed in the House as no 'mere private member' for her ability in satisfying almost everybody in turn. She herself was terse and modest. She paid appreciative tribute to the help of the Attorney General, Sir Donald Somervell, and his Department, without whom 'it would have been utterly impossible for so complicated a Bill to have been piloted through by a private Member', and thanked all Members 'who had subordinated their own views to the need for passing the Bill for ending a scandal to which all took exception'. In his turn, Somervell congratulated Ellen both for the way she had handled the situation in Standing Committee and the House, and on the patience with which she had conducted the arduous negotiations. The neatest tribute of all came from the redoubtable Tory individualist, Herbert Williams. Not only did he see 'the speed and manner of the Bill's final passage' as 'the most remarkable Parliamentary achievement for many years', but he also complimented Ellen for having 'formed a Popular

Front' in the House and 'completely enslaved the Attorney General and all the Government Departments concerned'.[98]

Ellen had reason to be satisfied. Even though she admitted that the Act was far from perfect:

> We got through a good deal more than some people had expected and on the whole it is better to get through a Bill commanding the widest measure of agreement with the trade than to force through a measure in the face of resentment.[99]

The Building Societies Bill

The Hire Purchase Act, which became law in July 1938, was not Ellen's sole venture into the field of consumer protection. She made one further foray, justified though unsuccessful, to protect house purchasers against jerry-building. In February 1939 she introduced the Building Societies (No. 1) Bill (drafted by Bill Sedley) designed to safeguard people who were buying houses through building societies but found that there was no adequate warranty if defects were found.[100]

In the early thirties when subsidies on council houses were virtually stopped, private building flourished. These new homes were bought mainly through Building Society mortgages, and to assist the purchasers of small means a scheme of dubious legality, 'The Builders' Pool', was devised. This enabled Building Societies to advance up to 95 per cent of the house price, so that a £500 house could, for example, be secured with a £25 deposit. The pitfall in this scheme was, as the famous case of Mrs Elsy Borders highlighted,[101] that Building Societies offered no guarantee of the quality of the properties purchased, and it was this that most interested Ellen. While the 'Borders' case was in train, Ellen's Bill, designed to protect tenants and to legalise the Pool retrospectively, came before the House. It provided that the amount of collateral security from the Builders' Pool should be known to the buyer before purchase and allowed the buyer to withhold mortgage on grounds of poor standards. 'Really it seems that Miss Wilkinson's Bill and the 'Borders' case together have made it impossible for the government to introduce a Bill legalising the Pool without safeguarding the buyer', *Time and Tide* commented.[102] But such optimism proved ill founded.

Ellen was outmanoeuvred. The day she presented her Bill Sir John Simon announced that the government was introducing its own legislation and the Building Societies (No. 2) Bill was speedily pushed through. The Pools were legalised retrospectively, no protection was conceded to the purchaser, and Ellen's proposal to issue a warranty as to the quality of the houses bought, was rejected as impracticable because 'the builders were the ones who knew these things'. Criticising the Bill 'for giving so handsome a present to the Building Societies but no protection to the victim', Ellen commented acidly that were she ever charged with the offence of murder she would enlist the services of Sir John Simon since 'he would not only prove to the world my innocence, but explain away the body as well'.[103]

Although she won some amendments in Committee Ellen could not stem the tide. The government had not only pre-empted Ellen's Bill and allowed the status quo to continue, but also had virtually legalised all the abuses that had been committed before her Bill had been introduced.[104] If she was disappointed over this, her Hire Purchase Act had been a real achievement. The forerunner of much consumer protection legislation, it was a landmark indeed, and it has been justifiably termed 'one of the few important measures of social reform inaugurated during the decade'.[105]

Notes

1. Michael Foot, interview.
2. *Manchester Guardian*, 7 February 1947.
3. Lady Rhondda, *Time and Tide*, 15 February 1947; Beryl Hughes, interview.
4. *The Star*, 12 April 1929.
5. Patience Ross, letter of 12 December, 1980.
6. Martin Lee (George Harrap), interview.
7. Winifred Holtby, *Sunday Times*, 9 June 1929.
8. Michael Thomas of A.M. Heath and Co., Literary Agents, interview.
9. *News Chronicle*, 13 December 1935.
10. *Sunday Times*, 20 May, 1945.
11. *Time and Tide*, 2 August 1930.
12. *Evening Standard*, 16 March 1931.
13. *The Clarion*, 9 June 1934.
14. *Time and Tide*, 21 December 1935.
15. *Sunday Referee*, 15 March 1936.
16. *Time and Tide*, 20 February 1937.
17. *Time and Tide*, 14 December 1935.
18. *Time and Tide*, 1 April 1933.
19. *The Times*, 4 May 1933.
20. *Time and Tide*, 3 December 1935.

21. *Time and Tide*, 14 January 1933.
22. *Time and Tide*, 18 December 1937.
23. *Daily Express*, 19 February 1932.
24. *Time and Tide*, 19 March 1938.
25. *Time and Tide*, 26 March 1938.
26. Beryl Hughes, interview.
27. Lady Rhondda, *Time and Tide*, 15 February 1947.
28. Much later Ellen tried unsuccessfully to help him obtain a lectureship in the Extra-Mural Department of Oxford University, and was extremely angry when the Delegacy failed to appoint him (H.D. Hughes, interview).
29. E. Wilkinson and Edward Conze, *Why Fascism* (Selwyn and Blount, London, 1934), p. 315.
30. *Cambridge Press*, 15 January 1932.
31. *Pearsons Weekly*, 5 December 1931.
32. *Newcastle Chronicle*, 14 May 1932.
33. *Cambridge Daily News*, 11 May 1932.
34. *News Chronicle*, 15 June 1932.
35. Paddy Scullion, interview.
36. *North Eastern Daily Gazette*, 12 December 1930; *New Dawn*, 6 December 1930.
37. *Daily Herald*, 23 April 1934.
38. *North Mail*, 26 March 1935.
39. In the mid-nineteenth century Charles Mark Palmer (1822–1907) had laid the basis for the shipyards (and his family's) great fortune by introducing the transport of coal by tramp steamers. See *Palmer's Shipyard and the Town of Jarrow*, compiled by Vince Rea (Bede Gallery, Jarrow, 1975).
40. Ritchie Calder, *Daily Herald*, 30 October 1936.
41. Ellen Wilkinson, *The Town that was Murdered* (Gollancz, London, 1939), p. 149.
42. Ibid., p. 192.
43. Ritchie Calder, *Daily Herald*, 30 October 1936.
44. Hansard, Vol 314, cols. 1263–70, 8 June 1936.
45. *Labour Monthly*, November 1936, quoting Goldsmith, 'The Deserted Village'.
46. Ellen Wilkinson, *The Town*, p. 196.
47. *North Mail*, 21 July 1936.
48. Ellen Wilkinson, *The Town*, p. 198.
49. Paddy Scullion, interview.
50. Jarrow Borough Council Minutes, 20 July 1936, 27/28 July 1936.
51. Wal Hannington, *Never on our Knees* (Lawrence and Wishart, London, 1967), pp. 314–18.
52. *Time and Tide*, 31 November 1936.
53. *The Times*, 2 November 1936.
54. *Time and Tide*, 31 November 1936.
55. Sammy Rowan, interview.
56. Betty Archdale, letter of 30 November 1977; known to the Wilkinson family by the affectionate nickname of 'Rumble', she is remembered as 'playing the Toreadors' song on the accelerator of Ellen's car while waiting for her' (Mrs Muriel Wilkinson, interview).
57. Labour Party Conference Annual Report, 1936, p. 228–9; press references are numerous, including *Bradford Telegraph, Northern Daily Mail, Birmingham Daily Despatch, News Chronicle*, all 8 November 1936.
58. Dalton was as anxious as Ellen to reinvigorate industry and promote employment. His report urged that work should be taken to the workers rather than the reverse. He proposed that a minister with special responsibilities for the distressed

areas should be appointed, with powers to insist that all new industry and factories must be established in the Development Areas, as they were eventually redesignated. Such powers he himself exercised six years later when President of the Board of Trade. One odd aspect of Dalton's obvious concern with unemployment — even more acute in his constituency of Bishop Auckland than in Jarrow — is the patent lack of co-operation or even consultation with Ellen. Dame Margaret Cole suggested this may well have been prompted by jealousy. Certainly he rarely mentions Ellen in the context of what was unquestionably a deep mutual concern.

59. After two meetings in Manchester "I rejoined the marchers, staying until October 18, when I had three meetings in Glasgow and one day's speaking to nurses in Leeds", after which she continued the trudge — letter from Ellen Wilkinson in *North Mail*, 26 October 1936.

60. *News Chronicle*, 2 November 1936.

61. *The Times*, 2 November, 1936.

62. Ellen Wilkinson, *The Town*, p. 208.

63. Eleanor Goodrich, letter of 13 January 1978.

64. *The Times*, 26 October 1936.

65. *Sheffield Independent*, 17 October 1936.

66. Ellen Wilkinson, *The Town*, p. 209; *Daily Mail*, 5 November 1936; *Yorkshire Telegraph*, 5 November 1936.

67. David Dougan, *The Jarrow March* (Bede Gallery, Jarrow, 1936), Appendix E.

68. *The Times*, 3 November 1936.

69. Ellen Wilkinson, *The Town*, pp. 209–10.

70. *Daily Herald*, 6 November 1936.

71. Minutes of Jarrow Borough Council, 1 December 1936.

72. Hansard, Vol. 317, cols. 479–80, 958–62, 11 November 1936.

73. *Manchester Guardian*, 13 November 1936.

74. Dougan, p. 80.

75. Paddy Scullion, interview.

76. Ellen Wilkinson, *The Town*, p. 230.

77. Ibid. pp. 211–13.

78. Letter to *The Times*, 2 October 1936.

79. The first industrial estate started in 1936 in the Team Valley Gateshead was an unqualified success. When Sir John died in 1973 (he had been Chairman of the English Industrial Estates Corporation) over 120,000 men and women were employed on such estates (*Newcastle Journal*, 25 June 1973).

80. For a detailed, scholarly analysis of the full economic implications see Dr D.A. Reid, 'Response to Misery — The Circumstances Surrounding the Jarrow Crusade' (Birmingham, 1970), unpublished thesis.

81. Post-war attitudes to unemployment changed rapidly from the thirties as the Barlow Report, the Royal Commission on the Distribution of the Industrial Population (CMD 6153–1940), the White Paper on Employment Policy (CMD 6527–1944) and the Distribution of Industry Act (1945) variously indicated. The fact that between 1945 and 1948 over half of all new industry was located in the development areas offers firm evidence of a fresh if too short-lived approach. See G.D.N. Worswick and P.H. Ady, *The British Economy 1945–1950* (Oxford University Press, Oxford, 1952), p. 267.

82. Ivy Davies (member, Womens Freedom League), interview.

83. *African Morning Post*, 5 November 1936.

84. Ellen Wilkinson, *Town*, p. 212.

85. The document conferring the Freedom of Jarrow upon Ellen is in the possession of her family, together with an embossed leather-tooled copy of *The Town that was Murdered*.

86. *Manchester Guardian*, 10 March 1937.

87. *North Mail*, 29 May 1937.

88. *North Mail*, 15 January, 1938.

89. Hansard, Vol. 245, cols. 1989–1991, 2 December 1930.

90. For a full analysis of the implications and ramifications of hire purchase operations see Aylmer Vallance, *Hire Purchase* (Nelson, London, 1939). It has not been bettered.

91. C.L. Mowat, *Britain Between the Wars* (Methuen, London, 1955), pp. 499–500.

92. Hansard, Vol. 330, cols. 729–48, 10 December 1937.

93. Ibid., col. 748.

94. Ambrose Appelbe, letter of 19 September 1978.

95. Hansard, Vol. 330, cols. 730–9, 10 December 1937.

96. George and Elsie Woods, interview.

97. Hansard, Vol. 330, cols. 727–49, 10 December 1937.

98. Hansard, Vol. 335, cols. 1195–1216, 6 May 1938.

99. *Yorkshire Post*, 1 November 1938.

100. Hansard, Vol. 344, cols. 211–12, 21 February 1939.

101. Mrs Borders was buying a house which proved to be excessively shoddy and dangerous, and accordingly withheld her mortgage repayments. When sued for arrears she argued that the Building Society had 'wilfully and fraudulently' misled her into believing that the house was soundly and efficiently constructed and had infringed its rules by lending money on a totally insufficient security. She conducted her case herself brilliantly, but it was thrown out. Later the Court of Appeal found in her favour, declaring that 'the Society's business was conducted fraudulently', but in May 1941 the Society was exonerated by the House of Lords. See N. Branson and M. Heinemann, *Britain in the Nineteen Thirties* (Weidenfeld and Nicolson, London, 1971), Panther Books edn, 1973, pp. 204–10.

102. *Time and Tide*, 25 February 1939.

103. *The Times*, 20 April 1939.

104. William Sedley, letter of 28 January 1979.

105. Branson and Heinemann, p. 261.

8 ACTIVITIES — 'THE POCKET PASIONARIA'

Anti-Fascism

The claims of justice transcend the boundaries of nationality — Ellen

Lady Rhondda was right about Ellen's commitments: they were varied and international. In the thirties two were paramount; the battle against unemployment — her first care was always for the people of Jarrow — and the struggle against international fascism, which she detested in all its manifestations. She saw it as the last stand of capitalist imperialism and recognised the dangers to democracy implicit in its war objectives. The authoritarian structure of the state which had place neither for trade unions nor socialism, led logically, she argued, to the total denial of human rights, the extermination of liberal ideas and the persecution of all who held them.

In the late twenties her personal links with the European underground had brought Ellen into contact with German socialists 'both the bigger noises and the ordinary folk'. She had early foreseen the inherent dangers of the Hitler movement.[1] NUDAW too had been one of the first unions to expose, in its journal and at its annual conferences, the implications of Mussolini's corporate state. By 1930 she was vigorously supporting a report — submitted to the Labour Party Conference by NEC member C.T. Cramp — concerning the fascist threats to Austrian socialism. Cramp had seen Vienna's splendid municipal housing schemes — the epitome of socialist achievement — and warned of the hostility such measures generated from the fascist Heimwehr, 'who were well supported with arms and money'.[2] Later Ellen visited Vienna to see the famous housing estates for herself, and in July 1932 was in Germany as a guest of the Social Democrats, prior to the Reichstag autumn elections. She was probably the first British politician to have appeared at any German hustings, and after a round trip ended up in Berlin addressing an eve-of-poll mass meeting of the Iron Front. Writing of this experience soon after, she greatly over-estimated the strength of the Front, which tried unsuccessfully to weld together all socialists under the sign of Three Arrows, a symbolic rejection of the Swastika.[3]

If Ellen was wrong over the impact of the Iron Front, she had no illusions about the destructive, repressive measures exercised by the Nazi Movement: 'Not only was the Communist Party declared illegal, even though in November 1932 it won 100 seats in the Reichstag, but also . . . any relationship between trade unions and political parties was forbidden.'[4] At NUDAW's annual conference Ellen developed this theme, attacking the German Social Democrats who 'could not recognise that they were in the throes of a class war', deploring 'their refusal to organise the workers who trusted them', and warning of the possibility of a world war. 'You should know what Fascism means to the unions. In my recent visit to Germany I saw men like yourselves whose eyes had been smashed with steel whips', and at this she broke down.[5] Conference passed a resolution protesting against fascist brutality, declaring undying solidarity with fellow-workers against Italian and German dictatorships, and instructed the Executive to assist in building a strong, united working-class front against the British government's drive to war and Fascism.

It was not, however, only the destructive cruelty of Fascism which incensed Ellen. Her feminism was revolted by policies perpetrated by the Nazis against women as women, excluding them from the universities and the professions, from public service and from politics. There was not one female member of the Reichstag and Jewish women in particular were subjected to appalling indignities.[6] Horrific accounts of Nazi brutality seeped into Britain. 'In Germany,' Ellen wrote bitterly,

neither personal eminence nor past public service could save a man if he be a Jew or a Socialist. The life of an Einstein is at the mercy of hysterical lads of eighteen or tough slum gangsters provided with revolvers with the warm approval of Captain Goering, President of the Reichstag.[7]

The liberal press tried in vain to stir the conscience of the nation.

Relief organisations, Jewish, Quaker and non-denominational, did however spring up, eager to disseminate factual information about and to raise funds for anti-fascist refugees. One such body was the British Committee for the Relief of Victims of German Fascism, founded by Willi Muenzenberg, the *éminence grise* and invisible organiser of the anti-fascist world crusade. It was an offshoot of the similarly named Paris-based body of which Albert Einstein was the President. Lord Marley chaired the British section, which attracted intellectuals from a wide political spectrum. Among active members, as well as Ellen, were Isabel Brown (Secretary), Dorothy Woodman, Kingsley Martin, Victor Gollancz, Sidney (now Lord) Bernstein, D.N. Pritt, Ivor Montagu and F.A. Voigt.[8]

Ellen's particular contributions to the Relief Committee were in fund raising, and propaganda. She addressed endless gatherings up and down the country and on one occasion clashed with the authorities of Oxford University. A meeting at which she was to have spoken on 'Hitlerism' for the University Labour Club was cancelled and had to be held under the auspices of the City Labour Association. This re-arrangement demanded by the University was within its powers, but implied that a pro-fascist bias existed in the Establishment. Oswald Mosley had already spoken in the City.[9]

Ellen's pen was as ready as her tongue to promote anti-fascist sympathy. *The Terror in Germany*, a pamphlet she wrote in 1933, was a trenchant account, carefully verified, of Nazi outrages against ordinary people. Its level tone was highly effective and exposed the frightening fact that people could no longer rely upon the police for assistance against thuggery. 'The erosion of judicial impartiality was one of the most alarming fascist symptoms of all.' Judges who refused to convict socialists or Jews brought before them on the flimsiest pretexts, were dismissed. In this pamphlet, which presented some horrific photographs, she appealed both for funds and hospitality for refugees. Less grim was a later pamphlet, *Feed the Children*, written after visiting the Saar. Again she pleaded for money to help feed both workers and children 'who can eat in the communal kitchen, though how much potato and how much ham in the kartoffeln salat depends on how much money comes from abroad'. The children, many of whose parents were dead or in concentration camps, needed more than food. The 'overriding solution to safeguarding their future is in adoption', she wrote, and for this she begged most earnestly.[10]

Part of her strength as a propagandist lay in the fact that she was a doer as well as a writer. Isabel Brown remembers being with Ellen and Otto Katz in Saarbrucken at a house which harboured children fleeing from the Nazis. Because the Saar plebiscite was imminent — 'The Nazi flags were hanging out in Saarbrucken' — the children had to be taken on to France for safety, and Isabel recalled a couple of people emerging from the forest at dawn with ten small war orphans. 'Somehow we got the children to the outskirts of Paris where they were cared for by the French Relief Committee.'[11]

The Reichstag Fire Commission

The most dramatic and politically important undertaking of the Relief Committee with which Ellen was associated, was the setting up of the Legal Commission of Enquiry into the burning of the Reichstag. This enquiry was close to Ellen's heart and the whole episode reads like a modern thriller.

Hitler, appointed Chancellor by Hindenberg, called elections for the Reichstag in March 1933, determined to secure a clear majority which would vote him into absolute power. To achieve this some exceptional episode seemed necessary which would discredit the communists and stampede the middle classes away from supporting the Social Democrats. The burning of the Reichstag on 27 February, immediately before the elections, did just that, but in circumstances too opportune to be accepted as spontaneous. Arrests were speedily made by the Nazis: a half-witted Dutchman, Van der Lubbe — who, found in the building, admitted to associations with both the Dutch Communist Party and the German Social Democrats — and four communists (Deputy Ernst Torgler, leader of the Communist Party in the Reichstag, and the Bulgarians, Dmitrov, Popov and Tanev). All were charged with arson. The British Relief Committee (probably inspired by Muenzenberg) suggested a factual enquiry into the outbreak of the fire, not to prejudice the pending trial in Leipzig of the five men, but to establish the factual circumstances leading to the outbreak. The unofficial enquiry was to be held in London by a group of practising and professionally reputable lawyers gathered from all over Europe who would consider and sift all available evidence and determine the true origins of the fire.[12]

In the face of intense propaganda before the trial in Germany for convicting the accused, and with the German papers demanding the death penalty for any witnesses daring to appear for the defence, this Legal Commission of Enquiry into the burning of the Reichstag was organised. It attracted backing from Dorothy Woodman, Kingsley Martin, John Jagger, Isabel Brown and Ivor Montagu, among many others, and legal sponsorship from Ambrose Appelbe, Stafford Cripps, D.N. Pritt and Neil Lawson (now a judge), who acted as secretary. Pritt, who chaired the investigation, had hesitated initially over assuming the responsibility, 'but it soon became clear to me that no progressive lawyer of any courage could refuse', he wrote.[13] Curiously, Bernard Shaw, who had been approached to speak at a meeting on the Leipzig Trial, refused because he believed that non-intervention should be the order of the day. The five prisoners, he pointed out, were not after all British citizens. Such a stance infuriated Ellen, who commented from the platform as chairman of the meeting that 'the claims of justice transcend the boundaries of nationality'.[14]

The Secretariat of the Commission usually met in Ellen's Bloomsbury flat and found her an exceptionally live wire. In Isabel Brown's opinion, Ellen proved to be a 'miracle worker': 'To have a former politician of national stature working with the Enquiry was wonderful. She proved superb at opening doors and cutting red tape.'[15]

The Secretariat had some 'diplomatic' obstructions to contend with. Ellen received an anxious letter from the Law Society, stressing the unofficial nature of their hall, which the Secretariat had hired for the hearing. This accommodation it was pointed out, had been let as a private booking but, 'as the subject seemed likely to attract so much attention the President of the Law Society thought it desirable to emphasise the unofficial character of the building where the proceedings will take place.'[16] There was strong suspicion that Ribbentrop, the German Ambassador to Great Britain, had also made overtures in high places to get the Enquiry cancelled. D.N. Pritt wrote of 'strong hostility from the British Government, pressed by the Nazi Government to prohibit it',[17] but the Commission would not retract. Neil Lawson refused to take back the cheque deposited for the hall and the hearing proceeded with the incident having provided some good publicity,[18] which was certainly needed.

At the outset there was a marked lack of sympathy from the British press, even though the Enquiry attracted both foreign and British observers.[19] After the first day, H.G. Wells, sent an indignant message to the chairman complaining that he 'had never attended a duller show'. To this Pritt replied that 'Wells could not have paid a more welcome compliment to the Commission's determination to hold the hearing in a sober and judicial atmosphere.'[20] Although she was not their press officer, Ellen exercised her sharp sense of news value. After the first day she arrived with a long face, bemoaning a bad press. Next day she was smiling: 'We have had,' she said to Pritt, 'wonderful publicity. Thank God you were presiding and not Jowitt. He would have read the papers and closed the proceedings.'[21]

From the Commission's intensive cross-examination of some 20 distinguished witnesses clear conclusions emerged.[22] Notably that the fire could not have been caused by Van der Lubbe alone (and he a half-blind simpleton). Carrying so much inflammable material openly into the Reichstag must have involved a number of people, who would most certainly have been detected in so well guarded a building. It also seemed likely that the material was taken into the Reichstag via the underground tunnel which connected the Reichstag with Goering's official residence.[23] The Commission exonerated the Communist Party, Dmitrov and the other Bulgarians from any complicity, but Van der Lubbe was not cleared.

The burning of the Reichstag was turned to political advantage by the National Socialists with suspicious speed. Close on the fire, extensive arrests were made in Germany and repressive measures introduced against the communists, freedom of speech, assembly and personal liberty. As Albert Phillipsborn, a Foreign Press Agency correspondent, had predicted, 'something was being planned near to the election, not soon enough to give the opposition time to prove the fraud, but not too late for the Nazis, if successful, to exploit it'.[24]

The Commission's report on the Fire was restrained and statesmanlike; their assessment clear and their statements qualified. Guilt was not directly attributed, but it is clear from the findings that grave grounds existed for suspecting that the Reichstag was fired by or on behalf of the National Socialists. The Report, though predictably denounced by the Nazis, received wide publicity in Paris, Moscow, London and New York and was even smuggled into Germany. Copies of the conclusions were in the hands of the judges and advocates at Leipzig from the opening day of the official trial, and the Public Prosecutor, both in cross-examination and in his final speech, dealt with much of the evidence submitted to the Enquiry.

When the trial ended in December 1933, during which Dmitrov made a brilliant speech in his own defence of great length and greater dignity — which rang round the world — , all but Van der Lubbe were acquitted. He alone, half-blind, half-witted, was condemned to death — these results were wholly exceptional, because the four men released were the only prisoners ever arrested by the Nazis who were brought to public trial and acquitted. The Relief Committee really was proving itself 'one of the real successes of the anti fascist movement in Britain'.[25]

If vindication of the Commission was necessary it came some years later in a deposition made by General Franz Halder, Chief of the German General Staff, which was read at the Nuremberg Trials on 18 March 1946: 'At dinner on the Fuhrer's birthday in 1942 we got talking about the Reichstag building. With my own ears I heard Goering call out, "I am the only man who really knows about the Reichstag — after all it was I who set it on fire." '[26]

There is a pleasing footnote to the Enquiry. The Commission had been splendidly served by its translators, Olive Budden (Mrs Robin Page Arnot) and Heinrich Fraenkel. Fraenkel's participation was particularly courageous because he had only recently arrived in England as an anti-fascist refugee. Later he became a close friend of Ellen's who in 1936 was a witness at his wedding, having been instrumental in helping his wife, a ballet dancer, to obtain permission to work in England.[27]

In the summer of 1934 Ellen went again to Berlin with John Strachey where a People's Court was to try yet more political prisoners. Herr Thaelmann and Ernst Torgler, the latter having been in prison since Leipzig in spite of his acquittal, were facing new political charges and 'we were empowered by the Relief Committee to arrange for legal assistance . . . which is more than any German citizen can do'.[28] The German authorities were not amused, and, although Ellen had been allowed into the country, the Nazis denounced her as 'a red-haired agitator', to which she laconically admitted, 'I must plead guilty.' Even when Hitler was firmly in power, anti-fascists contrived to meet her in perilous circumstances until the outbreak of war. They would slip out of Germany to France or Britain, to discuss tactics in their fight, and Ellen was always ready to help and advise. 'The German underground movement, the Spanish Republicans, the Italian anti-fascists, have a tale to tell of their long association and of her encouragement, help and friendship', wrote F.A. Voight after her death.[29]

Spain

If details of Ellen's personal work with the anti-fascist underground go largely unrecorded, those of her numerous investigatory missions to Spain do not. She first visited there in November 1934 on behalf of the Relief Committee, before the Civil War, with Lord Listowel and others. They went to investigate a revolt at Avieda and allegations that Moorish and Arab troops had been used against the 'rebellious' Asturian miners with great brutality. The visitors, highly suspect to the authorities, received cavalier treatment from Major Lisardo Doval who was in charge of disarming 'the rebels'. At Santander they were met by hostile crowds, and had to be escorted to the frontier by the National Guard, 'but only,' Doval alleged, 'after they had attempted to interview members of the Cortes'.[30]

This visit caused a furore because Ellen and Lord Listowel were regarded as intruders into Spanish internal affairs. Intruder or not, Ellen insisted that the Asturian miners had been victimised, foreign legionnaires had carried out mass executions, and left-wing journalists were being arrested.[31] As if a thoroughly cold shoulder from the Spanish authorities was not enough, Ellen and Listowel fell foul of their political masters at home. They had not been authorised to represent the British Labour Party in Spain, so the mission was denounced by the NEC as 'ill-timed and harmful' and both were officially censured.[31] For a while Ellen remained quiescent but undeterred, and when the Spanish Civil War broke had no doubts as to where her sympathies lay.

The causes of hostilities in retrospect are rarely pure and alignments are never simple, but to eager left wingers in the mid thirties the issues of the Spanish Civil War seemed crystal clear. Early in 1936 right-wing and centre parties won a small majority in the Cortes. A new moderate government, was supported by the left. The right took alarm and a 'National Government', headed by General Franco, and supported by the landowners, commercial classes, the Church and monarchists, was set up in Burgos, North-western Spain. The constitutional government ('Loyalists' or 'Republicans') held Madrid and other areas, including Valencia, Barcelona and the Basque and Asturian territories and was re-formed with a Socialist Prime Minister. The Nationalists saw this as a 'holy war of order against Communism'; to the Republicans it was 'a struggle for democracy against fascism'. Pro-Republican volunteers from the United States, Great Britain and France joined with anti-fascist refugees to form the International Brigade. In its ranks the humble and the high fought — and died — to defend the Spanish people.

At the outset the British government favoured neutrality, but from the mounting evidence of Italy's and Germany's aid to the Spanish Nationalists and with Leon Blum (head of the Front

Populaire government in France) being anxious to assist the Republicans, the policy of 'non-intervention' emerged. The great European powers and Russia agreed to suspend the export of war goods to Spain. In practice Italy and Germany continued as before and blantantly evaded the agreement.

The Labour Party was confused and uncertain over its policy towards Spain. Even the heartrending appeal for the Republicans at the Labour Party Conference in 1936 made by the dazzling 'Pasionaria', Senora Isobel de Palencia, failed, and in spite of opposition from Nye Bevan, Sir Charles Trevelyan and Philip Noel-Baker, Conference upheld the government's policy of non-intervention, *providing that it was made effective on both sides.*[33] One reason for the Labour Party's indecision was a fear of being accused of war-mongering — the ingrained pacifism of the party died hard. Moreover, the nation, prior to the 1935 general election, had unequivocally cast eleven million votes for disarmament and collective security in response to the Peace Ballot.[34]

Ellen saw the Spanish Civil War as part of the international struggle against Fascism, not as a clear cut issue of Catholicism versus Communism. It seemed important to her for people, 'not to be gulled by press propaganda', but to realise that 'Spain was 97 per cent Roman Catholic, and that there were as many Catholics on the side of the Government as on the side of the rebels.'[35] Democrat though she was, the outcome of the Peace Ballot had not allayed her own uncertainties. For the War posed a profound moral problem for socialists which her old pacifist colleague Gustave Regler voiced to her in Madrid. He had suffered imprisonment and persecution in Germany for his stand for Absolute Pacifism, yet when they met he was in uniform. 'I chaffed him a little at our mutual pacifist faith', she wrote soon after, 'and he said quietly, "a pacifist in face of fascism is, I think, a traitor to liberty." '

This meeting with Regler occurred in spring 1937 during a visit she made with the Duchess of Atholl, Eleanor Rathbone, MP and Dame Rachel Crowdy to study the work of relief bodies in Spain. 'It comforted the Spanish women that someone had come from the outside world . . . to witness the smouldering ruins of workers' areas where not one home is left standing', Ellen wrote, 'but my most personal memory of Madrid is the feeling of helpless choking rage as the shells fell, dealing death with their blind, stupid powers.' This visit fired the anger that stamped the Duchess of Atholl's searing book *Searchlight on Spain.* A thoroughgoing Tory, she was appalled by the

Nationalists' atrocities and horrified by the threat to Imperial communications.[36]

Earlier that year Ellen had been in Spain with Haldane Society representatives to help jobless anti-Nazi academics, and returned yet again in December with Major Clement Attlee, John Dugdale and Philip Noel-Baker. They stayed in Barcelona with Negrin, the distinguished socialist, met left-wing Catalan and Basque leaders, visited hospitals, saw bomb damage in Valencia and Madrid and inspected the International Brigade by torchlight. They talked with these volunteers, Attlee promised to do his utmost to end the farce of non-intervention and from then on No. 1 Company became known as the Major Attlee Company.[37] Their round of formalities evoked at least one social explosion. Attlee has described how:

> At a reception in Madrid a British Consular Officer was introduced to Ellen, whom she believed to be very pro-Franco. She drew herself up to her full height, looked at him with blazing eyes, made a deep curtsy, and turned away. It was most impressively suggestive of Queen Elizabeth meeting the French Ambassador after the massacre of St Bartholomew's Eve.[38]

Their physical difficulties were less easily dismissed. On a journey to Valencia, where Attlee was to address Republican soldiers, the hairpin bends flattened the men by car sickness, though 'Ellen was as bright as a button'.[39] Travelling to Barcelona in Negrin's plane, 'the pilot had to nose dive because there was an Italian fascist plane on our tail'. As if this were not enough, on the last lap back to England 'We made our own lightning flash at 100 miles an hour through the snow.'[40] Although she seemed 'dead tired' on arrival, the same evening Ellen was appealing for funds for food and milk for Spanish children: 'Do you really expect us to go to Spain and return impartial? No longer is it a Civil war, it is a fight between right and wrong.' Not without reason Philip Noel-Baker especially remembered her on that trip as 'a splendid spirit with a splendid soul'.[41]

Refugees

Anti-fascist refugees persecuted for their religion or their political beliefs evoked Ellen's practical help as well as sympathy. For while she mourned in the columns of *Time and Tide* that they were unpopular with the trade unions, 'who dread any influx of labour into an overstocked market',[42] she did far more than merely write. Ellen's table became 'swamped with piles of letters from professional men and women from Zurich, Vienna and Paris willing to work anywhere at any thing, if only they can get a permit'. Looking back to 1933, she recalled the years from then on 'in terms of different waves of refugees, and in the foreground, men with tight lips saying in Parliament "What have they to do with us? this is not our affair." '[43] To Ellen it was very much her affair. She raised cases (and Cain) in the House when she scented any suggestion of prejudice or injustice, and offered temporary asylum to many in her own small flat. She supported the German Refugees' Hospitality Committee and the Friends' Service Council, which sought shelter for children and employment for adults.[44] She was a member of Eleanor Rathbone's Parliamentary Committee on Refugees,[45] and capitalised on her experiences in Spain stomping up and down the country with Lord Listowel, JJ and Sir Richard Acland among others, appealing for funds, food and medical aid. 'The Spanish worker has every right to call on the workers of this country . . . Stretch out your hands and say we are with you to the end,' she urged.[46]

Such was the intensity of her concern that it is as the Pocket Pasionaria many still remember her. With her glowing hair, her burning sincerity and her divine anger, 'she was able to wring blood out of the Albert Hall'.[47] One particularly memorable triumph was scored when she persuaded Sir Samuel Hoare, a tough Home Secretary, to admit into England all the communist members of the Reichstag who had managed to evade Nazi persecution. This astonishing feat was wholly due, her friends remain convinced, to her fathomless charm to which the Home Secretary succumbed. Ellen persisted in seeking humane treatment for refugees and to this end secured an unexpected bonus during the war when she became Parliamentary Secretary in the Ministry of Home Security. Herbert Morrison, her minister, responsible for the internment of enemy aliens, often visited Twixtlands for the weekend with John Jagger, his PPS, taking piles of work. At times this meant that the case histories of refugees would be examined in great detail with a view to their being released and Ellen would intercede repeatedly for particular internees.[48] True to this image, her friend, Heinrich Fraenkel, recalls Ellen taking him to see Herbert Morrison soon after his own release from internment. 'She jubilantly led me into the Minister's office, tossed back her head and said defiantly "look Herbert, here is my friend Heinrich, one of your bloody victims." '[49]

Over the years Ellen continued to plead for and help innumerable people, mostly in unrecorded ways.[50] One particular incident illustrates her humane approach which was typically unconventional. It was described by an anti-Nazi refugee who had been marked down by the Gestapo as chairman of the socialist students at Prague University:

> My first husband had been killed just before the Normandy landings and amid the widespread distrust of foreigners prevailing I found it almost impossible to find either a roof for my baby and myself, or to gain employment. I had a degree . . . but although I wrote about two hundred applications for teaching posts I never got a reply. In desperation when Ellen became Minister of Education I sought her advice.

Ellen studied her case and decided to give her the training grant to which her husband would have been entitled. 'I launched myself into a modest, but happy teaching career.' Across the years she still gives thanks for Ellen's unorthodox act 'which not only rescued us from destitution, but restored my shaken belief in human values'.[51]

At the 1945 Labour Party Conference Ellen, as chairman, moved a resolution acknowledging the debt of the Labour Movement to those who had died in the concentration camps and to those who had survived fighting against Nazism:

> The service of these men, women and children to the common cause of human freedom will not be forgotten. These great souls, Socialist, Communists, Jews and a cross-section of all creeds, stood up to torture and . . . died in secret for the faiths that were in them . . . They went with their heads held high, each to face the fires of the crematorium.[52]

Conference passed the resolution, each and every delegate standing erect and silent.

The Bemused Thirties — Non-intervention

The 1930s were a period of economic and political upheaval. At

home the industrial and social anguish of unemployment was symbolised by Jarrow, and the parliamentary disarray of the Labour
Party was reflected in the 1931 election defeat when Ellen and many
political colleagues lost their seats. Abroad in Italy, Germany and
Spain Fascism was in the ascendant. Belief in the class war increased
and the use of parliamentary methods was seriously questioned.

Unity within the British Labour Party was lacerated by the innate
contradictions of its policies. The most abrasive challenges to
official Labour thinking came from Sir Stafford Cripps, initially
through his Socialist League formed in 1932 as a ginger-group. It
attracted a galaxy of talent — G.D.H. Cole, William Mellor, Frank
Wise, Sir Charles Trevelyan, D.N. Pritt, Harold Laski, Nye Bevan,
George Strauss — and for a few years really was an activating force.
Ellen, at first ambivalent towards the League, regarding it as 'too
intellectual', wrote caustically that the early discussions she attended
'made my bete noir among politicians [MacDonald] seem almost up
to date!'[53] However she soon joined, attracted by its positive
programme of thorough-going socialist action and its policy for a
united front against Fascism. The League enthused both individuals
and trade unions, of which NUDAW was one.

Before the Unity Campaign was in full flood Ellen had yet again
clashed with Herbert Morrison — at the 1933 Party Conference over
the bogey of Labour members fraternising with communists in such
bodies as the Anti Fascist Relief Committee. To many at Conference
the NEC appeared more concerned with fighting the communists
than with consolidating working-class opposition to fascism. Ellen
spoke bitterly and from the heart:

> I saw the rising tide of fascism . . . and in March this year, five
> days after the Reichstag had gone up in flames, I saw what
> fascism could do. Today German leaders are in concentration
> camps . . . largely as a result of divisions in the German working
> class . . . Why is Herbert Morrison going on the defensive? . . .
> Proscribed organisations flourish because our Executive acts too
> slowly . . . Why was the unmasking of a great conspiracy left to
> an unofficial committee?

Any suggestion, however, of an alliance 'with people unwilling to
unite with us, and negligible in numbers' was resisted successfully by
Herbert Morrison speaking for the NEC. He alleged that the division
within the German working class was engineered by the Communist

International. 'Ellen would be better occupied in concentrating her undoubted energy and drive on the forward work of the party.'[54] The official ban on the Relief Committee by the NEC sparked off widespread protest meetings in which Ellen often took part. One such at Bradford embraced a catholic platform of Vyvyan Adams, MP, J.R. Campbell, J.B. Priestley, Ellen and Dr Blunt, the Bishop of Bradford, who thundered against tyranny everywhere. This provoked allegations that the Bishop — and the Relief Committee — were under the influence of the Jews. To which the Bishop commented 'God help the Jew who tries to influence Ellen Wilkinson.'[55]

The international scene steadily darkened through the 1930s. Mussolini's invasion of Abyssinia, Hitler's assaults on Austria and the Spanish Civil War showed Fascism on the march in defiance of the vascillating democracies. Baldwin won the 1935 election on the strength of upholding the League of Nations. Yet if Britain was effectively to support it the issue of rearmament could not be evaded. On this the Labour Movement was still divided. Substantial trade union opinion and moderate socialists were harnessed by Bevin and Dalton behind collective security, sanctions and — eventually — rearmament, which the pacifists, the far left and certain unions opposed.

This internal conflict exploded at the party's 1935 Conference. George Lansbury, a life-long pacifist, resisted sanctions against Italy, but was savaged by Bevin and uprooted from the leadership. Dalton called on the government to support the League in preventing Italy's 'rapacious attack' on Abyssinia and won from delegates overwhelming support. But not before this line was bitterly attacked by Cripps, who, resigning from the NEC, expressed the view that the League of Nations 'was nothing but the International Burglars' Union,' and that 'Labour ought not to join without power in the responsibility for the capitalist and imperialist war that sanctions may entail'.[56]

If any single event helped to clarify Labour opinion it was the Spanish Civil War and particularly the blatant evasion of non-intervention by Italy and Germany. In October 1936 this had become so apparent that the PLP formally abandoned its support for non-intervention. A year later the party conference restated its support for the League of Nations, demanded the right for the Republican Spanish Government to buy arms and accepted the need for some rearmament. Left-wingers however remained doubtful that the Tory government could be trusted to use its weapons in a right cause.[57]

Ellen was as muddled as her party over rearmament. While still devoted to the League of Nations and supporting collective security, early in 1937 she vehemently denounced the idea of a rearmament programme. Six months later however she attacked Baldwin for 'torpoedoing the League' warning 'if you want peace to be realistic don't let us disarm this country'. She explained:

> You may be troubled because it seems that the Labour Party is going back on the pacifist programme preached since the days of Keir Hardie, but Labour is today faced with the new menace of fascism. Look what happened to the free people of Spain . . . remember Abyssinia and China . . . it is utterly impossible to leave our country defenceless.[58]

Ellen and like-minded colleagues carried the battle for Republican Spain into the House of Commons. They asked innumerable Parliamentary Questions, which ranged from the pitiful conditions of Spanish refugees in France, to the horrific bombing of women and children. Their probing became a constant irritant to the Tory right wing. Sir Thomas Jones has recorded how on occasion:

> at Cliveden after dinner the talk was on the mischievous continuous barrage of questions on foreign affairs in the House and the desirability of restricting it to one or two days [per week] . . . The Speaker told us that he daily ruled out dozens of questions but his powers were limited.[59]

Ellen made many well-briefed attacks on the government's overtures to the dictators — not to her was Franco a 'Gallant Christian gentleman' — and spoke with a force and accuracy that drew her compliments in the House from political opponents.

After the 1937 Labour Party Conference the NEC set up a Spanish Campaign Committee of which Ellen was a joint secretary. She redoubled her efforts and addressed Labour meetings throughout Britain, using every nuance of her skill in appealing for the people of Republican Spain, and in particular for the children. Their desperate situation deteriorated as Franco tightened his grip on the country, and when Ellen heard that Barcelona had fallen early in 1939 'she nearly broke down'. Soon after, she attacked the 'indecent haste' with which Chamberlain had recognised Franco when a large part of Central Spain was still held by the Republicans. A hostile government in Spain, she warned, was a real danger to our vital communications.[60] The final collapse of Republican Spain was a stunning blow to those on the left who like Ellen had worked so hard on its behalf.

The Left Book Club and *Tribune*

A development of major importance to the Labour Movement was the founding of the Left Book Club (LBC) by Victor Gollancz, pacifist and publisher, early in 1936. The Club was extraordinarily successful, helping to prepare the way for Labour victory in 1945 by publishing monthly books at the ridiculously low price (even then) of 2s 6d (12½p) — 'for those who desire to play an intelligent part in the struggle for world peace, a better social and economic order and against fascism'. The selectors, Victor Gollancz, Harold Laski and John Strachey chose some remarkable works — *The Road to Wigan Pier* (George Orwell), *Fallen Bastions* (G.E.R. Gedye), *Tory MP* (Simon Haxey), and later Ellen's own *The Town That Was Murdered*. Such books were manna for the minds of young socialists, as the ILP publications had been for Ellen in her political immaturity. Membership of the Club burgeoned and at its peak in 1939 was nearly 60,000 with flourishing local discussion groups and LBC Theatre Guilds. Club authors were in demand for speaking and inevitably Ellen took part. The LBC unequivocally supported United Front ideas and although later Gollancz's views changed materially, he never regretted the impact of the club: 'I shall always regard our participation in the Popular Front Campaign as my only possible passport to a problematical heaven.'[61]

Ellen was also associated with the founding of *Tribune*, a more permanent bequest to the Labour Movement than the LBC. This weekly paper, first edited by William Mellor, formerly of the *Daily Herald*, was conceived after the disastrous Labour Party Conference of 1936 from which the left had emerged 'despairing, dismayed but not in disarray',[62] and was a pungent protagonist of the Popular Front. Finances came mainly from Cripps and George Strauss, MP and its lively controlling Board included Brailsford, Cripps, Laski, Strauss and Ellen. The first issue, for which Ellen wrote a typically forthright piece on unemployment, appeared in 1937 and for a while she continued to contribute lively thoughtful articles. But the NEC dictat against Cripps, and possibly pressure from Morrison, had their effect. Ellen resigned from the Board in March 1939 and when she became a junior minister told Raymond Postgate, the editor, that as a member of the government she could no longer write for the press.

Unity and the Cripps Memorandum

Ellen knew well enough what she wanted in the international field, but her conception of effective political strategy at home was as confused — even as illogical — as that of the Labour Party as a whole. In the late thirties she must have been deeply torn by political motives and personal loyalties, since her intellectual inclinations tangled with her political ambitions and her personal feelings for Herbert Morrison.

Early in 1937 the Socialist League, the Communist Party and the ILP published a Unity Manifesto, signed among others by Cripps, Bevan, Laski and John Strachey. It proclaimed a campaign for a united front of working-class solidarity against Fascism, reaction and war. The Socialist League was promptly disaffiliated, declared a proscribed organisation and soon after disbanded itself.[63] A motion sympathetic to unity was swept away at the Labour Party Conference that year by a flood of 1¾ million hostile votes. Yet the rank and file, perverse as ever, returned avowed Manifesto supporters — Ellen, Cripps, Laski and Pritt — to the NEC, on which Ellen remained until her death.

The ruthless sequence of international events — the bombing of Guernica, Franco's successful offensives in Spain, and Hitler's pressure on Czechoslovakia — reinforced the case for a wider popular front of Labour, Communists, Liberals and Independents, designed to stop Chamberlain's policy of appeasement. Although the TUC continued to oppose the Popular Front, Ellen must have been heartened by, and doubtless partly responsible for, the line her own union took. At their conference in May, NUDAW delegates agreed, as Ellen wrote: 'that, as a large number of different political parties felt that the present government was a menace to peace and to democracy in Europe, they had better come to some amiable understanding before the next election and vote the government out'.[64]

The traumatic events of Munich, when Chamberlain signed an agreement with Hitler to divide Czechoslovakia, increased the clamour for his removal and for an alliance with France and Russia to halt Hitler's onward march. Ellen swiftly realised the significance of that famous 'scrap of paper' — 'We say to Neville Chamberlain we do not trust you. We believe you went to Germany to fix up the sale of the liberty of Czechoslovakia', she said speaking for thousands in Britain. 'It is not peace that has been purchased at Munich; only time has been bought by the sacrifice of the Czech people'.[65] Two months later she called for all people who loathed Chamberlain's policy towards Fascism to come together.[66]

To the left wing a further logical step was for unity in Parliamentary bye-elections: the idea of opposition to three-cornered contests 'when Unity might secure the victory of a non Tory' made good sense. It was tried out unsuccessfully that autumn at Oxford but vindicated at Bridgwater in Somerset when Vernon Bartlett of the *News Chronicle*, an authority on the League of Nations, stood in a by-election as an Independent with Liberal and constituency Labour backing and won. This was seen as a triumph for the left and a snub for the right-wing philosophy of the NEC.[67]

Cripps then produced his own proposals in his controversial memorandum submitted in January 1939 to the NEC; he called for a Popular Front to win an anti-Chamberlain majority in the next election, due within eighteen months.[68] These ideas were firmly rejected by the NEC, only Ellen, Laski and Pritt gave him backing, and Cripps immediately took action which made his expulsion from the Labour Party inevitable. He sent copies of the memorandum to all constituency Labour parties, which even to Pritt was an act of direct defiance, 'but I doubted,' he wrote, 'whether any lesser defiance of party discipline would have saved him . . . the right wing wanted to get rid of him . . . would have been glad to get rid of me . . . and perhaps Ellen Wilkinson . . . but found no opportunity'.[69] When late in January Cripps was expelled from the Labour Party, Ellen alone on the NEC voted against the decision — both Laski and Pritt were absent.[70]

Cripp's memorandum had been rejected for more than its procommunist sympathies; Pritt believed that there were also personal grounds. For in spite of his acknowledged ability and former high standing in the party, Cripps was not widely liked. Some feared him as a potential new Mosley, and he possessed 'an unhappy combination of aloofness, superiority and cockiness' which infuriated the NEC.[71] On the other hand he was admired by many intellectuals — to Harold Nicolson, for example, he was at this time one of the few fighting for the essentials of socialism: 'He is by far the most able man in politics today. Yet he is being countered by the dumb, drastic, fatuous opposition of Transport House.'[72]

Ellen was deeply distressed over the expulsion, but accepted the majority decision: 'I intend to remain a loyal member of the Labour Party, it must come first as a spearhead in the anti fascist battle'. She would no longer speak on all-party platforms, even on Spain, and issued a statement saying: 'As Sir Stafford intends to launch a great National [Petition] Campaign at Newcastle I feel it would not be in the interests of party unity, and as a member of the NEC I cannot possibly be present on his platform'.[73]

In the spring of 1939 the NEC made a further purge. It expelled Bevan, Strauss and Charles Trevelyan for supporting the National Petition. A proposal that the decision should be deferred until Party Conference was narrowly defeated, Attlee, Ellen and Morrison voting for deferment.[74] At the conference, Cripps made a long legalistic speech against his expulsion which alienated the sympathy of many delegates. Only NUDAW among the major unions supported him, and his speech, which so obviously lacked the common touch, was said to have killed the Popular Front idea in England.[75]

There is little doubt that Ellen must have been wracked with uncertainty during this period of her party's confusion. She admired Cripps as a powerful (if austere) intellect, yet admitted he knew too little of industrial life and of the Labour Movement. 'He forgets', she wrote, 'that party government is an essential instrument of political liberty in a democracy . . . Yet by his sheer honesty and self-lessness Cripps can always command loyalty. He is a bad leader but a magnificent lieutenant'.[76] While Ellen respected the democratic obligation of collective responsibility, in no way did she then share the NEC's antipathy towards left wingers, although at the time she was falling increasingly under the influence of Herbert Morrison.

Towards the outbreak of war, Ellen toned down her more strident left-wing activities. Certainly to Pat Strauss, who with her husband George (later Lord Strauss), was extremely active and close to Cripps, it seemed that 'Ellen was never really one of us in the Unity Campaign', although Sir Richard Acland and Billy Hughes thought that she strained her loyalty to the Labour Party almost to but never beyond breaking point.[77] Yet if Ellen was outwardly muted, at heart she still remained rebellious, and early in 1939 spoke with much of her old fire of 'two ghosts' metaphorically haunting Chamberlain's foreign policy. One was the fear of Bolshevism in Europe (a Conservative MP had said that if anything happened to Hitler and

Mussolini there would be Communism in Germany and Italy) the other was the fear for the stability of the City of London caused by the loans made by Britain to Germany.[78]

Chamberlain Must Go

Chamberlain's foreign policy culminated in Britain's abandonment of Czechoslovakia to the Nazis, and fuelled national anger into fury. If there was still a lingering feeling on the left that 'because we couldn't trust Chamberlain it was folly to build up arms, to be used against Russia', it was swept away in the surging hostility to the Prime Minister, which even his own side were beginning to share. Ellen spoke for her political colleagues early in 1939: 'Labour will not enter any government of which Neville Chamberlain is the head, and I speak of what I do know,'[79] adding soon after, 'We need a change in this tired House. The Messianism of Munich has oozed away . . . Churchill is now being seen as the obvious alternative.'[80]

She bitterly attacked Chamberlain in the House a few days after Hitler had marched into Czechoslovakia. The Czechs, Ellen said, had been left in the lurch although for years Britain and France had pledged them protection. The whole tendency of the Prime Minister had been to suggest that they were not worth helping.[81]

The Left was becoming war-minded. As the government moved towards peace with the dictators at almost any price and 'non-intervention and pacifism crossed over from the Opposition to the Government, "No War" became the slogan not of the Left but of the Right.'[82] In spite of its growing acceptance of war preparations, the Labour Party's distrust of Chamberlain was reflected in its opposition to conscription and to any element of compulsion in civil defence. These views Ellen shared. 'I believe in the voluntary system of ARP [Air Raid Precautions]', she declared, claiming somewhat naively that 'such a system is the best way to curb totalitarian aggression'. The Labour Party was nevertheless highly critical of the general sluggishness officialdom displayed over civil defence policy. After Munich, in the early autumn of 1938 Morrison, Citrine and Dalton met Chamberlain to discuss these matters. Morrison, deeply concerned for London, attacked the Home Office lethargy over ARP, and Horace Wilson, adviser to the Prime Minister, told Dalton that London had no modern guns to attack low-flying aircraft.[83] A few months later Ellen was expressing similar anxieties:

Enthusiasm [for ARP] has degenerated into the completest indifference . . . people won't even say what they have done with their gas masks . . . Herbert Morrison is taking his political life in his hands by appearing on the same platform [about London's defence] with Ministers of the Government, the same week as his Executive [the NEC] are threatening utmost penalities to any member seen in company with a liberal or a communist . . . Unless something is done to rouse the ordinary citizen to take his civic duties seriously, it is difficult to see how compulsion can be avoided.[84]

Not until Churchill held the reins of office was Labour prepared to change its attitude and then, ironically, Ellen herself was introducing compulsion into fire watching arrangements.

The cry to oust Chamberlain gathered momentum, and even after War had been declared the Labour Party refused to serve in any national government he headed. Ellen neatly interpreted the continuing refusal:

Whereas the Prime Minister saw the war as a fight against an individual and a group of men he could not trust, Labour regarded Hitler as a symbol of the powerful social and financial group who aim to bring down the country in order to secure the profits that the machine age can bring.[85]

Events finally forced the Prime Minister's hand, and hard on his moral defeat in the House over British naval strategy in Norway, Chamberlain, 'an incorrigible limpet', resigned. Ellen had long prophesied that 'when the bombs began to fall' Churchill would become Prime Minister. She admired Winston, in spite of his deserved anti-trade-union reputation, and was certain that he and not Lord Halifax should take over:

Parliament is quite aware that no House of Commons can control Churchill once he is well in the saddle, and so until the earthquake . . . Mr Churchill will not be Premier. But if that earthquake of war and disaster were to come, and with it inevitably a drawing together of the whole House to face the danger, I opine — to use his pet word — that Mr Churchill will be forced into the premiership whatever the Whips Office and the Carlton Club may say . . . When a real struggle is being waged events quickly change the men to suit the emergency.[86]

Attlee and Greenwood agreed to join a coalition government under Churchill early in May 1940, a decision which the party endorsed the same week at Annual Conference. Churchill treated Labour generously, they received a higher proportion of important offices in government than the party had seats in the House of Commons.[87]

Leadership Politicking

No one could call Ellen Machiavellian. She never had evil intent, but she was a plotter, as her persistent campaigning to make Herbert Morrison leader of the PLP testifies. Even so she was prompted by impetuous enthusiasm and loyalty rather than by innate deviousness; she was too forthright effectively to conceal her purpose.

Back in the 1930s Morrison was a name to conjure with in the Labour Movement; even Beatrice Webb stamped him with her approval.[88] Through disciplined energy and hard work he had shaped the London Labour Party into an excellent propaganda machine. Its efficient organisation coupled with his own positive policies and drive, enabled Morrison to achieve the singular triumph of winning the LCC for Labour in 1934,[89] and Ellen was deeply impressed by these achievements. She admired people who acted so positively and Herbert's ebullience struck a chord in harmony with her own liveliness. She hitched her political waggon to Morrison's star and never wholly severed the relationship, although there were many aspects of Labour Party policy over which they publically disagreed. Ellen was probably responsible in 1934 for the comment in *Time and Tide* that 'Morrison was now leader of the Labour Party by right of conquest.'[90] Certainly she approved of his 'having a training in administration few party leaders had troubled to acquire'. At the same time she also recognised Attlee's qualities. 'He had', she wrote, 'two fatal handicaps — honesty and modesty — but he is a subtle strategist who understands people and plays with his team.'[91]

When George Lansbury resigned and Attlee became acting leader in 1935 Ellen was deeply involved in the leadership elections. Hugh Dalton, at that time a Morrison supporter, noted in his diaries a dinner party at his flat to discuss tactics at which Ellen 'pretended to be not very keen on Morrison. She wrote to me afterwards that she *was* very keen, but feared one of my new boys would blab. I think he did.'[92]

At the PLP meeting amid strong emotional undercurrents there was great disinclination to propose Morrison, even among those who intended to vote for him. He survived the first round when Greenwood was eliminated, but Attlee was overwhelmingly elected as the bulk of Greenwood's votes were switched to him. This support both Dalton and Morrison attributed to the Masons, since a number of MPs and some Transport House officials belonged to the same Masonic Lodge,[93] but some contemporaries thought this explanation unreliable.[94] After his defeat Morrison refused to stand for the deputy leadership 'as he would be too busy on the LCC'. This was undoubtedly a tactical error, and at the time Dalton felt that 'we had lost the strongest personality and by far the most efficient politician of the three', but with hindsight he admitted, 'I was wrong . . . I wholly underestimated Attlee . . . He grew out of all knowledge as the years passed.'[95]

How deeply Ellen was involved in schemes over the years to oust Attlee is not clear. Manny Shinwell recalled 'taking her to task at a party meeting for her attack upon him' (in 1935) though he did concede that 'her diatribe was mainly the culmination of considerable plotting by various other members of the party.'[96] Anti-Attlee manoeuvres continued. In December 1938 'Four Winds' (of which Ellen was known to be one) had written in *Time and Tide* that:

> More than the left wing are feeling that Mr Attlee ought to show more fight . . . the star of Herbert Morrison has risen so appreciably in this Parliament that the socialists have a really good alternative if they decide that they would like a change.[97]

An attempt to oust Attlee when he was ill in June 1939 caused fireworks in the PLP, sparked off by an article Ellen had written in the final issue of the *Sunday Referee*.[98] Again she boosted Herbert Morrison for the leadership, and named Dalton, Greenwood and Cripps as his 'able lieutenants'. Dalton enlarged upon these events in his unpublished papers:

> I had some words with Ellen and HM. I think we are not observed together meeting after the House has adjourned in the little room behind the Speaker's Chair. . . . At the party meeting A.G. raised from the chair . . . the question of Ellen's article . . . saying that the NEC thought it very wrong . . . to express lack of confidence in a sick leader. The discussion was angry and confused. Ellen is

not popular with most of the men at the best of times, and on this occasion she had infuriated the Masons and all the loyal little Attleans. She did not make a very good defence . . . Jagger who watches the wind as skilfully as most men, and is a great friend of Ellen's, made no attempt to defend her article but did in a semi-humorous speech argue against a vote of censure on her.

Morrison spoke briefly saying that he had had nothing to do with inspiring the article, had he seen it beforehand he would have advised against it. He would support a resolution of confidence in Attlee, but if a censure vote on Ellen were pressed he would abstain, and in the event the pro-Attlee motion was carried *nem. con.* Ellen did not vote. As Dalton commented, it had been 'a queer episode'. Morrison went further, whispering to him later on the Front Bench 'that was a queer double meaning debate we had this morning'.[99]

As the war clouds gathered discussions over the international situation and internal party tactics superseded the leadership wrangle. Arthur Greenwood continued as Deputy Leader to guide the party — in Dalton's view — 'admirably', and in September Attlee was back. 'As his health returned and as the war situation grew graver, he rose to the full height both of his duty and his opportunity.' By mid-November all leadership doubts within the PLP had abated. Attlee was unanimously re-elected.[100]

The following May when the Labour Party agreed to enter the war-time coalition, Attlee stirred party conference by an uncharacteristically emotional speech:

We have to stand today for the souls in prisons in Czechosolovakia, Poland, Germany. We have to fight for the freedom of the human spirit. Life without liberty is not worth living. Let us go forward and win and establish that liberty for ever on the sure foundation of social justice.'[101]

His sentiments were overwhelmingly endorsed.

Attlee's judgement was not only as astute as Ellen's was fallible, it was also generous. For when Churchill formed his government Ellen was included, as Dalton wrote:

Talked at lunch with CRA who is in good form. I think he has made his selections and omissions for government posts very well. A balance has to be made between bourgeois and working class

MPs — he has got quite a lot of our people in. Winston was very keen on Ellen — and so was he.[102]

A halt had been called to politicking.

Notes

1. F.A. Voigt, *Manchester Guardian*, 7 February 1947.
2. *New Dawn*, 25 October 1930.
3. *Labour Magazine*, August 1932.
4. *New Dawn*, 6 April 1933.
5. *New Dawn*, 6 May 1933.
6. *Sunday Referee*, 21 May 1932.
7. *Time and Tide*, 1 April 1934.
8. C.H. Rolph, *Kingsley* (Gollanz, London, 1973), Penguin edn, 1978, pp. 1–193. Koestler *The Invisible Writing*, (Hutchinson, London, 1954, Danube edn) (pp. 242–6) writes sardonically of the 'World Committee Willi founded . . . with its branches all over Europe and America . . . camouflaged as a philanthropic organisation, which had in every country a panel of highly respectable people . . . Great care was taken that no Communist should be connected in public with the Committee.' For a more sympathetic account see Cockburn, *I, Claud* (Penguin, Harmondsworth, 1967), p. 129.
9. *The Times*, 4 May 1933.
10. Ellen Wilkinson, *The Terror in Germany* (for the British Committee for the Relief of the Victims of German Fascism) pamphlet, n.d.
11. Isabel Brown, interview.
12. Judge Neil Lawson, interview.
13. D.N. Pritt, *From Right to Left* (Lawrence and Wishart, London, 1965), p. 53, and Pritt, unpublished papers (Marx Memorial Library) p. 161.
14. *Birmingham Post*, 23 September 1933.
15. Isabel Brown, Ivor Montagu, interviews.
16. E.R. Cook, letter of September 1933 (undated) to Ellen Wilkinson (Marx Memorial Library).
17. Pritt, *Right to Left*, p. 56.
18. Judge Neil Lawson, interview.
19. These included George Lansbury, H.J. Laski, H.G. Wells, J.B. Priestley and Ernst Toller.
20. D.N. Pritt, *Right to Left*, pp. 57–8.
21. D.N. Pritt, unpublished papers.
22. D.N. Pritt, *Right to Left*, p. 58.
23. Ibid., pp. 59–60.
24. D.N. Pritt, unpublished papers.
25. Rolph, p. 193.
26. D.N. Pritt, *Right to Left*, pp. 62–3. Sceptical criticism about the Enquiry rumbled on for years. Not surprisingly, Sefton Delmer, a former foreign correspondent of the Daily Express, took a diametrically opposite view from Pritt: The 'Hitler-Göring-Göbbels did it' legend, he contended, had been thoroughly exploded by Fritz Tobias in his account of the Reichstag Fire published in Germany in 1959 (*Trail Sinister* (Secker and Warburg, London, 1961), p. 199). Four years later, however, Delmer's theory was demolished by Constantine Fitzgibbon in a review of the English version of Tobias's book: in arguing that van der Lubbe alone was respon-

sible for the arson, 'Tobias', he wrote, 'ignores expert testimony either by omission or by denigrating the experts.' He agreed 'that a convincing case was made for van der Lubbe's ignorance of being manipulated by the Nazis'. However, 'Tobias fails to convince this reader that the Nazis did not know that van der Lubbe was going to fire the Reichstag: and more important, he has similarly failed to convince the more responsible German historians.' (*Observer*, 17 November 1963). After which, there was silence.

27. Herman Fraenkel, Ivor Montagu, interviews.

28. *Time and Tide*, 21 July 1934.

29. *Manchester Guardian*, 7 February 1947.

30. *Evening Standard*, 15 November 1934; *Manchester Guardian*, 16 November 1934; *Time and Tide*, 24 November 1934.

31. *Manchester Guardian*, 24 November 1934.

32. *Manchester Guardian*, 7 December 1934. The whole episode caused much huffing and puffing in Labour Party circles, but correspondence between Jim Middleton, then Assistant Secretary to the Labour Party, William Gillies the International Secretary, and Ernest Robinson, a source of information based in San Sebastian, does suggest some grounds for Robinson's decrying the visit as 'badly conceived and much worse in execution'. If they had merely come to find out facts they should have come quietly, for people were too frightened willingly to volunteer information. The time of the visit was also unpropitious because the government had lately instructed all provincial governors to examine minutely the papers of all foreigners, and any irregularity would result in their immediate extradition. Robinson's assumption that 'the investigators had only come to Spain as a joyride at some other people's expense so they could return to England, talk about it and make fees from lecturing' was as spiteful as it was unsubstantiated. Gillies, unpublished papers (Labour Party Library, London, 1934), WG/SPA/*i*, dated 15–29 November 1934.

33. Labour Party Conference Annual Report, 1936.

34. The great Peace Ballot of autumn 1934-June 1935 was a unique event. It was a house-to-house canvas by volunteers, conducted by an *ad hoc* body, the National Declaration Committee, chaired by Lord Robert Cecil, President from 1923 to 1945 of the League of National Union. The questions may well have been 'tendentious' as has been suggested, but they certainly reflected the aspirations of those 11½ million British citizens who signifying support for the League favoured an all-round restriction in armaments, economic/non-military collective security in the face of aggression, and the use of collective military measures only in the last resort — C.L. Mowat, *Britain Between the Wars* (Methuen, London, 1955), pp. 541–2.

35. *Hampstead and Highgate Express*, 3 October 1936.

36. *Time and Tide*, 1 May 1937; Duchess of Atholl, *Searchlight on Spain*, (Penguin Special, London, 1938).

37. H. Thomas, *The Spanish Civil War* (Eyre & Spottiswood, London, 1961), p. 639.

38. C. R. Attlee, *As It Happened* (Heinemann, London, 1954), p. 94.

39. Philip Noel-Baker, interview.

40. *Daily Express*, 10 December 1937.

41. *Daily Herald*, 10 December 1937; Philip Noel-Baker, interview.

42. *Time and Tide*, 28 May 1938.

43. *Time and Tide*, 11 June 1938.

44. Mrs Guerney Taylor, letter of 23 August, 1978.

45. Mary Stocks, *Eleanor Rathbone* (Gollanz, London, 1949), pp. 283–4). This Committee which drew together disparate organisations was formed to challenge — and mitigate — the methods by which genuine anti-Nazi refugees of every calling were indiscriminately arrested and interned after the outbreak of War

under Defence Regulation 18b; Bertha Bracey, letter of 19 April 1978.
46. *Manchester Guardian*, 1 July 1936.
47. Judge Neil Lawson, interview.
48. Beryl Hughes, interview.
49. Heinrich Fraenkel, interview. (He became a most distinguished chess correspondent for the *New Statesman* and contributed to *Time and Tide* on central European affairs under the pen-name of Cinna.)
50. One humble tale is representative of many. Lola Humm Sernau was secretary to Lion Feuchtwanger, the great writer, for seven years. She came to know Ellen in the mid-thirties through Professor Emil Gumbel. 'I had a friend (M. Fanta) in Paris who, during the war, became separated from his wife who was in England and couldn't get permission to leave'. Ms Humm Sernau wrote to Ellen explaining the situation. 'She answered at once saying she'd do everything in her power to help. Within a very short time Mrs. Fanta, overjoyed, received her exit permit.' (Ms Lola Humm Sernau, letter written from near Locarno, Switzerland, February 1979.)
51. Mrs Steinhardt, letter of 8 May 1978.
52. Labour Party Conference Annual Report, 1945, p. 150.
53. *Time and Tide*, 28 January 1933.
54. Labour Party Conference Annual Report, 1933, pp. 221–2.
55. *Manchester Guardian*, 25 September 1934.
56. Mowat, p. 551.
57. G.D.H. Cole *A History of the Labour Party* (Routledge and Kegan Paul, London, 1948), p. 332.
58. *Dudley Herald* and *Wallsall Observer*, both of 25 September, 1937.
59. T. Jones, *Diary*, p. 358.
60. Hansard, Vol. 344, col. 1142–3, 28 February 1939.
61. S. Hodges, *Victor Gollancz* (Gollancz, London, 1978) pp. 130–40.
62. *Tribune*, 1 January 1977; M. Foot, *Aneurin Bevan* (MacGibbon and Kee, London, 1962) Palladin edn, 1975, vol. 1, p. 233.
63. G.D.H. Cole, pp. 347–8.
64. *Time and Tide*, 7 May, 1938.
65. *Rotherham Advertiser*, 5 November 1938.
66. *News Chronicle*, 27 January 1939.
67. B. Pimlott, *Labour and the Left in the 1930s* (Cambridge University Press, 1977), p. 167.
68. The life of the 1935 Parliament would in normal times have had to end by Spring, 1940, but in the event it was extended until July, 1945.
69. D.N. Pritt, *Right to Left*, p. 104.
70. B. Pimlott, p. 173.
71. D.N. Pritt, unpublished papers, p. 299.
72. H. Nicolson, *Diaries and Letters 1930–39* (Collins, London, 1966), p. 389.
73. *News Chronicle*, 27 January 1939; *The Times*, 4 February 1939.
74. B. Pimlott, p. 178; H. Dalton *The Fateful Years — Memoirs 1931–45* (Muller, London, 1957), p. 217.
75. B. Pimlott, p. 178; H. Dalton, *Fateful Years*, p. 219.
76. *Sunday Referee*, 4 June 1939.
77. Pat Strauss, H.D. Hughes, interviews, Sir R. Acland, letter.
78. *Manchester Guardian*, 10 February 1939.
79. *Tribune*, 29 March 1939.
80. *Sunday Referee*, 14 May 1939.
81. Hansard, Vol. 345, cols. 480–6, 15 March 1939.
82. C.L. Mowat, p. 578.
83. *Methodist Recorder*, 16 May 1939; H. Dalton, *Fateful Years*, p. 182.
84. *Time and Tide*, 28 January 1939.
85. *Scunthorpe Star*, 2 December 1939.

86. *Time and Tide*, 2 March 1940.
87. H. Dalton, *Fateful Years*, p. 318.
88. B. Webb, *Diaries*, 12 and 15 November 1935.
89. Donoughue and Jones, Ch. 14 *passim*.
90. *Time and Tide*, 6 October 1934.
91. *Sunday Referee*, 18 October 1936.
92. H. Dalton, *Fateful Years*, p. 80.
93. Ibid., p. 82; Lord Morrison, *An Autobiography* (Odhams, London, 1960), p. 164.
94. George Strauss, Lord Manny Shinwell, interviews and letters.
95. H. Dalton, *Fateful Years*, pp. 82–3.
96. E. Shinwell, *Conflict without Malice* (Odhams, London, 1955), p. 133.
97. 'Four Winds', *Time and Tide*, 31 December 1938.
98. H. Dalton, *Fateful Years*, pp. 224–5.
99. H. Dalton, unpublished papers (Dalton Collection, British Library of Political and Economic Science), Part I, Diaries, Vol. 20, 14 June 1939, pp. 64–7.
100. H. Dalton, *Fateful Years*, p. 281.
101. Labour Party Conference Annual Report, 1940, pp. 123–5.
102. H. Dalton, unpublished papers, Part I, Diaries, Vol. 22, 18 May 1940, p. 80.

9 WARTIME COALITION GOVERNMENT — PARLIAMENTARY SECRETARY

Ministry of Home Security

> I prefer Ellen Wilkinson's realism . . . she said to me: 'You deal with ideas and one can never see how an idea works out. I deal in water closets and one can always see whether it works or not.' I do so like the little spitfire — Harold Nicolson

> I remember Churchill telling me when the Coalition came into being in May 1940 that he had formed the widest based government ever made in Britain. 'It stretched from Lord Lloyd of Dolobran on the Right to Miss Wilkinson on the Left' — Harold Macmillan

Churchill's wartime government was formed in May 1940 with full Labour co-operation at a time when the western world was crumbling before the German onslaught. As Holland, Belgium and France fell in swift succession during that burning summer, the invasion of Britain seemed imminent. Dunkirk was evacuated — over 330,000 troops, British and French, were extricated in a saga that made history — and Churchill vowed to prosecute the war with the utmost vigour in the face of total national unpreparedness. As sectarian argument and political in-fighting receded before the urgency for safeguarding Britain's survival, few on the Left doubted that the purpose of the War was to defeat Fascism and to preserve democracy. The issues seemed crystal clear and wholly different from the imperialistic rivalries which, to many socialists, ignited the First World War. Even so those claiming conscientious objection in 1939 were four times greater than in 1914 — and were more tolerantly treated.[1]

In the wartime coalition government Ellen was first appointed a Parliamentary Secretary to the Ministry of Pensions. There for a few months she undertook the back-stop duties of answering Parliamentary Questions, presenting policy in public speeches, and coping generally. Although she enjoyed her responsibility for Hardship

Tribunals, no one could pretend that Pensions was either the most scintillating of Departments or of obvious relevance to the war effort. Certainly the job was out of joint with Ellen's restless sense of urgency: she yearned to tackle work where something more positive could be achieved.

She did not have to wait long. When London's uneasy calm was broken at the end of the 'Spitfire Summer' by the blitzkrieg the devastation and administrative chaos that ensued made radical reorganisation of the war effort imperative. Churchill appointed Herbert Morrison Home Secretary and Minister of Home Security. In this, Morrison, with his deep rapport with Londoners, was to prove an outstanding success, and Ellen joined Osbert Peake and (Sir) William Mabane in his team of Parliamentary Secretaries. It is a revealing comment on the cautious security of the day that when after taking up his appointment Morrison asked to see the Department's personal files on himself and Ellen, he was told, 'Minister, they were destroyed yesterday!'[2] Ellen was made responsible for air raid shelter matters and for a new Standing Committee on Shelter Policy. This was an inspired appointment, as into it Ellen channelled her concern for people and her determination to find immediate solutions to gruelling problems.

Initially the blitz was concentrated on the London Docks and the East End; later it spread to Britain's great industrial cities. Main services were emasculated and industries pulverised. Fires, injuries, homelessness and death had to be tackled by local authorities who, even if they had the will, too often lacked the resources to cope. Shelter policy became a prime political issue. Official arrangements were less than adequate. Local authority 'rest centres' were usually opened in schools and as their name implied offered relief but little protection from bombs. For 'domestic use' the government had made available 'Anderson' shelters (basically trenches dug in the gardens with corrugated roofing) and street brick shelters: neither was designed to provide substantial protection under sustained air attack. So it was that the public adopted their own deep shelters and took themselves to the Chislehurst Caves in Kent, or to the Underground Railway Stations in London. Night after night families queued to get their 'pitches' on the tube platforms, eating, cooking, sleeping there, and even staying down during the day. The 'Tube Movement' gave rise to families enduring a troglodyte existence, which created great camaraderie, but was dangerously deficient in basic facilities and sanitary provision.

Inevitably the lack of amenities and potential health hazards aroused bitter criticism. Winds howled through the tunnels, lice went from head to head, the stench could be frightful.[3] Of the multifarious muddles and hazards Ellen became well aware. 'I have visited a large number of shelters nightly during the past few weeks; at present it is five-sixths of my job,' she told the House, adding that improvements would be effected and speedily. By the end of November (1940) she was able to announce at Oxford that a tremendous programme of new equipment and reorganisation was under way and 'any suggestion that nothing substantial has changed in the last two months is either malicious or ignorant or both'.[4] A Parliamentary Secretary is not a policy innovator. But as Ellen insisted on seeing bomb damage for herself and talking with the homeless and the bereaved, her reports bore a stamp of immediacy which made great impact. Night after night she went round London's blitzed areas consoling survivors with almost foolhardy disregard for her own safety. One evening, for example, she went down a tube leaving her officials above ground. Sirens sounded: more people descended; the Minister did not reappear. Frequent messages indicated that she was about to emerge, this she did — but not until 4am! She liked giving officials the slip, but was also concerned for their safety. She feared putting her chauffeur at risk and would often drive herself, though in the raids this could be a hair-raising operation as she was an erratic driver.[5]

Ellen had 'nerves of fire and steel'[6] and would visit sites — such as the Cafe de Paris in Piccadilly, London — soon after serious attacks. Often she was accompanied by Admiral Evans 'of the Broke', famous in the First World War and now one of the Regional Commissioners for London. He always wore full 'canonicals' — dress uniform, decorations and white gloves — and like Ellen was a wonderful morale booster.[7] Laski, who also visited the shelters, recalled the eager encouragement and words of comfort she offered: 'That word of praise from a Minister, say to a shelter marshal, was like an accolade and you realised the warmth and generosity of mind that was Ellen.'[8] As air attacks were extended to major industrial centres so Ellen directed her visits all over Britain. Once in Glasgow she and her party saw first hand the havoc caused when German bombers mistook a main road, bright in the moonlight, for the Clyde and systematically destroyed not warehouses, but countless homes.[9]

A sympathetic listener, Ellen was able to capitalise on her own experience and always got through to people. For she too knew what losing a home entailed, having been bombed out of Guilford Street in October 1940 and rehoused at Hood House in Dolphin Square, Pimlico.[10] In that instance she suffered no direct physical hurt, but in time the war took a heavy toll of her health. Irregular meals, long working hours, harrowing investigations and curtailed sleep — she had a bed in her office and refused to use the deep shelters provided for Members of Parliament[11] — drained her emotionally and lowered her resistance.

Ellen 'saw things fresh and raw that the rest of us preferred to push out of our consciousness', wrote Lady Rhondda. 'She told me of a foot that she had seen by itself which haunted her because no one knew to what body it belonged. She could not take that memory out of her mind.'[12] In spite of the horrors and the heartbreak Ellen did not wallow in sentiment. Rather she galvanised people into taking fresh initiatives — forming welfare committees of 'locals' who knew their areas, or after visiting bombed Merseyside, instructing the Regional Commissioner to use Birkenhead stations for deep shelters.[13] No experience was ever wasted upon her.

During her early days at the Ministry she exercised uncharacteristic caution over the popular pressure for deep shelters. She warned those agitating for such provision that, although the Minister would consider any form of new proposals, he was not prepared 'to have haphazard and irresponsible deputations making such demands without understanding the geographic and scientific problems involved'.[14] This was an uncharacteristically blinkered misrepresentation of the widespread clamour from supporters of scientist Professor J.B.S. Haldane, the distinguished communist exponent of deep shelter provision. The issue was 'a hot potato' and Ellen's attitude can only be explained by her having to walk a political tightrope as a new minister. The citizens of London had, however, established a claim which could not be denied and by the end of September nearly 200,000 people were sleeping nightly in the London tubes — without any organised facilities.[15] Late in 1940 the Cabinet, which had feared that a 'deep shelter mentality' would breed defeatism, formally reversed its policy and allowed the use of tubes as deep shelters. Various disused stations were opened, and an uncompleted tube extension became so vast a shelter that a visiting American 'walked for half a mile and literally after each step had to find a place to put the next foot down without stepping on something human'.[16]

A special committee on shelter improvement was set up (in September 1940) under Lord Horder. Its members included Father John Groser, 'the turbulent priest' well known in the East End, elegant Rose Henriques, wife of (Sir) Basil Henriques, Warden of the Bernhard Baron Jewish Settlement, and Alderman Charlie Key, MP for Bow and Bromley, with K.B. Paice 'an urbane civil servant' as secretary.[17] Many of their recommendations Ellen, chairing the appropriate inter-departmental committee, implemented. Chemical buckets were installed; bunks were provided; canteen facilities and mobile food trolleys, even education classes, were introduced. Buskers and itinerant groups, some from Unity Theatre, gave 'plat-form' entertainment; calamity generated good fellowship in this 'subterranean society'.[18] Ellen could never suffer fools gladly and even less so in time of crisis. It was typical that when, during discus-sions on the installation of earth-closets, an over-cautious Treasury official suggested obtaining additional quotations she furiously rapped out that decisions were to be made and acted upon then and there, or she would appeal to the Prime Minister.[19]

In spite of the presumed security of the tubes, many Londoners preferred to sleep in their own homes. Ellen therefore had to consider indoor provision, a need speedily met by the 'Morrison' shelter devised by (Sir) John Baker, then working in the Home Security Research Division.[20] This was a neat comfortable contrap-tion with wire-mesh sides and a steel-plated top usable as a table, which Ellen announced early in 1941. By the end of the year half a million such shelters had been distributed and she travelled round popularising their use and handling endless complaints. One from Manchester was typical: 1,400 shelters had been delivered but none could be assembled because there were no spanners! Ellen assured her audience that the boy scouts who helped to erect shelters would be issued immediately with monkey wrenches![21]

Both Morrison, the innovatory administrator, and Ellen, dis-pensing 'hygiene and cheer', were humane and able ministers. It was therefore surprising that Churchill transferred all matters con-cerning 'the health and comfort of shelterers' to the Ministry of Health and made Morrison's Department responsible only for shelter construction.[22] Ellen accepted the change with equanimity, aware that she could thus better tackle matters of national shelter policy, although Londoners, commented *Time and Tide*, 'will greatly miss the dynamic energy with which she dealt with the capital's special needs.'[23] In practice she continued her visits around

London whenever time allowed. Arranging structural improvements to shelters became one of her responsibilities and offered useful experience in the difficult inter-departmental negotiations over the allocation of scarce materials.

The Fire Services

The London blitz, with all its tragedy, starkly exposed the inefficiency of Civil Defence arrangements. Bitter criticism was provoked, none more formidable than that from Ritchie Calder, a colleague of the Jarrow Crusade and a prominent radical journalist. His scalding articles in the *New Statesman* (and subsequent book, *Carry on London*) called for deep shelter provision, exposed London's unpreparedness and attacked the pathetic parochialism of local authorities whose fire-fighting powers ended legally at their borough boundaries. These accurate exposes displeased authority and he was summoned to an audience with — of all people — Ellen. She pointed to a copy of his book on her desk and commented reproachfully 'This is not the work of a friend.'[24] Criticism made impact and early in 1941 Morrison introduced substantial changes. The local unco-ordinated fire services were reorganised into the National Fire Service (NFS) and Ellen, serving under Morrison on the Fire Service Council, assumed responsibility for the well-being of personnel. Further, it was widely recognised that if incendiary bombs were tackled promptly enough, lethal fires could be restricted — Parliament itself was severely damaged by reason of inadequate fire precautions — so fire watching arrangements were strengthened and some compulsion introduced. From early 1941 every male became liable for 48 hours' fire watching or other civil defence duties each month, either at work or at home.

The conscription of young unmarried women for work of national importance or for the 'auxiliary' Civil Defence services followed. This was the first time conscription of women had been introduced into any European country and was effected in face of Churchill's opposition. Then, in August 1942, everyone, including women from 20 to 45, not doing alternative war work were made liable for fireguard duties. Ellen was wholly in favour of everyone undertaking Civil Defence. Before the war she had angrily suggested that the Women's Auxiliary Services were too exclusive, salary earners were being overlooked for commissions in favour of women with titles, whereas, 'efficiency and merit, not titles ought to be the prime consideration'.[25]

For a while Ellen faced unprecendented unpopularity over this policy. Fire watching on works premises was disliked for the extended burden it imposed on family life and for imposing the principle of compulsion on women. Infuriated wives actually complained to the Regional Commissioner for London that their husbands were being seduced by women civil servants during fire watching duties![26] Yet Ellen was unshakeable. She showed little sympathy for the large numbers of people seeking exemption: 'Some are already doing their full share of Civil Defence and some have enrolled in the Home Guard . . . I appeal to all citizens not to claim exemption and to put in a spell of fire watching this winter.'[27]

While defending compulsion, she understood women's domestic commitments, and made sure that those with young children or working excessive hours were exempt. In spite of being a temporary 'Aunt Sally' Ellen energetically boosted morale and defended her department's policy. So much so that she is credited with having actually created the army of five million fire watchers herself,[28] an exhausting but tough achievement for a frail fiery particle!

With some abatement of bombing, the official visits Ellen had to make to defend 'compulsion' and inspect defence arrangements became slightly less grisly, but they were still physically exhausting. Travelling in the blackout was tedious, unhealthy and tiring. Yet in spite of frequent attacks of bronchitis and asthma and several accidents — *The Times* from mid-1942 onwards is peppered with references to her indifferent health — coupled with great personal distress over the unexpected death of John Jagger — Ellen drove herself unremittingly. In January 1943 she faced the horrors of visiting both a London school and a London tube which had received direct hits.

Her ministerial work demanded not only hard application and sheer grind, but also much niggling argument. In 1942 she assumed additional responsibilities from her colleague William Mabane, who was transferred to the Ministry of Food, and later that year when restructuring of the Fire Watching Services was approved,[29] Ellen chaired an inter-departmental Fire Operations Committee which worked out details of the changes, and handled numerous objections from local authorities.[30]

Ellen's understanding of administration matured with experience.

In the infrequent debates on Home Security matters she would acquit herself well, displaying a solid grasp of Civil Defence detail (and there was an immense amount to master within the ever-changing structures). In one debate, the question of recoupment by local authorities of expenditure on shelters and bomb damage was raised. Ellen was on familiar ground — that of inequitable rates burden — which she had so often raised in connection with unemployment benefit. Now she defended the government's policy to reimburse local authorities fully irrespective of the extent of their bomb damage, 'though I fully recognise that there are unequal areas of suffering . . . and that some authorities have had 400 bombs to the acre, others less than two'. The only real solution as she saw it was in reappraising 'the financial relationship between local and central government'.[31]

During the summer of 1943, back 'in splendid fighting form' after absence through illness, she introduced a full-scale debate on Civil Defence. Her wide survey, ranging from the reorganised Fire Service to completed deep shelters, gave an impressive picture of 'our Fourth Arm — Civil Defence — of which Britain should be so proud', but she confessed: 'I get worried about the amount of things our people are expected to do. We are cutting and cutting into their leisure and human beings must have some leisure and recreation other than sleep.' She referred to the NFS, to which women had contributed much: 'now they are working in control rooms, making decisions on which life may depend. They have come a long way from serving tea to the exhausted male as their role was once conceived!'[32]

As the intensity of air attacks abated Ellen continued to visit Civil Defence establishments, to encourage personnel in leisure activities and she jubilantly opened an exhibition of paintings by firemen which included her own portrait. Additional Home Office duties made her responsible — nice irony — for dealing with the electoral register. This undertaking prompted her to deny any sympathy, official or personal, with proportional representation.[33]

The Release of Mosley

The war reduced though it did not eliminate disharmony within the Labour Movement, and late in 1943 Ellen faced a bad patch politically. She came under more bitter criticism from Labour colleagues than at any time in her whole career; this was because she supported her minister's decision to allow the release of Sir Oswald Mosley, leader of the British Union of Fascists, from detention under the wartime Defence Regulation 18b. This evoked sustained public outcry, and nine out of ten people felt it should not have been permitted.[34] Morrison as the minister responsible was severely censured by the TUC and the NEC; a bitterly critical motion was only narrowly defeated in the PLP, and protest meetings culminated in a massive rally in Trafalgar Square.[35] Morrison was adamant. He vigorously resisted his critics in the furore of an adjournment debate and Ellen stood by him. Additional evidence now available had shown, he said, that Mosley was no longer a 'national security risk'. His decision had been made on a judicial basis and it would be totally wrong for him to have been influenced by political considerations. Mosley's continued imprisonment was a threat to his health.

Labour members were furious: 'The Government has flouted the popular belief that this is a war against fascism', John Parker argued, 'and anyway 18b is a political not a judicial instrument.' Dan Chater, whose East End constituents had been threatened by fascist thugs long before the blitz, was equally incensed, and Sidney Silverman suggested that extraneous pressures had weighted Morrison's decision. Silverman had examined all the medical evidence made available to him and, he said, it had not implied anything serious about Mosley's health.[36] Any of these critical speeches Ellen herself might have made. Publicly however, much as she must have detested its implication, she defended Morrison's action on the grounds that although loathing all Mosley stood for, she understood that he was 'bedridden, remained under strict guard and had kept within the law'.[37]

Members of her union censured this stand.[38] Although a resolution demanding Ellen's employment be terminated was withdrawn before the 1944 NUDAW Conference, her unpopularity lingered. She was unable to attend the Conference, being in a nursing home to clear up the effects of heavy bronchitis aggravated by returning to work too soon, but she defended her action in a letter read to delegates. Mosley had been, she wrote, an undoubted security risk, but now the notoriety of his release was over, 'the big blackshirt became a nonentity'. Moreover she questioned the right of a trade union to 'control the vote of their MPs'. This she regarded as an 'impossible constitutional doctrine'. Unions and the Labour Party leaders had the right 'to expect MPs and ministers to act in accordance with the

general principles for which we stand', and she had voted in the
Mosley debate in accordance with the majority decision of the PLP.
However,

> the implication that in a Labour Cabinet trade unionists should
> receive telegrams of instruction as to how they should vote on
> important issues and be threatened with future financial penalties
> if they were disregarded, is constitutional nonsense. Under such a
> system no trade unionist could ever become a Minister of the
> Crown, nor in fact could one ever have a Labour Government.[39]

Ellen must have agonised over this whole conflict, yet the stand she
took was prompted by something deeper than 'characteristic
impetuosity' (as one NUDAW delegate had suggested). She knew
the temperature of public opinion well enough — ministerial mail
about Mosley's release arrived in sackfuls[40] — but she allowed personal and ministerial loyalty to override her most profound convictions and supported Morrison in the voting lobby. Resignation
would have been the only alternative.

Her stand over Mosley's release indicates that Ellen's politics were
taking a rightward turn, and over this Morrison's influence cannot
be discounted. She drew back from speaking on the United Front,
and resigned from the boards of Tribune and LRD. More significantly, she defended a ban on the *Daily Worker* in the face of opposition from her union. 'The matter of the ban should be left in the
hands of those who do not want to see . . . irresponsible people running campaigns such as the *Daily Worker's* peace at any price campaign,' she said in an untypically stilted statement.[41] The need to win
the war and loyalty to her Minister had dictated her stand over a
number of politically delicate matters. Ellen was learning that politics really is the art of the practical.

Privy Councillor

As the grey days of war dragged on, Ellen's health was at a low ebb.
Mr MacLellan, a consultant surgeon and close friend, whom she
always called 'my doctor', remembers visiting Penn at Christmas
1944 during a snowstorm. 'She was confined to bed, and her spirits
were sunk below zero', he wrote,[42] but something had happened to
offer personal cheer. In the New Year's Honours List she was to be

made a Privy Councillor, together with Florence Horsbrugh.[43] At the time she displayed little enthusiasm: 'I feel neither right nor honourable' she said to Mr MacLellan. Yet it was an exceptional honour for outstanding work then paid to only two other women: Margaret Bondfield and Lady Astor. Ellen had travelled a long way in experience and achievement from the days when she had been warned off teaching!

In a Ministry that had had to grapple with the impact of the blitz, the shortcomings of local government, and the creation of a national Civil Defence network, Ellen tackled responsibilities with fearlessness and humanity. Even so, to her civil servants she was far from faultless. One had to walk warily with her; she could explode with anger and become hurtfully spiteful. She upset people by being outrageously rude, though more often than not her remarks flowed from impatience to get things done. Her tantrums were wholly unmalicious, and when told she had caused offence she would immediately write a contrite note of apology.[44]

Ellen was certainly a galvanising force and a good publicist for her department and, as even her most grudging critics conceded, she was 'a useful prodder and supplier of all round energy'. The waspish comments that 'she rarely made any useful [written] contribution on a file'[45] implies rightly that she was a doer rather than a desk-based administrator. She injected a sense of real urgency and doubtless led her minister in a direction that was healthy for the department — and the country. The senior staff in Home Security, aware of her closeness to Herbert Morrison, were originally apprehensive lest she would interfere in policy matters — but of this there is no evidence at all.[46]

All in all, Ellen made a success of an exhausting job. During the blitz she heartened thousands, shared in their suffering, planned for their shelter comfort and later in the face of much hostility created a vast new fire watching force. Toughly courageous, brave and hard working, in spite of her physical frailty, Ellen Wilkinson, PC, MP, had a war record of which she could be proud, but it was a record earned unquestionably at the expense of her health.

No Short Cut to Paradise

During the years of acute national need, Ellen's ministerial commitments naturally took precedence over party work. When official pressures eased however her political obligations became far more demanding. Even before she assumed the chairmanship of the NEC in 1944 after the unexpected death in mid-term of George Ridley, Ellen was deeply involved in clarifying the party's plans for the future. By 1941−2 she was serving on the Party's Committees for Post War Reconstruction and for Press and Publicity. The former, particularly high powered included Dalton, Morrison, Attlee, Laski and Noel-Baker under the chairmanship of Manny Shinwell. In 1943−4 she undertook more responsibilities and by the following session was on the Election Campaign, Party Organisation, Policy, International Affairs and Finance and General Purposes Committees. She also represented the NEC on the National Council of Labour[47].

The wartime coalition remained in being until May 1945 and was followed briefly by a Tory government. Both Ellen and Herbert Morrison were among those who, anxious for the Labour Party to reassert its independence, had favoured an early break up of the coalition; Bevin, Dalton, and Attlee preferred its continuing at least until November. In the run-up to the summer general election the Conservatives pledged an end to all wartime controls, but the Labour Party held that their retention was as essential to the nation's well-being as the nationalisation of major industries, advocated in their election manifesto.

Chairman of the Labour Party during the election year Ellen vigorously presented the party's programme:

> Tinkering around with the social system [was just not good enough] . . . The planning machine built up during the war must not be scrapped in the interests of 'freedom and plenty'. If we do we shall only present the speculators and monopolists with the freedom to exploit the community for private profit and make a Third World War certain.

In short, people must 'decide between the break up of national planning, and national needs being met by the ethics of the poker table, or by trained and tested intelligent planning'.[48] The lessons of Jarrow were still branded on her mind. To secure social justice, nationalisation, including that of the steel industry, was imperative, and even if the Labour Party did not intend to nationalise ship-building straight away it must have an overall plan.[49]

During the long weary war Ellen's hopes, like those of many, were by no means exclusively materialistic. 'I have noticed while moving around in my civil defence work that whereas people grumble, they seem to have a curious hunger for some kind of community life'. For in spite of exhaustion and personal despair (or perhaps because of it), in June 1945 the electorate chose a party pledged to plan for the community and to retain rather than abolish controls. There was indeed a new unselfishness in popular attitudes to politics, a feeling that suffering could be reduced if only it could be shared. 'Winning the peace need not be a grim job', Ellen wrote, 'it can be a new crusade inspired by a high sense of adventure and service to the community.'[50] Her election address to Jarrow demanded that all people should have 'a sense of hitherto little known security in their lives', as Beveridge had spelt out in his report. She also gave high priority to the creation of a world security organisation and pledged herself to fight for jobs for all and to extend public ownership. Ellen had never pretended that peace time would be easy and had once said during the war: 'No one should expect to get a Socialist State tied up in pink ribbon as an armistice present from Winston Churchill — it has to be worked for.'[51]

Chairing the Labour Party Conference at Blackpool in election year she gave a stirring and decisive lead; but again injected a warning: 'A Britain without unemployment cannot be built on the shifting foundations of monopoly capitalism . . . The whole resources of the country [must be] efficiently organised in the interests of the community . . .' Socialists wanted millions of homes, jobs for all, social security, educational opportunity and a state health service:

> These must be obtained and paid for by . . . a highly efficient industry and properly planned agriculture. There must be no illusions. The Labour Party does not offer a short-cut to paradise. We know that peace, like war, must be won . . . [but] we will fight and fight for power.[52]

For this stirring cry to action she received a great ovation. 'It was', as Philip Noel-Baker remarked, 'Ellen's finest hour. No one will ever forget the nerve, the verve, the wit, the confidence and the joyful challenge with which she led the Conference.'[53]

An End to Kingmaking

The imminent election and the demands which office imposed did not deter Ellen from further 'kingmaking'. According to Hugh Dalton, she approached him and 'doubtless others' at Blackpool in May 1945, and 'earnestly pressed . . . that Attlee should now step aside before the election campaign began, and let Morrison become Leader of the Party'. Yet this attitude, in view of Attlee's standing in the country, showed a singular lack of sensitivity to public reaction and opaque loyalty to Herbert. As Dalton commented, 'this was out of the question. Apart from everything else the timing was quite impossible.' Harold Laski, the party's chairman-elect, pursued a line similar to Ellen's. 'They tried hard to substitute Morrison for me but failed to get any response', Attlee later observed.[54]

Labour won a landslide victory. The electorate returned 393 Labour Members on a 76 per cent vote cast in burning summer weather. The new PLP contained an exceptional wealth of talent, which coupled with the size of Labour's majority and general political optimism gave an impetus to social change. Against this background Morrison wrote to Attlee saying that he intended to stand for the leadership. He proposed that Attlee should refuse to form a government until the new PLP had met to decide upon a leader.[55] Laski took the same view, but Attlee disagreed. 'If invited by the King to form a government you do not say that you cannot reply for forty-eight hours,' he retorted briskly. 'You accept the Commission and you either bring it off or you don't.'[56] The idea of this temporary deferment had also been pressed by Maurice Webb — lobby correspondent for the *Daily Herald* — Cripps, Bevan and Ellen. Ernest Bevin was bitterly opposed, and rang Morrison to say, 'If you go on mucking about like this you won't be in the bloody government at all.'[57] Yet even after Attlee had been to the Palace, Morrison was still trying to persuade the new MPs that the leadership issues had yet to be decided. He buttonholed John Parker at a Fabian celebration, and urged that 'we cannot have Attlee as leader'. Such overtures however were 'out of time'; Attlee announced at a massive Victory Social the same evening that he had undertaken to form a government and he received a ringing ovation.[58]

Ellen did not readily concede defeat and even after some ministers had received their seals of office she was still agitating on Morrison's behalf. A newly elected MP, Leah Manning, an old friend of Ellen's, wrote of her conspiratorially seeking support for Morrison at a meeting of the PLP the following morning: 'I was very fond of Ellen, but to challenge Clement Attlee's leadership seemed a dirty bit of chicanery — and I told her so.'[59] Attlee, retaining his imperturba-

bility throughout these machinations, made some shrewd appoint-
ments. He included several 'combative personalities' in his government, and Ellen became Minister of Education. Thereafter plots
faded. Shinwell added a revealing postscript: 'I mentioned to
Attlee,' he wrote, 'that a number of plotters had been given jobs. He
laughed, perfectly well aware of what had been going on. It is not
bad tactics to make one's enemies one's servants.'[60]

Not all hatchets were so easily buried. The antipathy between
Bevin and Morrison which dated back to when Morrison was
Minister of Transport, was in no way diminished by the Prime
Minister's game of diplomatic chess. Francis Williams recalled how,
soon after he had been appointed Attlee's adviser on public rela-
tions, Bevin sent for him. 'I'm glad you're coming to look after
Clem,' he said. 'You keep an eye on 'Erbert when I'm not here,
Francis. Let me know if he gets up to any of his tricks. I wouldn't
trust the little bugger further than I could throw him!'[61]

Ellen's role as a so-called plotter cannot readily be explained on
the simplistic analysis that her heart ruled her head, though it often
did and she allegedly still 'worshipped' Morrison. Certainly her
affection was compounded with admiration for his political and
administrative flair; he was after all a proven 'doer' as she had had
occasion to observe first hand. Yet more than that, the contrast
between Attlee and Morrison — the quietly retiring seemingly
colourless middle-class barrister, and the warmly approachable
extrovert cockney — was inescapable. Moreover, within the PLP
preference for one candidate over the other had nothing to do with
either contestant being 'right' or 'left' wing — as Michael Foot,
then a newly elected MP, recalled, 'Morrison just seemed the more
positive and personable of the two.'[62]

In all fairness there were mixed factors prompting Ellen's obstinate attitude. The tensions of wartime, the strain of overwork,
which had intensified her attacks of asthma, may well have mis-
directed that never over-reliable judgement. They explain — at least
in part — why she so greatly underestimated the warm opinions
Attlee had earned throughout the country as Churchill's unobtrusive
rock-like deputy. To Ellen, Herbert, her ex-minister, was the
achiever *par excellence*: the majority of the PLP judged otherwise.

Notes

1. A. Calder, *The People's War* (Jonathan Cape, London, 1969), p. 495.
2. Beryl Hughes, interview.
3. A. Calder, p. 185.
4. *The Times*, 23 November 1940.
5. John Parker, Kenneth Witney, Beryl Hughes, interviews; John Parker was Ellen's Parliamentary Private Secretary, 1940–2.
6. Mrs Muriel Wilkinson, Mrs Kathleen Wilkinson, interviews.
7. John Parker, interview.
8. H.J. Laski in *Reynolds News*, 9 February 1947.
9. John Parker, interview.
10. This was a flat she reputedly loved because from its height she could see the House, and St Stephen's Tower (Amy Wilde, interview).
11. Beryl Hughes, interview.
12. Lady Rhondda *Time and Tide*, 15 February 1947.
13. Mrs Bowrie Mensler, interview.
14. *The Times*, 28 October 1940.
15. B. Donoughue and G.W. Jones, *Herbert Morrison* (Weidenfeld and Nicolson, London, 1973), p. 283.
16. A. Calder, p. 184.
17. Beryl Hughes, interview.
18. Lord Sorenson, unpublished papers (House of Lords Library, London).
19. John Parker, interview.
20. Donoughue and Jones, pp. 290–1.
21. *The Times*, 28 April 1941.
22. PRO.HO/205/143.
23. *Time and Tide*, 11 January 1941.
24. Lord Ritchie Calder, interview.
25. *Hansard*, Vol. 340, col. 399, 3 November 1938.
26. Beryl Hughes, interview.
27. *The Times*, 6 June 1941.
28. *Spectator*, 24 August 1945.
29. PRO.HO/187/661.
30. *The Times*, 9 August 1943.
31. Hansard, Vol. 370, cols. 1795–9, 10 April 1941.
32. Hansard, Vol. 390, cols. 1643–58, 30 June 1943.
33. Hansard, Vol. 793, cols. 730–1, 759–63, 3 November 1943.
34. A. Calder, p. 551
35. *The Times*, 27 November 1943.
36. Hansard, Vol. 393, cols. 461–78, 1 December 1943.
37. *The Times*, 27 November 1943.
38. *The Times*, 4 May 1944.
39. *New Dawn*, 20 May 1944.
40. Donoughue and Jones, p. 304.
41. *Scotsman*, 12 May 1942.
42. Edward MacLellan, letter of 1 May 1980.
43. Florence Horsbrugh (MP, Dundee 1931–45, Moss Side Manchester 1950–4 and Minister of Education 1951–4).
44. Mrs Bowrie Mensler, Beryl Hughes, Kenneth Witney, interviews.
45. Sir Austin Strutt, interview.
46. Kenneth Witney, interview.
47. Labour Party Conference Annual Reports, 1942, 1943, 1944 and 1945.
48. Ellen Wilkinson 'Socialism and the Future of Britain' (Fabian Lecture, 1944);

The Times, 5 March 1945.
49. *The Times*, 30 June 1945.
50. Ellen Wilkinson, *How the People will win the Peace* (Labour Party, London, 1945), pamphlet.
51. *Daily Herald*, 6 October 1942.
52. Labour Party Conference Annual Report, 1945, p. 150.
53. Labour Party Conference Annual Report, 1947.
54. H. Dalton, *The Fateful Years* (Frederick Muller, London, 1957) p. 460; C.R. Attlee, *As it Happened* (Heinemann, London, 1954), p. 145.
55. Dalton, *The Fateful Years*, p. 467.
56. F. Williams, *Nothing so Strange* (Cassell, London, 1970), p. 213.
57. Dalton, *Fateful Years*, p. 468.
58. John Parker, interview; Dalton, *Fateful Years*, p. 474.
59. L. Manning, *A Life for Education* (Gollancz, London, 1970), p. 164.
60. E. Shinwell, *Conflict Without Malice*, (Odhams, London, 1955), p. 134.
61. Williams, *Nothing so Strange*, p. 218.
62. Michael Foot, interview.

10 MINISTER OF EDUCATION THE RT HON. ELLEN WILKINSON PC, MP, MA, LLD(HON.)

In all that Ellen Wilkinson did or said as Minister one could not detect any element of self-interest or self-advancement. She was fighting for others all the time — Neville Heaton

No time is ever regarded as ripe for reform, but by standing firm in Cabinet Ellen saved the Education Act. — Lord Alexander of Potterhill

Appointment and Background Issues

After the election victory Ellen scaled political heights. Attlee (some would say generously, others astutely) gave her, as Minister of Education, a seat in the Cabinet, which indicated the importance he attached to the office. The department, facing the monumental task of reconstruction and of implementing the 1944 Education Act, had at its head for the first time a woman educated within the state system. On grounds of her 'previous performance' Ellen's elevation was no surprise: the actual department allotted to her was. Once she had frivolously opted for the Ministry of Labour when the likelihood of any preferment was remote,[1] but when opportunity came she was undoubtedly delighted with Education. She told H.D. ('Billy') Hughes, her PPS, it was an appointment she had genuinely wanted.[2] It had been rumoured that she had set her heart on the job,[3] although the suggestion that Ellen dashed down from Jarrow to Westminister to ask Attlee for the Ministry[4] is highly speculative, and even if true was unlikely to have been the overriding reason for her appointment. The Prime Minister, who in John Parker's opinion proved so adept at harmonising the disparate abilities in his team,[5] was far too shrewd a judge to be swayed by emotional cajolery even though he regarded Ellen highly, as a creature of spirit and forgave her a lot on that account.[6] Chuter Ede, who as Parliamentary Secretary to R.A. Butler had been closely involved with drafting the 1944 Education Act, was widely tipped for the job.[7] He had, however, much experience in other fields of local government and he was a known NUT figure, whereas Ellen was wholly uncommitted to any pressure group. As Attlee wrote later: 'I needed a man of particular quality for the Home Office which is a post where mistakes can easily be made [and so appointed Chuter Ede] . . . Ellen had done well as a junior minister and I knew she was an enthusiast for education.'[8] Maybe, but only in the sense of a general keenness for improvement. In no way was Ellen an educational expert, nor did she ever pretend to be.

The appointment was widely welcomed. 'She will bring to the job personal knowledge of the public system, the warmest sympathy with children and young people, and a great capacity for decisions and dynamic energy', declared *The Times Educational Supplement*.[9] Vera Brittain (mother of Shirley Williams, a future Minister of Education) expressed the feminist's jubilation in her congratulatory letter:

> The Ministry has long needed a woman and you are THE woman. Given time, I know you will clear away many existing anomalies and inequalities . . . How I wish Winifred Holtby, who admired you so much, were here to back your work with voice and pen.[10]

It was nevertheless in some ways a surprising appointment because Ellen had so few positive ideas about Education. Of course she was aware of the socially divisive nature of a system which denied secondary education to all. She abhorred the wastage of well over 80 per cent of the school population leaving at fourteen, and had long regarded it as 'one of the tragedies of life that poorer children had to leave school and go to work when beginning to appreciate what school can do for them'.[11]

It is only fair to admit that questions of inequality of educational opportunity and wasted potential had roused little public attention pre-war, other than from specialists. Parliament in those days usually discussed education on Derby Day or similar social occasions when government benches were virtually empty.[12] Even at Labour Party and TUC conferences motions on education were usually relegated to the end of the agenda. Yet Labour experts believed that educational change was essential to the building of a just society. Specialists ranging from Sir Charles Trevelyan, Professor R.H.

Tawney and Chuter Ede to Barbara Drake, Margaret Cole and Harold Shearman[13] over the years worked in the Labour Party's Advisory Committee on Education, the Fabian Society, the National Association of Labour Teachers (NALT)[14] and the LCC Education Committee, examining general ideas for achieving that change. Yet although the broad aims of a socialist educational policy were clear enough there was no agreed detailed blue-print.

The quintessence of Labour's educational thought was embodied in a long resolution moved for the NEC by Harold Clay and accepted in 1942 at the Labour Party Conference. He sought to establish real equality by substituting for 'the greasy pole' of education a broad highway of opportunity for every child. This meant extending nursery schools, improving primary education, making school canteens and free meals a reality and establishing free secondary education for all (with adequate maintenance) on the basis of the 'common school principle'. This unified or multilateral system, later called comprehensive, was to embrace all secondary pupils — of grammar, technical and secondary-modern abilities — under one roof, to provide a wide variety of courses for pupils of different aptitudes and to plan for flexibility of transfer between courses. Since nearly half of all pupils were educated in higher elementary or all-age elementary schools, all too often leaving school with the rudiments of the three Rs but little else, these schools, Clay insisted, should be reorganised without delay. All secondary schools must be accorded equality of status and have a common code securing similar standards of staffing, accomodation, equipment and salaries. No longer should grammar schools receive preferential treatment. Above all, high priority should be given to raising the school-leaving age to fifteen immediately hostilities ended (and to sixteen within three years) and to developing part-time education until eighteen.[15] Support for introducing the multilateral school was repeated at the Labour Party Conference the following year, and in 1945 when Ellen was chairman Alice Bacon accepted this policy on behalf of the NEC, agreeing that 'newly built secondary schools were to be multilateral where possible'.[16]

Labour's thinking had influenced the 1944 Education Act with its stated intent to ensure education for all children according to age, aptitude and ability. The Act as (later Sir) Harold Shearman wrote, was a landmark in English educational history[17] and transformed the old Board of Education into a Ministry, with powers to impose duties on all Local Education Authorities (LEAs). The key note of the Act was a unified approach organised in three progressive stages — primary, secondary and further; and it became the duty of LEAs to contribute 'to the moral, mental and physical development of their community' by making that education available. Secondary education moreover was to be free, but there was no lead as to the form it should take, which was the inherent weakness of the Act.

There was no doubt about Ellen's broad intentions as minister. She was determined to 'improve the lot of underprivileged children and to make secondary education much more than elementary education with frills'. But she had not thought through the implications of basic educational change, let alone how it should be achieved. It was a serious, if wholly explicable, weakness that Ellen had had so little contact with socialist educationalists — not even with the vocal and intelligent pressure group NALT, which had expounded the concept of multilateral schools since the late 1920s.[18] So it was that, with no positive political remit other than the monumental charge 'to implement the 1944 Act', weary from excessive war pressures, and even then unwell — 'she was desperately ill at least during twelve of her eighteen months in office'[19] — Ellen initially had to rely heavily on her civil servants.

From the outset she established a warm rapport with her senior staff, reared though they were to a man in the public school tradition.[20] Had Ellen's relationship with the senior civil service been more abrasive her impact as minister might have been different, for even though she 'never hesitated to make her views known',[21] it was difficult for her persistently to disagree with officers she held in esteem and who were a prime source of her information. After initial uncertainty, the department came to regard her warmly. The civil servants were used to ministers 'with no background to educational policy', but they had been apprehensive 'because she had the reputation for being fiery, aggressive and successfully combative',[22] and they were unsure as to the government's education intentions.

Ellen, still prone to fall into hot water not always of her own boiling, again did just that. According to the civil service grapevine the retiring Permanent Secretary, Sir Maurice Holmes, 'who deserved as much acclaim for the 1944 Act as R.A. Butler',[23] was to be succeeded by an internal appointee who had been unofficially 'named' before Ellen took office. The gentleman in question however aroused Ellen's intense dislike and she demanded instead a 'replacement who was both a good administrator and not establishment minded'. In due course Herbert Morrison (Lord President of the Council) released Sir John Maud (later Lord Redcliffe-Maud) to Education from the Ministry of Reconstruction (the 'little think-tank which had been Winston's sop to those wanting to develop post war planning', where he had been working under Lord Woolton). This proved a happy translation and an easy relationship evolved between the minister, her permanent secretary and Mr (later Sir) Antony Part, Ellen's Principal Private Secretary. They worked in 'close harmony' together at their Belgrave Square headquarters in London. Billy Hughes was an admiring and devoted PPS; but with David Hardman, who succeeded the ailing Arthur Jenkins as Parliamentary Secretary, Ellen had absolutely no rapport.[24]

Ellen gave and received great loyalty. She was found to be far less aggressive, more sensible, than had been anticipated and she was willing to be influenced by the facts. She worked immensely hard, attained and expected exactingly high standards, and was intolerant of inefficiency, although in the House she would tenaciously defend her department. In general, Ellen adapted more readily to her job than many had supposed possible, but was clearly more interested in policy than in administrative minutiae. She delegated well, was eminently approachable, had little sense of protocol, and preferred to talk with the person 'who knew'. Lord Redcliffe-Maud reflected that 'Unlike Dick Crossman, Ellen trusted her civil servants, recognised they offered her a fund of goodwill and was angelic in assuming that they would help rather than obstruct. She therefore accepted rather than resisted advice . . . [and] as Minister learnt rather than led.'[25] While this pleased her civil servants it became on occasion the despair of, even the cause for attack by, political colleagues.

If the personal circumstances of Ellen's appointment and her departmental relationships were comfortable, the economic background was one of unmitigated gloom. Britain had fought and won a total war, cut exports dramatically, and survived economically only by selling foreign assets and receiving Lend Lease Aid from the USA. This had enabled her to obtain imports without immediate payment, but it had also meant that huge debts accumulated and that by the end of the war serious problems in restoring foreign trade had to be faced.

The Treasury calculated that if all went well, equilibrium in the balance of payments could be established by 1949 — four years after the conclusion of hostilities. But while negotiations over Anglo-American trade relations were in train, within three weeks of the Labour government's taking office, and totally without prior warning, President Truman announced the cancellation of Lend Lease. The cabinet, like the country, were stunned. Michael Foot has described the position:

> The question was how the British people were to be fed and British factories supplied with raw materials. If no loan was forthcoming as a substitute for Lend Lease, the nation would have to endure a period of harsher austerity than it had known even in the war. Worse still, all the Government's plans for reconstruction would have to be re-shaped on a much less ambitious basis.

Keynes, toiling for the Treasury, did his 'brilliant best'. A loan was negotiated but had strings. The Americans demanded — and secured — an undertaking that sterling should be made convertible within a year of the loan coming into force! The amount was much less than had been hoped for. Austerity remained the order of the day.[26] Such were the economic tensions behind what many had anticipated would be a period of socialist reconstruction and innovation. It was an era fraught with uncertainties, which makes Ellen's departmental achievements all the more remarkable.

Raising the School-leaving Age and the Emergency Training Scheme

The first public pledge that Ellen gave after becoming minister was to raise the school-leaving age (ROSLA) and as she wrote to Sir Charles Trevelyan, 'I am making it my first major job'.[27] She regarded the 1944 Act as one of the greatest achievements of the Coalition Government and its implementation as 'work for a generation', but within this framework she accorded ROSLA top priority. Cumulative shortages and inter-ministerial competition for skilled labour and scarce raw materials offered formidable threats to its introduction. But lack of determination had never been one of Ellen's failings, and in September she confidently announced that the school-leaving age would be raised to fifteen on 1 April 1947, and later to sixteen.[28]

This had not been done lightly. Ellen had demanded a prompt decision from the cabinet so that LEAs could make the necessary preparations, but from the outset she had argued that ROSLA could be introduced by April 1947, the date fixed by the 1944 Act, and the requirements for teachers and accommodation met, provided manpower and materials were allocated. In this she was strongly supported by Chuter Ede who argued that postponement would dishearten progressive LEAs, and convince the less adventurous that ROSLA could be postponed indefinitely. Nye Bevan also supported Ellen, although as Minister of Housing he was apprehensive about the implications for his department.[29] At this stage Herbert Morrison was also sympathetic:

> As a test of the Government's sincerity we must stick to the date in the Act if humanly possible and not a moment must be lost in extracting skilled technicians from the forces. For a time, the public will have to accept imperfect conditions, but the first steps can and should be taken.[30]

The cabinet, reassured by Ellen that 'really active steps were in train to increase training college places', agreed that 'material shortages did not justify postponement'.[31]

Once the decision on ROSLA had been made, the question of teacher supply assumed priority. Low war-time recruitment into, and imminent retirements from, the teaching profession widened the gap between the Act and the Fact. To help meet the anticipated shortage, the Emergency Training Scheme (ETS) was introduced — an enlightened innovation, devised by some 'original and brave officers' in the department during the War. The identity of the originator is unclear, but the scheme was piloted at Goldsmith's College.[32] Responsibility for its administration is associated with Sir Gilbert Flemming (a senior civil servant) who found it 'one of the most challenging and satisfactory jobs I ever undertook'.[33] Its sensible simplicity won Ellen's enthusiastic support.

Under the ETS, temporary colleges were set up which offered a one-year course in teacher training (followed by two-years' probation and part-time study) to ex-servicemen and women. No formal academic attainments were required, and selection was by interview, based on personal qualifications, war-time experience and enthusiasm. The response was overwhelming and the quality of applicants, which surpassed expectation, allayed any professional apprehension of 'dilution'. For the first time people with broad experience were entering the teaching profession, and their influx brought in a 'breath of fresh air'.[34] At its peak the scheme attracted well over a thousand applications each week; by the end of 1946 over 37,000 men and women had been accepted and as many rejected.[35]

The ETS became a victim of its own success. Oversubscribed, understaffed, overcentralised, and with a shortage of college accommodation, it was beset with administrative difficulties. Students had to wait twelve to eighteen months after acceptance before a place in college was available and had to face long delays before receiving their grants. In the House the ministry came under repeated angry questioning over which Ellen stonewalled. The shortages of essential materials for necessary adaptations were real enough, but 25,000 demobbed candidates were eagerly awaiting placement in September 1946. The apparent apathy and complacency afflicting the minister and her civil servants exasperated their critics.[36] There is no indication that the minister intervened to improve procedure, although she did secure some additional staff. However, had her work pressures been lighter, her familiarity with the work of the department greater and, above all, her health more robust, Ellen might well have acted more aggressively. She certainly seemed more prepared to bully administrators when she was Herbert Morrison's Parliamentary Secretary than when minister in her own domain; though in all fairness inter-ministerial competition for resources must have been fierce.

Yet to Ellen's credit, however hard pressed in the House she would always tenaciously defend her department. When under severe censure for the tardy progress of the ETS she never blamed her civil servants, as others did:

If the Minister and the Parliamentary Secretary had been led to see for themselves and to exercise their own judgement instead of accepting that of their admirable but possibly unprogressive civil servants . . . it is unnecessary to look further for explaining the alleged slowness.[37]

The outcome of ETS exceeded all expectations. When the scheme ended in 1951, over 35,000 men and women whose seriousness of purpose and maturity of mind enhanced their profession had been trained. No one pretended that the national teacher shortage had been solved, but it had been substantially eased and qualitatively improved.[38]

The minister consistently urged LEAs from the outset to adopt every possible means for accelerating the provision of accommodation for ROSLA and for schools in new housing developments.[39] This meant hard inter-departmental fighting up to ministerial level, to secure the necessary building resources. It was a tribute to Ellen's persistence that she was able to announce at the end of 1946 that the year's capital expenditure of about £7 million for the educational building programme would be increased to £24 million for 1947 with a long-term objective of £70 million.[40] To save on scarce materials and skilled manpower the classrooms were mass-produced under the Hut Operations for Raising the School Leaving Age Scheme (HORSA), organised by the Ministry of Works led by its energetic minister, George Tomlinson. Good ideas, however, did not guarantee delivery. By September 1947 less than half the needed accommodation had in fact been delivered.[41]

ROSLA Threatened

In spite of dogged work by the government, 1946 was not a year of miracles and ROSLA again came under threat. Arctic-like weather and fuel and food shortages, intensified by the ending of Lend Lease aggravated economic stringency and the general feeling of despondency. The mutterings that ROSLA might have to be postponed welled into a two-pronged threat, from a panicky Scottish Secretary of State on one hand and from the Chancellor of the Exchequer, Sir Stafford Cripps, demanding economies, on the other.

The former, alarmed by the projected shortfall of accommodation in Scotland, predicted part-time schooling for mid-1947 if ROSLA were not postponed and threatened to approach the cabinet direct — a suggestion that Ellen scotched as being 'quite improper'. The Chancellor's Economic Review for 1947 was far more ominous and late in December he recommended postponement of ROSLA until September 1947. This Ellen adamantly resisted, though privately the department conceded that it would be a miracle if the building programme was completed on time — 'too many LEAs had retreated into a defeatist mood' — but she and Sir John Maud were at one, no one must get the impression that their ministry faced a hopeless task.

Ellen therefore submitted a reassuring document to the Lord President. In this was spelt out that the real crunch from ROSLA would not come for eighteen months. Then, by September 1948, the total teaching strength was likely to be 200,000, and might even facilitate some reduction in class sizes. Moreover, over 86 per cent of the extra age group would by then be housed in existing premises or in the HORSA prefabricated hutments and the balance of pupils would be accommodated in new light timber and steel permanent construction on existing school sites or in new housing estates. 'I am satisfied', Ellen wrote, 'that accommodation plans can be largely completed by the relevant dates provided that . . . the degree of priority promised us is in no way reduced.' Above all ROSLA was a first major step in educational reform, and delay, she concluded, would so shake public confidence that the whole operation of the Act would be endangered. The Committee of Ministers agreed that there should be no postponement.

The final battle was joined in full cabinet on 16 January, only three weeks before Ellen's death. She reminded her colleagues that in every harassed government education had always been the first casualty and that the weakest element, children, always went to the wall. 'We shall gain more by saying that the Government will not sacrifice them, whatever else goes, than we shall from justifying the very speculative productive capacity [on the labour market] of those youngsters.' She further recalled how in 1945 when LEAs were wholly sceptical about ROSLA:

> I pledged the honour of the Government that 1 April 1947 would be the date. Just because I made the country believe that the Government meant to keep its word, the phased programme is now ready enough to do its job: we shall never get the same intensity of effort to a date again, and those to suffer most by deferment will be precisely those working class children whose education has already been so seriously interrupted by the war.

She added a threatening coda: 'As a trade union official I am fully prepared to use my union, public platforms and the press to argue the case.'[42] In fact her PPS had already been lobbying back-benchers for support. Had an adverse decision been reached a revolt within the PLP would have been highly probable.[43]

Ellen carried the day and the cabinet agreed 'that the educational and political advantages of introducing ROSLA on 1 April outweigh any possible economic gain from deferment'. It was not a unanimous decision. Attlee, Nye Bevan, Ernest Bevin, Chuter Ede, George Tomlinson, among others stood firmly behind Ellen, but Herbert Morrison, anxious over the administrative as well as the economic implications agreed with Cripps. Some suggest that Ellen was deeply hurt by his unsupportive attitude, but she too could face practicalities and George Tomlinson remembered how after the final decision had been taken in cabinet 'she left immediately to issue the prepared press notice.'[44] So it was Ellen triumphed; however, 'there is no doubt whatever that had she been defeated she would have resigned'[45]

A Visit to Germany

During her early months in office Ellen visited Germany — Hamburg, West Berlin, Frankfurt and Dusseldorf — to study de-nazification and educational conditions in the British zone, where she found the phoenix-like progress astonishing. In some four months an acceptable administration had been established and in Hamburg a high proportion of schools and two-thirds of the damaged university building were re-opening.[46] At a lighter level Sir Antony Part recalled Ellen's meeting a Control Commission Brigadier, whom she insisted on calling Captain. When Sir Antony tactfully remonstrated, she replied 'Oh well — I only know the ranks in the Fire Service!'[47] 'Remarks such as these,' commented Billy Hughes, 'utterly captivated the Generals!'

Ellen warmed especially to the German teachers she met who had spent long years in concentration camps yet who were making plucky attempts to educate the young. Her visit proved particularly useful in a way of which she was perhaps unaware, but would doubtless have approved. The Control Commission was anxious to assemble strong teams of educationists, particularly women, to work in all the Länder (state) capitals. Yet only a few women volunteered, because under the Nazis they had fared so badly that their self-confidence and willingness to assume responsibility had been undermined. Ellen's appointment and her visits in her capacity as minister strengthened the hand of the Control Commission by proving to hesitant Germans that Britain practised what she preached.[48]

The minister also met senior educational staff. One official recalled Ellen's 'prodding' over the delay in re-opening schools:

> I explained the sheer physical difficulties; lack of classrooms, of fuel for school boilers, and of food in the children's stomachs . . .
> Soon after that, through Ellen's intervention, a modest school

meal was introduced, only a plate of milk soup, but it was a beginning.[49]

The United Nations Educational, Scientific and Cultural Organisation

One of the noblest conceptions of the post war world — George Thomas

Unless we can put standards of values into the minds of youth we cannot have a great civilisation or a great country — Ellen Wilkinson

Domestic affairs had, of course, first call on Ellen's attention, but she made further official visits abroad — to Gibraltar, Malta and later to Prague, in addition to Germany — and also strengthened the international role of her department by her cherished connection with the United Nations Educational, Scientific and Cultural Organisation (UNESCO).

UNESCO had grown from the United Nations Organisation — UNO — whose birth Ellen had witnessed in San Francisco during the spring of 1945 when a member of the British delegation led by Sir Anthony Eden. Later she endorsed to the full the sentiments of the King's Speech, 1945, that 'the horrors of the atom bomb, so vivid in men's minds, emphasise afresh that the nations of the world must abolish recourse to war or perish by mutual destruction'.[50] To this theme Attlee returned when he welcomed in London representatives from forty countries for the First Plenary Session of UNESCO over which Ellen presided jointly with Leon Blum: 'Since war begins in the minds of men, it is in the minds of men that the defence of peace must be concentrated.' Historic words, which Archibald McLeish the American poet enshrined in the prologue to the Constitution of UNESCO at Ellen's suggestion.[51] The aspirations for UNESCO, defined in Ellen's official speech to that Plenary Session, coincided with her personal hopes. These aimed above all to develop in children a concept of international citizenship instead of nationalism. 'In the field of education which is our concern', she said, 'the national and international can most readily be fused for the common good.'[52]

The future boded well. Early in 1946 (later Sir) Julian Huxley suc-

ceeded Sir Alfred Zimmern as Executive Secretary, and later became
Director General of UNESCO:

> When Sir John Maud asked me whether I would like to become
> Secretary of the Preparatory Commission I was flabbergasted,
> but I promised to think it over . . . John Maud did not let the
> grass grow under his feet. He got Ellen to invite me and him to
> dinner at the House . . . I was persuaded to accept. I felt like one
> of those early Christians who were kidnapped and compelled to
> become Bishops.[53]

Soon after Ellen announced that the UNESCO Secretariat was to be
based in Paris. This was rumoured to have been a quid pro quo for
Leon Blum's support of Huxley's appointment, for on this Ellen had
insisted before she would agree to Paris being the centre for
UNESCO.[54] Sadly, however, she was unable to attend the first
anniversary conference at the new headquarters and was intensely
disappointed. Allegedly this was due to work pressures arising from
ROSLA;[55] in reality, the conference was being held too soon after
the visit to Prague, where Ellen had been taken seriously ill. As Sir
John Maud commented, 'We could never publicly admit that the
Minister was unwell.'[56]

During a subsequent brief Parliamentary debate on UNESCO
— 'one of the noblest conceptions of the post war world', — Ellen
optimistically projected her hopes:

> We are trying to build up out of poverty and misery . . . so that
> UNESCO shall raise the banner of what I believe is the essential
> thing . . . the sense that there are such things as standards, that
> there is a difference between right and wrong, that intellectual
> needs are not luxuries. Unless we can put standards of values into
> the minds of youth we cannot have a great civilisation or a great
> country. It is because the men and women in UNESCO have real-
> ised the values of the human spirit that I believe UNESCO will do
> great things.[57]

This was one of her last speeches in the House.

Colleagues in UNESCO considered Ellen's personal contribution
towards its establishment as 'really important'. Julian Huxley was
'always enthusiastic about her clear mindedness and strength in dealing with people and problems', wrote Lady Huxley, and Archibald

McLeish warmly acknowledged Ellen's enormous help in shaping the seminal London Conference. 'From her vivid self, her humour, her passionate commitment, the fruits have grown,' he wrote.[58]

School Milk and Meals

The provision of free milk and meals to school children, long advocated by the Labour Party, was a reform on which Ellen felt keenly. She understood the correlation between low income and malnutrition (and under-achievement in school) which Sir John Boyd Orr's pre-war report — *Food, Health and Income* (1937) — had underlined, and she was also well aware of the contrast in physique between pupils in Local Authority and Independent schools, which research had confirmed statistically. This imbalance, much as she might have wished, Ellen could not radically rectify, but she could and did instigate the means for its steady improvement.

Since 1906 LEAs had been empowered to provide meals for school children, but only during the Second World War had such provision become an integral part of the Education Service, and this the minister wanted to extend. She authorised the issue of one-third of a pint of milk free to all pupils under eighteen — an innovation welcomed in those days of austerity — and she regarded it rather oddly 'as a culmination of our promise to do away with class distinction'. 'Free milk will be provided in Hoxton and Shoreditch, in Eton and Harrow. What more social equality can you have than that?' Ellen declared at the 1946 Labour Party Conference.

The provision of free school meals, however, was impossible until canteen and central kitchen facilities were adequate and she instructed LEAs accordingly. Nevertheless, dinners were essential to the corporate life of the school, and although accepting that the scheme could not succeed without willing co-operation from the teachers, Ellen unequivocally insisted that it was part of their duty to share in the roster of supervising mid-day meals. A working party, set up to examine attendant difficulties, recommended the employment of auxiliary helpers. This suggestion temporarily allayed anxieties, but Ellen did not foresee the heritage of resentment to which her well-intentioned scheme gave rise. Nevertheless progress exceeded all expectations. By October 1946 well over 90 per cent of all school children were taking up their free milk; and school meals, which in 1944 had benefited half a million pupils, were served to 1.8 million in February 1946, to 2.3 million in October, and the following year topped 2.5 million.[59]

Further and Higher Education

The expansion of further and higher education had been another of Ellen's broad hopes. She pledged herself to introduce County Colleges to provide day release courses for sixteen to eighteen year olds. 'I want', she wrote to Sir Charles Trevelyan, 'to get good permanent buildings for the County Colleges because I think it most important that the young people should have attractive places to come to.'[60] Sadly, for economic reasons, the relevant section of the 1944 Act (as with its parallel in the 1918 Fisher Act) was disregarded for years. On the university front, entrance was highly restrictive. Owing to economic and social barriers, only a minuscule number of students from working-class homes obtained higher education, as Ellen only too well appreciated and was anxious to rectify. At the end of the thirties (and indeed up to the end of the war) about one child in eight — according to the Spens Report of 1938 — went from elementary to secondary school and about one boy in 170 reached university — and the girls had even less chance.[61] The Further Education and Training Grants Scheme of 1943 had done nothing to ease these radical difficulties, but within limits had been generous. The scheme had benefited men and women invalided out of the services, and after the war had assisted ex-service personnel whose further education had been interrupted. It also encouraged admission to universities on a less rigorous basis — but again only for ex-service personnel. The scheme did not broaden opportunity for pupils still at secondary school.

Ellen could not eliminate social barriers but she did make sure that no suitably qualified student lost a university place on financial grounds. At the time the universities' own awards and state scholarships (the latter made by the Ministry) were highly competitive and many LEAs only grudgingly exercised their powers to grant 'major awards' for higher education. The minister improved this by regulations which laid down that state scholarships were to be more generously administered, and also tried to persuade LEAs to grant major awards more liberally. She could not direct, but she strongly encouraged awards being made to students who had not won scholarships, but who were good intellectually and seemed likely to complete a course at university or elsewhere with credit. 'A wide field will thus be open to LEAs within their approved schemes of Major Awards and the Minister is confident that they will be ready to pursue a generous policy.'[62] She thus paved the way for the subsequent radical reform of mandatory awards, whereby no student who gained a university place would be prevented on financial grounds from taking it up. She brooded too on the need for more university places. Universities she knew were overcrowded, 'though not all to the same extent. Should Oxford and Cambridge be extended?' she asked, thinking aloud on a minute sheet. 'My view is yes . . . Should there be a new university? My view is York . . . and what other extensions to Redbrick? There is room in the south-west.'[63] Had she lived she would clearly have supported the subsequent university expansion.

The relationship between universities and teacher training colleges or Colleges of Education examined in the McNair Report on Teacher Training, 1944, also had to be tackled. McNair had recommended that, in order to break down the isolation of training colleges, 'centres' on an area basis should be established, to bring universities, training colleges and LEAs close together. Ultimately Area Training Organisations (ATOs) were devised, based on Institutes of Education. It was the Minister's responsibility to bring these ATOs into existence — which she did in June 1946 — after agreeing that 'some diversity of organisation should be permitted', but only after months of vascillating. In all fairness, negotiations, particularly with London University, had been difficult.[64]

Occasionally Ellen would express wholly unorthodox opinions. For example, she observed that the personnel of the University Grants Committee was 'too safe and inbred', and urged Vice-Chancellors to 'throw their net wider'. The fact that the suggested nomination to the UGC of Professor P.M. Blackett — 'who is vigorous, wide-minded, and in short a personality' — was opposed by the Treasury annoyed her greatly.[65] Her most injudicious intervention was perhaps seeking the resignation of Lord Soulbury, Chairman of the Burnham Committee on teacher's salaries, so that she could appoint someone more politically congenial.[66] This incensed both teachers and LEAs and to Sir Frederick Mander, then General Secretary of the NUT, 'It was entirely wrong for the Minister to put her small but clumsy feet into the affairs of the Burnham Committee'. Ellen told Lord Soulbury that her actions had been dictated from a 'higher level' and that she hoped he, as a politician, would understand the desire of her party to have all the political plums.[67]

The Burnham ranks closed against the minister and after her death George Tomlinson retained Lord Soulbury in office until 1949.

Secondary Education for All

There is a tendency to disparage Ellen's term as minister because she did not actively promote multilateral or comprehensive education. She was said to have been too sympathetic to grammar schools and to the old tripartite system of separate grammar, modern and technical schools because this path had led her to personal success.[68] This seems to underestimate her 'sincere desire to do at all times what she genuinely considered to be in the best interests of the underprivileged',[69] the economic tribulations of the time and the fact, on her own admission, that she was not opposed to comprehensive education, but intended to avoid dogmatism. 'I wanted to make it clear', she told the House, 'that there is no antagonism in my mind to the idea of multilateral or bilateral schools . . . but I do want to see the proposals are properly worked out and that the schools do not become unreasonably large.'[70]

Ellen was totally committed to establishing secondary education for all. She wanted to enable pupils to follow courses suited to their aptitudes and abilities; but by what means she was unsure. The new secondary-modern schools which would help to make this possible 'were to be modern in aim as well as name and in no sense dumping grounds'.[71] Yet how did this fit in with the call by Labour educationists for the Common School?[72] It is not surprising there were inconsistencies in her thinking. She was no elitist in that she wanted equal opportunity for all children, yet she respected the grammar school seeing it as the main source of university entrants and constantly opposing any intention to destroy it.[73] Direct Grant grammar schools should fit into any new structure. She wanted variety and flexibility between grammar and technical schools, yet thought it was the 'multilateral or bilateral' schools which made it easier for children to switch courses.[74] Above all she wanted to avoid wasting talent — but how best to do it when over one million children were still being educated in unreorganised elementary schools?

In all fairness, there was no groundswell of enthusiasm for multilateralism within the Labour Party as a whole. NALT had certainly published a thoughtful and constructive pamphlet *Education — A Policy* (1929), revised in 1938, explaining its implications, and the party's Education Advisory Committee expressed support for multi-lateral schools as early as 1939,[75] but the concept was neither clearly understood nor widely discussed. Party Conferences had passed resolutions in favour of the 'common school principle', but in the 1945 election manifesto — *Let us Face the Future* — reference to education was pitifully thin and the common school issue was ignored. As Lord Goronwy Roberts remembered, 'to most new MPs eager to build socialism it seemed important to create secondary education for all rather than to reform machinery. The idea of multi-lateral schools was remote and esoteric and familiar only to a few educational experts'.[76] Ellen in effect had no mandate other than to 'implement the Act by forging ahead immediately with ROSLA and the expansion of school meals'.[77]

In no obvious way was Ellen prompted by her officials to examine the multilateral idea. On the contrary, there was a traditional bias within the ministry towards the tripartite system, which had been crystallised in the much discussed pamphlet *The Nation's Schools* published by the department during R.A. Butler's regime, but for which her critics held her responsible. It is easy to be wise with hind-sight, but there was justification for the department's 'thinking cautiously.' The academic validity of comprehensive schools was under question, and within the ministry the idea that all secondary school children could study a common core of subjects from eleven to thir-teen was viewed sceptically. No one had then *proved* the comprehen-sive principle in England. As Lord Redcliffe-Maud said, 'At the time the grammar school was still regarded as the "way-in" for the bright boys.'[78] Moreover, as Sir Edward Britton (former President and General Secretary of the NUT) said, 'a policy of comprehensive schools was just not practical then; there were neither sufficient buildings, nor staff'.[79] So it was that Ellen did not exhort LEAs to think along comprehensive lines, and even those authorities who regarded this pattern as crucial to the development of secondary education in their areas (under the Act all LEAs had to submit development plans to the Minister) proceeded cautiously. The pre-eminently progressive authority, the LCC, whose ideas for com-prehensive education in London were worked out in principle by officers and Members during the war in basement shelters,[80] did not present their plan until March 1947. It was not finally approved by the department until 1950.

Ellen was bitterly attacked in the House for her lack of incisive action and tacit acceptance of the tripartite system. Yet even W.G.

Cove MP, her most vituperative critic, was confused over the role of grammar schools in a multilateral system. He supported the latter while deploring any restriction upon grammar school places[81] and even as late as November 1947 wrote in *Modern Education* — the official organ of NALT — 'Let it be clearly stated that those of us who accept the principle of multilateralism will not tolerate any lowering of the status and dignity of secondary grammar schools.'[82] He and Ellen in many ways exemplified the confusion over educational policy that existed within the Labour Party. For they were attracted to the equality of opportunity associated with unhindered access to the grammar school, yet recognised the inequality implicit in the existing system. In physical conditions, poor staffing ratios, salary scales, allocation of books and equipment and overcrowding, most of the 'secondary' schools were glaringly inferior to the grammar schools. Raising their standards was a necessary first step in improving secondary education even if later they might become part of a multilateral system. The parity of esteem which the Labour Movement demanded and Ellen sought to effect was at that time largely an empty dream.[83]

The ministry faced immense pressures. A baby boom accelerated demand for primary places and blitzed school buildings clamoured for reconstruction. In the LCC area alone by the end of the war over two-hundred 'educational institutions' and schools were unusable and additionally well over a thousand were damaged. There were also one million damaged houses in London alone, and not surprisingly, in the face of intense shortages of raw materials and manpower, labour was first directed to 'home revival'.[84] Ellen saw the problem in perspective. Generous minded as ever — and politically astute — she wrote to Sir Charles Trevelyan:

The question of building permanent schools must wait until the housing situation has eased . . . It has taken all the weight I could bring to bear upon the Cabinet to get the extra provision for [HORSA] classrooms, but I should not myself find it within my conscience to take away labour from housing when we could manage with prefabricated huts.[85]

With so many issues clamouring for attention and with ROSLA taking precedence, it is not surprising that Ellen appeared to evade the issue of multilateralism and to accept the tripartite philosophy which permeated her department. For this she was severely attacked at the party conference in 1946 and in the House by W.G. Cove for not disclaiming *The Nation's Schools* and the implicit tripartitism it upheld. Backed by the NEC, but opposed by conference grassroots, Ellen's stand was condemned even though, as Harold Clay told conference, the offending pamphlet was out of print — and Ellen assured delegates that she had forbidden reprinting in its present form.

In the event the pamphlet was succeeded by the *New Secondary Education*. This described 'work in progress' and plans for the future as an answer to the pessimists who feared that the 1944 Act might, like the Fisher Act, become the first casualty of peace when the cry for economy was raised. It was published after Ellen's death, but she had contributed a foreword which, vigorous and full of hope, is important for 'reflecting something of her real self'.[86] She welcomed plans 'designed to suit different *children* not different income groups' and the fact that they 'aimed at educating the child by the awakening of interest', a technique she herself had so effectively adopted in her pupil teaching days.

'No child', Ellen wrote, 'must be forced into an academic education which bores it to rebellion, merely because that type of grammar education is considered more socially desirable by parents who can afford to pay for it.' There must be parity of esteem between the different types of school — but this would remain merely a phrase unless there was:

> some parity of social esteem for the avocations to which the children go from the schools. The British people are learning the hard way how dependent is a civilised community on its farmers, transporters and miners, its manual and technical workers . . . I am emphasising this because it is the answer to those who think that secondary education for all must mean a grammar school education for all and that the secondary modern and secondary technical schools are merely devices for keeping intact a class system of education . . . Until education in the State secondary schools is as good as the best that money can buy outside the State system, so long will inequalities remain.

The concluding paragraph warmly expressed Ellen's life-long affection for children and might well be regarded as her educational testament:

Everything to do with children must have room to grow . . . Schools must have freedom to experiment, and variety for the sake of freshness . . . Laughter in the classroom, self confidence growing every day, eager interest instead of bored uniformity, this is the way to produce the Britons who will have no need to fear the new scientific age, but will stride into it, heads high, determined to master science and to serve mankind.[87]

Had her critics bothered to know Ellen better, or at least tried to probe her intentions, their outbursts in the House might have been less raucous. During 1946 Cove's unprecedentedly spiteful personal attacks must have been deeply hurtful to one so caring. To accuse Ellen of believing 'neither in the capacity of the ordinary child nor in an egalitarian system of education', was completely to distort her fundamental beliefs. Cove's moving a reduction in the minister's salary — tantamount to a vote of censure — was repudiated by Ralph Morley, who stressed 'the excellent impression' Ellen had created at the recent NUT conference, and concluded 'the Minister who has a very difficult task . . . is giving great attention to detail . . . doing her work with enthusiasm . . . and [shows] a real love of children'.[88] Leah Manning, like Ralph Morley an NUT sponsored member, also resented Cove's attack which 'can only have been caused by jealousy,' she wrote, adding, 'His unwarranted attacks on Ellen could only have been motivated by her success as a woman.'[89]

The core of criticism directed against Ellen has been that she impeded rather than promoted the comprehensive principle, particularly because her official circular of December 1945 suggested that about 70 to 75 per cent of secondary education places should be of the modern type, the remainder being earmarked for grammar and technical provision. Yet in her defence the circular did add that, while for immediate purposes LEAs would have to think in terms of three types of secondary schools, *in time*, 'the conception of secondary schools might well, through the development of modern schools, gradually replace the classification of schools into grammar, technical and modern.' The creation of multilateral and bilateral schools had to depend 'on local circumstances' and large schools were not at that time viewed favourably, but some LEAs '*might* want to combine two or more types of secondary education into one school'.[90] Undeniably the circular was imprecise — the new 'bilateral or multilateral' school must 'not be such as to prejudice the position of other maintained secondary schemes in the area' — but options were kept open. Ellen subsequently seemed to favour bilateral schemes for she appreciated the country's need for technicians and saw new schools with a technical stream 'as doing for industry what the grammar schools had done for the professions'.[91] Clearly her ideas were moving towards sympathy with multilateralism.

Mr Squeers Across the Years

Evidence of that sympathy is discernible in the blistering comments she wrote after reading a departmental draft on secondary-modern schools from which the *New Secondary Education* pamphlet eventually emerged. They suggest not only that Ellen's awareness of the needs of working-class children was as sharp as ever, but also that she was churning over in her mind some of the tangled questions about secondary schooling to which the multilateral idea might offer answers:

> I wondered why I felt deep down angry having read the draft. Then I realised that Mr Squeers had given me a quizzical look across the years . . . this pamphlet is fundamentally phoney because it subconsciously disguises the real question that has to be answered, namely, 'What shall we do to get miners and agricultural workers if a hundred per cent of the children able to profit from it are offered real secondary education. Answer [of the draft] . . . give the real stuff to a selected 25 per cent, steer the 75% away from humanities, pure science, even history.'

She strongly objected to this and also to suggestions for fostering qualities in young people which employers wanted to find, to be achieved by the pupils being freed from external examinations and acquiring practical experience (in ways she regarded as 'glorified Squeers'). The idea of boys, 'building pig stys, or making beehives and wheelbarrows and of girls doing laundry work or catering' infuriated her. 'For the rest of their lives 95 per cent of the girls who marry will have to do all those things. Can't their precious three years of secondary education be at least a relief from all *that*?' she demanded, 'Can't Shakespeare mean more than a scrubbing brush — can't enough of a foreign language be taught to open windows on the world a bit wider — I learnt French verbs saying them as I scrubbed floors at home.' Proposals for the development of bodily skills she found acceptable but she deplored the condescension implicit in the suggestions that merely 'something of the sciences, maths and the arts might be taught'. The final indignity lay in 'history being banished as too difficult . . . or was it possibly too dangerous if an intelligent child asked awkward questions? (Don't worry how we got India, let's go and do some nice work at the forge!)'.

In further minutes she was more positive ('Mr Bevin advised me never to criticise without being constructive'):

> If we are committed to three types of schools one grand thing about the scheme is that it won't work — at least not peacefully: it would hit the middle classes who would scream . . . Pupils of grammar or technical abilities (with high IQs) should be separated on a functional basis, not by going to physically different/ separate schools . . . let the lower IQs find their level in separate classes; arouse [their] interest by a practical side to their tuition; but don't let the stigma of lower IQs attach itself to the whole school.

She added (with a typical Ellen flourish), 'The higher IQs will become intolerable little wretches if stamped from eleven as being superior!' As to modern schools:

> Lateral transfers must be made possible, but these schools must not be the only one of the three types not taking external examinations . . . The practical side must not be overstressed in the curricula . . . Some LEAs only need a nod to do all the overstressing themselves . . . certain cultural subjects should be included . . . art and music . . . and I would like to add French. These have always been high school subjects . . . their inclusion would encourage parents to accept the 'good all-round standards' of the modern school, and the advantage of leaving their children there until 16.[92]

These spontaneous remarks in which fires of the old Ellen of the Jarrow Crusade still flickered have been quoted at length because they are the only critical thoughts on secondary education she wrote down while minister which are extant.

Direct-grant Schools

A politically delicate issue which Ellen inherited was the future of the direct-grant schools whose status was under review. These 242 secondary schools, some denominational, were the remnant of those which in 1926 had opted to receive their grant from the then Board of Education instead of from the LEAs. They were spread unevenly over the country, were effectively part of the local grammar provisions and in some cases the sole provider. LEAs therefore relied heavily upon them to supplement the general deficiency in grammar schooling. The direct-grant schools valued their freedom from LEA control, though the LEAs for their part resented this, and to many Labour critics they were socially exclusive bastions of privilege.

Negotiations over payment, and the availability of places to LEAs had been in train long before Ellen took office. R.A. Butler had rejected the abolition of fees recommended by the Fleming Committee in 1943, but proposed that an increased number of places should be taken up by LEAs. The governors of the direct-grant schools, as the Bishop of London told him, feared however that this would threaten their independence.[93] A *modus vivendi* was ultimately reached, and Ellen introduced revised regulations: governors were to make available up to 50 per cent of their places for the LEAs if they so required.

She also reduced the number of approved direct-grant schools to 155, though not before 'the protracted discussions had caused as much fuss as if the entire system was to be abolished',[94] and raised the income level below which children could be admitted to them free. These revisions she genuinely considered were an attack on social privilege and claimed that since 'in many cases the direct-grant schools provide the only available grammar school education in an area, it seems wrong to place the opportunity for such free education beyond the reach of [a substantial number of] qualified pupils'.[95] In fact because grammar schools were in such short supply and held in such high esteem, this 'revision' accentuated the competition for free selective places and left a tangled legacy. Their right to cream off bright children (Manchester Grammar School for example could comb through the whole north-western conurbation) severely hampered future comprehensive schools from recruiting an intake of balanced ability.[96] The Fabian Society warned the minister in a memorandum against the danger of allowing certain schools 'receiving money from public funds to stand outside the maintained sector', as this would 'make the planning of secondary education by LEAs much more difficult'. Ellen took no action, but she shared the Fabians' unease and certainly hoped for the eventual abolition of fees in all direct grant schools.[97]

Reconstruction Before Reform

Ellen's singleminded determination to introduce ROSLA with minimal delay saved the Education Act which in itself is a monument to her memory.[98] Yet more than that, she secured resources for her Department to carry through the ETS (essential to ROSLA), limited the direct grant system, widened opportunity for university entrance, expanded the provision of milk and meals for school children and, as a long-standing international socialist, helped to create UNESCO. To dismiss these achievements as negligible after less than eighteen months in office, is to underrate the difficulties Ellen faced in the aftermath of war, the economic blizzard which swept the country and her own crippling ill-health. The slowness of the ministry's administrative machine also hampered progress,[99] even though 'most of the civil servants were keen, able and eager to make the Act work'. The job was formidable enough to have daunted a tougher, more experienced minister, yet 'Ellen's drive and imagination was such that had she been at her physical best she would undeniably have made education one of the leading departments in the post war social revolution.'[100]

The suggestion that Ellen was a failure as a minister because she made no frontal attack on the tripartite system and did not push the comprehensive principle is unfair.[101] Even if her attitude was muddled, she never positively opposed the idea, and reiterated her belief that 'experiments are justified and desirable in working out a new conception of secondary education for all'.[102] In all fairness Ellen saw her job as one of reconstruction before reform. As the Chief Education Officer for Essex commented 'Our Minister knew that while many people talked about "secondary education for all" the phrase was meaningless while so many young people left school at fourteen.'[103] It was nevertheless true that while Ellen was firm on socialist basics and would fight for them to the death — which she literally did — she was unclear on long-term education policy and so relied perhaps too heavily on departmental advice.[104]

Many people felt that the job was too big for her; certainly pressure was such that she had to take first things first. Yet she held to her priorities and worked like a daemon, even during the last few weeks of her life when she was too ill to be at the ministry.[105] Perhaps her obstinate resolve to carry on regardless emanated from a sense of failure, of being under fire for not being on top of her job.[106] Yet apart from the constant handicap of nagging illness, Ellen had little opportunity to stand back and *think* in the face of insistent departmental demands for swift decisions and swifter action. Not for her was there to be that 'generation in office' which she had envisaged as essential for implementing the 1944 Act.

Richard Crossman once mourned the fact that certain 'former firebrands', including Ellen, Bevan and Cripps, had abandoned the theory of revolution to achieve social change in favour of reformism,[107] implying that Ellen's political fires had waned. Yet this was not so, and a more perceptive assessment was made by Lord Redcliffe-Maud: 'All her political life', he said, 'she had been on the other side of the barricades, protesting to, and arguing with, the Government of the day. As Minister she was building up and learning the importance of collective responsibility. Always her attitude was "Build, don't break down" '.[108]

Always too, her care was for working-class children: Ellen never forgot their needs or her own grass-roots origins, even if she did recognise merit in the tripartite structure she had climbed on her road to success.[109] After her death, the *Times Educational Supplement* wrote:

Had she lived longer, there is little doubt that the children of England and Wales would have had reason to bless her name. She would have made mistakes; she would have provoked bitter antagonism; but she would have seen to it that in fact, as well as promise, no child would be denied the opportunity that was his due.[110]

No Minister of Education could have desired a warmer epitaph.

Notes

1. J.L. Hodson, *News Chronicle*, 13 December 1935.

2. H.D. (Billy) Hughes (MP, Wolverhampton West, 1945–50; Principal, Ruskin College Oxford, 1950–80), interview.

3. *Times Educational Supplement*, 11 August 1945.

4. *Times Educational Supplement*, 8 February 1947.

5. John Parker, interview.

6. Kenneth Harris, interview.

7. According to Sir Ronald Gould, past President, National Union of Teachers, and former General Secretary, Chuter Ede was 'much disappointed'. He was, however, philosophic and remarked to Gould: 'You must play where the Captain directs.' Sir Ronald Gould, letter of 11 January 1979.

8. C.R. Attlee, *As It Happened* (Heinemann, London, 1954), p. 153.

9. *Times Educational Supplement*, 18 August 1945.

10. Vera Brittain, letter of 4 August 1945 (McMaster University Library, Canada).

11. *Daily Herald*, 19 November 1928.

12. Kenneth Lindsay, Dame Margaret Cole, interviews.

13. (Sir) Harold Shearman, Education Officer, WEA 1935–45, Academic Adviser University of London Tutorial Classes, Chairman LCC Education, Member Robbins Committee on Higher Education, and much else. He was a life-long socialist, devoted to education.

14. The predecessor of the Socialist Education Association.

15. Transport and General Workers' Union official; long-standing member NEC and sometime Chairman of the Labour Party.

16. Labour Party Conference Annual Report, 1942.

17. Harold Shearman, *The New Education Act* (Workers' Educational Association, 1944).

18. *Education — a Policy (1929, revised 1935)*, National Association of Labour Teachers, London.

19. Professor Harold Dent, Lord Redcliffe-Maud, and others, interviews.

20. Several months after she had been working with Lord Redcliffe-Maud (then Sir John Maud), her Permanent Secretary, the minister asked him to what school he went. 'I replied, "Eton, but as a charity boy, my father couldn't afford the fees." But that didn't deter her at all — she was wholly unprejudiced about it!' Lord Redcliffe-Maud, interview.

21. Lord Redcliffe-Maud, interview.

22. Sir Antony Part, interview.

23. 'At the official level the 1944 Act was the work of a team of which Maurice Holmes was the incomparable leader. But they would have got nowhere without R.A. Butler to see them through the religious, political and Parliamentary morasses', Neville Heaton, interview; Sir Antony Part, interview.

24. Lord Redcliffe-Maud, Sir Antony Part, H.D. Hughes, interviews.

25. Lord Redcliffe-Maud, interview.

26. M. Foot, *Aneurin Bevan* (MacGibbon and Kee, London, 1962), pp. 49–52.

27. Letter, 1 October 1945, (Trevelyan papers, University of Newcastle), CPT 161.

28. *Times Educational Supplement*, 6 October 1945; Ministry of Education Circular 64, 27 September 1945.

29. PRO Cabinet Conclusions, CM 25(45) 23 August, 1945.

30. PRO CP/45 (140), 1 September 1945.

31. PRO C/CON 28 (45), 4 September 1945.

32. 'Who first suggested the ETS is doubtful. I always believed S.H. Wood, Head of the Teacher Training Branch was the originator. I heard SH claim this . . . Gilbert Flemming was chairman of the Departmental Committee which worked out the structure of the Scheme, but I never thought of him as administering it. R.S. (later Sir Robert) Wood the Deputy Secretary did a lot in the early stages and David Hardman (Parliamentary Secretary) travelled all over the country seeking suitable sites.' (Professor Harold Dent, letter of 6 May 1979); 'Gilbert Flemming who was brought

back from the Cabinet Office was responsible for making the necessary preparations for the ETS and for supervising its administration when put into operation. S.H. Wood concentrated on the ordinary training colleges and Departments of Education' (Neville Heaton, letter of 18 August 1980).

33. Sir Gilbert Flemming, letter.

34. H.D. Hughes, interview.

35. *Education in 1947* (HMSO 7426) pp. 42–3.

36. *Times Educational Supplement*, 25 May 1946.

37. H.M. Burton, *Times Educational Supplement*, 22 June 1946.

38. *Education in 1947*, p. 43.

39. *Ministry of Education Circular 64*, 27 September 1945; *Times Educational Supplement*, 6 October 1945.

40. *Ministry of Education Circular 134*, 19 December 1946.

41. *Education in 1947*, p. 51.

42. PRO.ED 136/727 (spanning 5 December 1946 to 16 January 1947).

43. H.D. Hughes, interview.

44. Fred Blackburn, *George Tomlinson* (Heinemann, London, 1954), p. 168.

45. Lord Redcliffe-Maud, interview.

46. *Times Educational Supplement*, 13 October 1945.

47. Sir Antony Part, interview.

48. An amusing piece of sophisticated gossip tells of Ellen giving a short talk to educationalists on 'Independent Thinking'. After this she was approached by an enthusiastic woman teacher who with her colleagues had been so impressed that she asked for a 'few guide-lines for such an approach'! This subsequently hit the headlines of a German satirical 'cabaret chat' as 'we cannot even feel secure in our own guilt complexes' (Heinrich Fraenkel, interview).

49. A. Hearndon (Ed), *The British in Germany* (Hamish Hamilton, London, 1978), pp. 98–9.

50. For details of the aims and structure of UNESCO see Kenneth Lindsay, UNESCO, in *United Nations Association Year Book, 1948* (Hutchinson, London 1948), pp. 276–82.

51. Archibald McLeish, letter; Blackburn, p. 134.

52. *Times Educational Supplement*, 3 November 1945; PRO-ED/136/616. It is interesting that the original concept of UNECO had excluded matters scientific. Under pressure, however, from Julian Huxley, Joseph Needham, Ritchie Calder and others, the composition was revised — with Ellen's approval. Scientists, she accepted 'could no longer remain dissociated from the social complications of their discoveries' (*Times Educational Supplement*, 17 November 1945).

53. Julian Huxley, *Memoirs* (George Allen and Unwin, London, 1973), vol. 2, p. 14.

54. Philip Noel-Baker, interview.

55. Hansard, Vol. 428, cols. 1220–3, 5 November 1946.

56. 'Almost the last talk we had, had been about UNESCO. She was bitterly disappointed that ill-health prevented her from going to Paris' (Lord Butler, *The Times*, 7 February 1947).

57. Hansard, Vol. 430, cols. 1229–30, 22 November 1946.

58. Bobby Carter, Lady Huxley, Archibold McLeish, letters.

59. *Education in 1947*, p. 56, paras. 13–14.

60. Letter to Sir Charles Trevelyan, 1 October 1945, Trevelyan Papers, CPT/161.

61. David Rubenstein, 'Ellen Wilkinson Reconsidered' in *History Workshop* (Spring 1979) p. 161; B. Drake, *Education for Democracy* (British Association for Labour Legislation, 1941), pamphlet.

62. *Ministry of Education Circular No. 104*, 16 May 1946.

63. PRO-2197/2, 5 September 1946.

64. PRO-C/112, June 1946; Professor H.C. Dent, Neville Heaton, interviews.

65. PRO-2197/2, 5 September 1946.
66. Ronald Gould, *Chalk Up the Memory* (G.P. Alexander, London, 1976), p. 49.
67. Sir Frederick Mander to Sir William Brockington, letter of 27 November 1946 (Burnham Archives, Box 19). (Mander was General Secretary of the National Union of Teachers — 1931–47 — and leader of the teachers' panel on Burnham. Brockington was leader of the Local Authorities' Panel. They were joint secretaries of the Burnham Main Committee.)
68. B. Simon, *The Politics of Educational Reform, 1920–1940* (Lawrence and Wishart, London, 1974), p. 284; David Rubenstein, pp. 161–7.
69. N. Heaton, interview.
70. H.D. Hughes, interview, and Hansard, Vol. 424, cols. 1811–2, 1 July 1946.
71. *The Times*, 27 January 1946; Labour Party Conference Annual Report 1946.
72. The early phrase, 'the Common School', was coupled with, then superseded by, the term 'multilateral' until the mid-forties, and linked with 'bilateral' in ministry circulars. It is difficult to establish precisely when the term 'comprehensive' became used exclusively. NALT was highly suspicious of the changed nomenclature, believing that 'the official element adopted a device which might have been calculated to spread confusion in the ranks of opponents [by] the device of changing the labels of the babies in their cradles . . . the term multilateral was retained to describe a school with three entirely separate streams — a tripartite system on one site.' More than one local authority, as NALT saw it, 'had walked into the trap of planning the ministerial tripartite multilateral school in the belief it was implementing Labour's policy!'. *The Comprehensive School*, (NALT, London, 1948), p. 11.
73. Fabian Society lecture, 26 October 1945; *Times Educational Supplement*, 9 March 1946.
74. *Times Educational Supplement*, 1 July 1946.
75. Barker, *Education and Politics 1900–51* (Oxford University Press, Oxford, 1972), p. 73.
76. Lord Goronwy Roberts, interview.
77. H.D. Hughes 'In Defence of Ellen Wilkinson' in *History Workshop* Spring 1979, pp. 157–9; H.D. Hughes and Dame Margaret Cole, interviews.
78. Lord Redcliffe-Maud, interview.
79. Sir Edward Britton, letters and interview.
80. M. Cole, *Servant of the Country* (Dobson, London, 1956), pp. 187–94.
81. Hansard, Vol. 424, cols. 1831–2, 1 July 1946.
82. W.G. Cove, in *Modern Education*, November 1947, p. 213.
83. It is true that there were some good modern schools notably in Cambridgeshire and Leicestershire among others in existence and that when the 1944 Act came into operation, new regulations laid down common standards for premises and class sizes. But the fact remains that improvement was slow; reorganisation of all-age elementary schools had not been completed by the end of the decade, and many thoroughly bad schools were still retained; in January 1947 over one million children — one-fifth of the total school population — were still being educated in all-age schools. (*Education in 1947*, p. 99, Table 2.)
84. Hansard, Vol. 424, cols. 1849–50, 1 July 1946; P.H. Gosden, *Education in the Second World War* (Methuen, London, 1976), pp. 63–4; PRO.Ed. 10–308.
85. Trevelyan Papers, CPT.161, 1 October 1945.
86. Neville Heaton, interview.
87. *The New Secondary Education — Forword* (HMSO, London), Pamphlet No. 9, 1947.
88. Hansard, Vol. 424, cols. 1831–7, 1 July 1946.
89. L. Manning, *A Life for Education* (Gollancz, London, 1970), pp. 203–4.
90. *Ministry of Education Circular 73*, 12 December 1945.
91. *Manchester Guardian*, 13 March 1946.

92. PRO-ED/136/788; this undated outburst, from internal evidence, was probably made in early March 1946. It was provoked directly by a draft submitted by Sir Martin Roseveare, the ministry's Senior Chief Inspector. Ellen's Minutes were prefaced by an ambiguous, unsigned, undated note: 'This may be regarded as the toned-down headings of the speech Ellen Wilkinson MP would make from a back bench to the present Minister of Education on the issue of this pamphlet with a gracious foreword from her.'

93. Gosden, p. 357.

94. H.D. Hughes 'In Defence of Ellen Wilkinson', *History Workshop*, no. 7 (Spring 1979), p. 158.

95. *Hansard*, Vol. 415, cols. 1709–9 November 1945.

96. Factual material in this section was supplied by Neville Heaton: the conclusions are the author's own.

97. PRO.ED. 136/209, undated.

98. Dame Margaret Cole, Dame Evelyn Denington, Lord Alexander of Potterhill, interviews.

99. *Times Educational Supplement*, 12 October 1946.

100. H.D. Hughes, interview.

101. D. Rubinstein 'Ellen Wilkinson Reconsidered', *History Workshop*, no. 7 (Spring 1979), p. 167.

102. Ministry of Education, Circular 73, 12 December 1945, and Circular 90, 8 March 1946.

103. Dr Bernard Lawrence, Chief Education Officer, Essex from 1939 to 1965.

104. Lord Alexander, Dame Evelyn Denington, Sir Edward Britton, interviews.

105. Neville Heaton, interview.

106. Edward MacLellan, Dame Evelyn Denington, Lord Alexander, Sir Edward Britton, interviews.

107. *New Statesman*, 15 June 1946.

108. Lord Redcliffe-Maud, interview.

109. B. Simon, *The Politics of Educational Reform 1920–1940* (Lawrence and Wishart, London, 1974), p. 284.

110. *Times Educational Supplement*, 8 February 1947.

11 ADIEU

Accidents and Ill-health

Accidents and ill-health hampered Ellen's career and progressively drained her vitality. She would bounce bravely back, enthusiastic for work, but there is no doubt that as crippling illnesses affected her concentration of thought her effectiveness as a minister declined, and 'the burdens of office weighed heavily on her frail shoulders'.[1]

During the blitz her ministerial obligations to see and be seen, hard work and overall strain set up nervous tensions which accelerated her asthma. Moreover, Ellen had long been accident prone. Various falls and car mishaps had not in the past been serious, but soon after John Jagger's death she sustained a slight fracture of the skull in a car crash,[2] and from then on her mishaps became more frequent and incapacitating.

Not least disruptive to her work, was the ill fated accident in January 1943 in which she was involved, together with General Frederick 'Boy' Browning (hero of Arnhem) and a clutch of MPs who had been invited to see the effectiveness of gliders in action. As Vernon Bartlett, wrote:

> When we got to Salisbury Plain although there was too much wind, Boy Browning took us up in two large gliders. Both crashed. I was not in the same glider as Ellen which suffered more than ours. She had a broken ankle and I remember one of the Tory MPs remarking on her courage and cheerfulness. When it became obvious that we too were about to crash one MP looking out of the window said . . . 'there are going to be a hell of a lot of bye elections!'[3]

The broken ankle Ellen dismissed nonchalantly, but there were protracted repercussions in a series of operations and enforced absences from the House. Even more seriously the accident triggered off the bronchial asthma which now beset her with increasing frequency. During 1944 these attacks intensified and in December severe pneumonia prevented her from chairing the Labour Party

Conference or from returning to work before late January 1945.[4] By that time Ellen's health, affected by the tempo at which she drove herself on endless party commitments, was causing concern, as she looked 'really worn'.

Like many colleagues who 'had been working flat out during the war and were exhausted when they did get into Government', the minister's failing health from the beginning was all too apparent to her department. Lord Redcliffe-Maud observed: 'In my experience she seemed always ill, though not at any stage ever at the end of her tether, or weary of life. She was just thoroughly fed up with that nagging bronchitis and asthma.'[5] Close friends were becoming deeply worried. Muriel Nichol recalls attending a party at India House with Ellen late in 1945: 'We went together in a taxi: Ellen was breathing so badly she could hardly get up the great stairway — and during the party was so ill we had to return home.'[6] Margaret Bondfield too remembered how 'tired and spent she was, particularly when off guard . . . I gave her a motherly warning about her need for rest of mind and nerves. This as usual she cheerfully disregarded.'[7]

During the minister's official visit to Prague for the Anglo-Czech Film Festival in the autumn of 1946, Ellen's failing health became alarming. As this was the first time since the end of the war that any cabinet minister had officially visited eastern Europe, it was an undertaking which she had most eagerly anticipated.[8] She had been unwell even before they started, and became gravely ill in Prague. Sir Antony Part remembers her determination to open the Festival and how she was given an injection to enable her to make her inaugural speech.

Ellen, wearing an apple-green dress, was just fit enough . . . to be carried to the prompter's corner; and was ill in full view of the Prague Symphony Orchestra. She was able to get to the centre of the stage to speak briefly, but after walking back she collapsed. The Czechs, afraid that the Minister might die, offered to fly her home, but she was too ill to go immediately. Ellen plaintively remarked, 'I don't lack courage, but I simply cannot do it'.[9]

Her tenacity won grateful acknowledgement from the Czechs and on balance the festival was a great success. The Czech press appreciated Ellen's presence, 'in spite of her marked indisposition', and Paul Rotha, the distinguished documentary film producer, remembers how 'several of us — Anthony Asquith, Richard Winnington, Ralph Bond, Muir Matheson, talked with her about the possibility of a return visit to London of the Czech film makers. She agreed to sound out the Treasury and the Foreign Office, although she never thought she would get any help; but she did. An example of her fighting spirit. Ellen died before the return Festival took place, but the event would not have been possible without her effective pressure on official sources when she was so desperately ill.[10] It was not surprising that later that autumn a parliamentary journalist observed, 'At the height of her career Ellen Wilkinson seems to be an ailing woman. If she should leave the Government in the near future her illness will be no diplomatic excuse.'[11]

Although January 1947 heralded the bitterest of winters, the weather did not deter Ellen from fulfilling her last known public engagement — that of opening the Old Vic Theatre School on 25 January. A photograph of the occasion shows her looking drawn and tired; yet obstinate as ever, rather than escape from sitting in the icy building, blitzed into heatlessness and open to the sky, she elected to stay and caught penumonia. A member of the Old Vic staff has said they had long thought that this opening ceremony had been directly responsible for Ellen's death. A view shared also by the Wilkinson family.[12]

Early in February Ellen was taken from her flat at Hood House in Dolphin Square to St Mary's Hospital, Paddington, and on 6 February at the age of 55 she died from 'heart failure following bronchitis'. Her funeral, small and simple, was at the parish church in her much loved Penn. The plain headstone to her grave, made at the Eric Gill Workshops at Naphill, was simply inscribed:

Ellen Wilkinson 1891–1947

Inexplicably, Herbert Morrison, admittedly in hospital himself, sent no flowers.[13] To the end he remained — selfishly — discreet.

Parliament and the nation paid their tribute to Ellen. First from the floor of the House she loved, where Winston Churchill, among many, testified to the 'earnest zeal and sympathy with which she did her work in the administration of which I was head', and later at a memorial service in St Margaret's Westminster which, as she would have wished, was attended by the humble as well as the high. The Prime Minister read the Lesson: 'because the preacher was wise he still taught the people knowledge. He sought to find out acceptable words and that which was written was upright even in the words of truth' — an apt choice. 'Red Nellie' Wilkinson had travelled far from that small humble home in Coral Street.[14]

Ungenerous Gossip

This was not however the finale to Ellen's eager, restless, purposive life. An inquest was held and her death gave rise to ungenerous gossip about suicide. The Coroner, Dr H. Neville Stafford, quelled speculation by recording the verdict that she had accidentally taken an overdose of the drugs which had been prescribed for her attacks of asthma and bronchitis and had died from heart failure following emphysema, with acute bronchitis and bronchial pneumonia, accelerated by barbituric poisoning. 'I want to make it perfectly clear', the Coroner said, 'that there is no shred of evidence that these substances were taken deliberately by Miss Wilkinson. Persons who take these drugs may inadvertently take an overdose.'

For about nine months before her death, it emerged at the inquest, Ellen had been taking a combination of two drugs (Theamine and Amital) prescribed for her asthma, together with Medinal for her insomnia. According to the Home Office pathologist, Dr Roche Lynch, the post-mortem examination had revealed quantities of barbituric acid. Dr W. Brooks, the Assistant Physician at St Mary's agreed that 'a strong-willed person who finds that taking a prescribed dose of medicine does not have the desired effect, may take it into their heads to take a little more'. No facts were elicited which threw doubts on Dr Neville Stafford's positive conclusion.[15]

Yet there are still those who aver that Ellen killed herself because she was dissatisfied with her showing as minister and felt the job overwhelming. Donoughue and Jones in their biography of Herbert Morrison concluded that Ellen did commit suicide, though they cite no positive evidence other than 'She had always suffered from ill health, especially asthma, and kept going on drugs. Her appointment as Minister presented a burden which her frail frame could not carry.'[16] On the other hand, her friend Edward MacLellan, a consultant surgeon, totally disagreed — 'I doubt very much that she took her own life' — and in this he was not alone: Ellen's family, friends and political colleagues who knew her well, have expressed similar views. Time and again they have commented independently that the easy way out was entirely out of keeping both with Ellen's characteristic courage and with her love of life. 'Suicide just did not belong to her make-up. She loved life too much.'[17] As Paddy Scullion said, 'she was too brave a woman to kill herself.'

On occasion Ellen did show hypochondriacal tendencies. She would become agitated when she ran out of her sleeping tablets;[18] she tried (unsuccessfully) to persuade a member of her private office to obtain additional tablets for her when she was in hospital; and she would get so impatient with her illness that she tended to over-treat herself.[19] There is no proof, however, that she had ever relied excessively on drugs. Moreover she had been warned against over-medication, notably by Mr MacLellan who 'knew all the secrets of her heart as well as her health':

> Towards the end of her life she began to ask, even to demand, injections of Adrenalin to enable her to make after dinner speeches, when I knew that she was quite unfit to go anywhere except bed. I told her that this would destroy her and that I could play no part in her destruction.[20]

The totality of the evidence in no way suggests suicide.

The most likely explanation of Ellen's death is that, intensely overwrought and overworked, she muddled her medicines through sheer exasperation and confusion. Frequently, when busy, she would forget how many, if any, pills she had actually taken and would say to her secretary — 'I cannot remember whether I have had them or not, so I'll take a double lot now.'[21] It was in line with her characteristic impatience, that resentful over recurrent illness and anxious to return to her ministry to grapple with work, she would take too many pills in an attempt to expedite a quick recovery. Fearlessness was as steel in her soul; Ellen would never retreat from what she thought to be right and even though she may have felt she had not been as successful a minister as she had wished, she possessed a courage that would never concede defeat. The easy escape by suicide was totally out of keeping. Ellen was not a quitter.[22]

Farewell

I can assure you that Ellen Wilkinson was a very lovable person — Arthur Koestler.

She was the product of her age: full of steel and guts, yet charged with high emotionalism — James Margach

No one who met Ellen ever forgot her. The burnished hair was as distinctive as her minute stature, her charm and her vitality — 'One couldn't not notice her'.[23] A bundle of concentrated energy she was as rock-like in her socialist idealism as in her feminism, abounding in mercurial anger yet overflowing with generosity of intent. 'Ellen', wrote Susan Lawrence, 'was a flame-like spirit, giving life and light to thousands. She had one of the quickest and surest minds I have ever met and leapt instantaneously to the heart of a problem.'[24]

By sheer ability and a driving capacity for hard work Ellen won her way from a humble background to Parliament, the Privy Council and the Cabinet; but behind that ability lay a strength of purpose derived from the Methodist precept to 'go for those who need you, especially those who need you most.' As an excellent parliamentarian she gave the highest priority to her constituency, and loyal to her working-class origins, defended the exploited, the voteless, and the hounded anti-fascists of Europe. Always the downtrodden evoked a wrath expressed through speech and pen: 'Wherever trouble was, there was Ellen, battling with stars in her eyes'.[25]

It has been suggested that Ellen was a thoroughly calculating creature whose political progress was one of premeditated design. Certainly she was ambitious and she did trim her sails; her determination to stay in the Labour Party (and on the NEC), gave latterly a rightward swing in her behaviour which was unquestionably reinforced by her relationship with Herbert Morrison. Yet she never lost her resolute independence of thought and sought power not for self glory but to succour the weak of the world. 'With Ellen . . . action followed thought with a lightness and swiftness, without a shadow of calculation as to whether this or that would be to her own personal advancement.'[26]

As a politician she did of course take advantage of opportunities. With her journalistic flair and her stunning platform appeal, she would secure publicity for her causes, her constituents, her campaigns. And if she did 'make scenes in the House to impress',[27] and the publicity rubbed off on her, they were created with unselfish intent.

Certainly though she was not without fault. Overcommitment made her muddled and confused: disciplined efficiency was never Ellen's hallmark. Gullibility made her 'too ready to accept undigested ideas, without letting them simmer', and she was prone to assume that the Left was right just because it was the Left.[28] Further, her intense impetuosity could make her hurtful; when temper exploded into bitchiness, her tongue could flail, though instantly she would apologise and cajole with a charm that lingered. Disagreements rarely degenerated into alienation, for Ellen had a gift for friendship that reached across the political spectrum.[29] Susan Lawrence was not alone in finding her 'the kindest and most generous friend that anyone had the good fortune to possess'.[30]

Powered by a driving urge to get things done, Ellen was always in a hurry to right the wrong, haunted by the spectre of an all-too-real time shortage. Politics were her life and spinsterhood the logical if unpremeditated outcome. Had Herbert Morrison been willing to free himself from his matrimonial obligations, the outcome might have been different. As it was, in Harold Laski's words, 'she took the whole world of people, in pain and sorrow, to her heart, giving her whole self to the service of socialism. Pride in her own achievement was always set in the perspective of the Movement's victory.'[31] It has been said, not unfairly, that in her political career, which was her life, Ellen illustrated the broad evolution of Labour views and attitudes over the past quarter century.[32]

A feminist rooted in her trade union, she progressed from being 'little Miss Perky' to 'Our Ellen' and eventually 'Our Minister', and justifiably has been termed 'the most interesting political woman of her generation'.[33]

Beatrice Webb, shrewdly prescient, described Ellen in her early thirties 'as being neither vain nor self conscious [but] . . . direct, devoted, public spirited — free from malice — and . . . peculiarly lacking in personal vanity', adding, 'She will not alter the policy of the Labour Party by hard thinking or new observation or spiritual insight — she will be an interpreter of other people's thoughts and intentions.' Astutely she predicted that Ellen would be 'moulded for the Front Bench and eventually for office . . . if she does not wear herself out by rattling over the country addressing mass meetings'.[34] This was exactly what she did do: the 'Mighty Atom' burnt herself out.

From the distance of decades, Beatrice Webb had written prophetically; Lord Redcliffe-Maud, close to his minister until her death, spoke from first-hand experience. 'She was', he wrote, 'an heroic and lovable figure, with integrity and first rate moral and physical courage, but with a body, at least for the last twelve months of her life, quite inadequate to serve the generous purpose of her spirit.'[35]

Vivid and resolute, Ellen drove herself like a fury, bringing colour and courage to the Labour Movement she loved: her life force was rooted neither in egotism nor in the desire for power as an end in itself. 'Quite simply it arose from the urge of compassion for mankind and a vision of the world that might be.'[36]

Notes

1. Professor H.C. Dent and Heinrich Fraenkel, interviews.
2. *The Times*, 15 August 1942.
3. Vernon Bartlett, letter of 15 May 1978.
4. *The Times*, 1 December 1944 and 22 January 1945.
5. Lord Redcliffe-Maud, interview.
6. Muriel Nichol, interview.
7. Margaret Bondfield in *Labour Woman*, March/April 1947.
8. H.D. Hughes, interview.
9. Sir Antony Part, interview.
10. Paul Rotha, letter.
11. J.W. Murray, *Parliament*, October 1946.
12. Molly Sole, Mrs Muriel Wilkinson, Mrs Kathleen Wilkinson, interviews.
13. B. Donoughue and G.W. Jones, *Herbert Morrison, Portrait of a Politician* (Weidenfeld and Nicolson, 1973), p. 392.
14. 'Active, courageous, accessible, she had many traits which ministers of every government and every party have been taught to aim at. Vital and fearless, she also had a great pride in our country. She always wished to see this island great and capable of offering a decent home to all its people.' (Winston Churchill, Hansard, Vol. 432, col. 1984, 6 February 1947); Ald. T. Meehan, *Middlesbrough Evening Gazette*, 6 February, 1947.
15. *Manchester Guardian*, 1 March 1947.
16. Donoughue and Jones, p. 392.
17. Among the many who expressed such opinions were the Wilkinson family, Betty Archdale, Maud Bickford, Isabel Brown, Dame Margaret Cole, Lord Fenner Brockway, Lord Ritchie-Calder, Heinrich Fraenkel ('totally out of keeping'), Margaret Gibb ('she loved life'), Kenneth Harris, Ivor Montagu, Amy Mitchell, Muriel Nichol, John Parker, MP, Dame Mabel Tylecote and Lord Redcliffe-Maud.
18. Mrs Kathleen Wilkinson, interview.
19. K. Witney, Beryl Hughes, interviews.
20. Edward MacLellan, letter of 23 April 1980.
21. Beryl Hughes, interview.
22. Lord Redcliffe-Maud, interview.
23. Robin Page Arnot, interview.
24. Betty Archdale, letter; Susan Lawrence, *Fabian Quarterly*, March, 1947.
25. James Margach, letter.
26. Susan Lawrence, *Fabian Quarterly*, March 1947; Betty Archdale, Isabel Brown, Ivor Montagu, Amy Mitchell, Paddy Scullion, Dorothy Elliott, Harry Weate, Arthur Blenkinsop and others, interviews.
27. Lord George Strauss, interview.
28. Dame Margaret Cole, interview.
29. Kingsley Martin, *Picture Post*, 22 June 1940; Lady Rhondda, *Time and Tide*, 15 February 1947; many others spoke of her capacity for friendship.
30. Susan Lawrence, *Fabian Quarterly*, March 1947.
31. *Reynolds News*, 10 February 1947.
32. *Times Educational Supplement*, 8 February 1947.
33. H.D. Hughes, interview.

34. B. Webb, *Diaries — 1924–1932* (Longmans Green, London, 1936), pp. 132–3, 7 February 1927.

35. *The Times*, 8 February 1947.

36. Jack Lawson, MP, *Methodist Magazine*, April 1947.

APPENDIX I: PARLIAMENTARY ELECTIONS

1923
Ashton under Lyne

Sir W. de Frece (Con)	7,813
H.T. Greenwood (Lib)	7,574
Miss E.C. Wilkinson (Lab)	6,208
(Con majority)	239

1924
Middlesbrough East

Miss E.C. Wilkinson (Lab)	9,574
P. Warde Aldam (Con)	8,647
Penry Williams (Lib)	6,688
(Lab majority)	927

1929
Middlesbrough East (enlarged electorate)

Miss E.C. Wilkinson (Lab)	12,215
E.J. Young (Lib)	9,016
J.W. Brown (Con)	8,278
(Lab majority)	3,199

1931
Middlesbrough East

E.J. Young (Lib)	18,409
Miss E.C. Wilkinson (Lab)	12,080
(Lib majority)	6,329

1935
Jarrow

Miss E.C. Wilkinson (Lab)	20,324
W.G. Pearson (Con)	17,974
(Lab majority)	2,350

1945
Jarrow

The Rt Hon. E.C. Wilkinson (Lab)	22,656
S. Holmes (N/Lib)	11,649
(Lab majority)	11,007

Source: F.W.S. Craig, *British Parliamentary Election Results 1918–49* (London, Macmillan, 1977)

APPENDIX II:
COMPOSITION OF THE
HOUSE OF COMMONS

	Labour	Independent Labour	Communist	Liberal	Conservative & Nat. Unionist	Others
1923	191	–	–	158	258	8
1924	152	–	1	42	415	6
1929	288	–	–	59	260	8
1931	46	6	–	72	475	16[1]
1935	154	4	1	(54)[2]	390	12[3]
1945	394	5 •	2	(25)[2]	202	12[4]

[1]Including Coalition Labour and others
[2]Liberal National plus Independent Liberal
[3]Including Coalition Labour, Sinn Fein and others
[4]Including Coalition Labour, Sinn Fein, Commonwealth and others

BIBLIOGRAPHY

Allen, Lady (of Hurtwood), *Memoirs of an Uneducated Lady*, London, Thames and Hudson, 1975

Archdale, B., *Indiscretions of a Headmistress*, London, Angus and Robertson, 1972

Atholl, Duchess of, *Searchlight on Spain*, Penguin Special, 1938

Attlee, C.R., *As It Happened*, London, Heinemann, 1954

Barker, R., *Education and Politics 1900–51*, Oxford, Oxford University Press, 1972

Benedict, L., *The Refugees*, London, Hogarth Press, 1938

Berkeley, H., *The Myth That Will Not Die*, London, Croom Helm, 1978

Blackburn, F., *George Tomlinson*, London, Heinemann, 1954

Bracher, S.V., *The Herald Book of Labour*, London, Labour Publications, 1923

Branson, N. and Heinemann, M., *Britain in the Nineteen Thirties*, London, Weidenfeld and Nicolson, 1971

Branson, N., *Poplarism*, London, Lawrence and Wishart, 1979

Brookes, P., *Women at Westminster*, London, Peter Davies, 1967

Browne, M., *Too Late to Lament*, London, Gollancz, 1955

Bussey, G. and Timms, M., *The Women's International League for Peace and Freedom*, London, Allen and Unwin, 1965

Calder, A., *The People's War*, London, Jonathan Cape, 1969

Cockburn, C., *I, Claud*, London, Penguin, 1967

Cole, G.D.H., *A History of the Labour Party from 1914*, London, Routledge and Kegan Paul, 1948

Cole, G.D.H. and Postgate, R., *The Common People 1746–1938*, London, Methuen, 1938

Cole, M., *Makers of the Labour Movement*, London, Longman, 1948

——, *The Life of G.D.H. Cole*, London, Macmillan, 1971

——, *The History of Fabian Socialism*, London, Heinemann, 1961

——, *Growing Up Into Revolution*, London, Longmans, Green, 1926

——(ed.), *The Road to Success*, London, Methuen, 1936

243

Courtney, J., *Women of My Time*, London, Lovat Dickson, 1934

Dalton, H., *Call Back Yesterday 1887–1931*, London, Muller, 1953

———, *The Fateful Years — Memoirs 1931–1945*, London, Muller, 1957

Davies, S., *North Country Born*, London, Routledge and Kegan Paul, 1963

Delmer, S., *Trail Sinister*, London, Secker and Warburg, 1961

Donoughue, B. and Jones, G.W., *Herbert Morrison, Portrait of a Politician*, London, Weidenfeld and Nicolson, 1973

Dougan, D., *The Jarrow March*, Jarrow, Bede Gallery, 1976

Drake, B., *Women in Trade Unions*, London, Allen and Unwin, n.d.

Eastwood, G., *Harold J. Laski*, London, A.R. Mowbray, 1978

Elliott, D., *Women in Search of Justice*, unpublished papers *c*. 1960

Esterick, E., *Stafford Cripps*, London, Heinemann, 1949

Fawcett, M., *The Women's Victory and After*, London, Sidgwick and Jackson, 1920

———, *What I Remember*, London, Fisher Unwin, 1924

Fenwick, I.G.K., *The Comprehensive School (1944–1970)*, London, Methuen, 1976

Foot, M., *Aneurin Bevan*, London, MacGibbon and Kee, 1962

Gershon, K., *We Came as Children*, London, Gollancz, 1966

Gilbert, M. (ed.), *Plough My Own Furrow*, London, Longmans, 1965

Gosden, P.H., *Education in the Second World War*, London, Methuen, 1976

Gould, R., *Chalk Up the Memory*, London, G.P. Alexander, 1976

Hallsworth, J., *Trade Board Rates, Standard Rates and Wages*, Manchester, NUDAW, 1922 (pamphlet)

Hammond, J.L. and B., *The Town Labourer*, London, Gollancz, 1937

———, *The Bleak Age*, London, Pelican, 1947

Hamilton, M.A., *Remembering My Good Friends*, London, Cape, 1944

———, *Margaret Bondfield*, London, Leonard Parsons, 1924

———, *Women at Work*, London, Labour Book Service, 1941

Hannington, W., *Never on Our Knees*, London, Lawrence and Wishart, 1967

Heardon, A. (ed.), *The British in Germany*, London, Hamish Hamilton, 1978

Hellman, L., *An Unfinished Woman*, USA, Little, Brown, 1969

Hodges, S., *Victor Gollancz*, London, Gollancz, 1978

Horrabin, J.F., Postgate, R. and Wilkinson, E., *A Worker's History of the General Strike*, London, Plebs League, 1927

Hughes, E., *Keir Hardie*, London, Allen and Unwin, 1956

Huxley, J., *Memoirs*, London, Allen and Unwin, 1973

Jennings, W.I., *Parliament*, Cambridge, Cambridge University Press, 1939

Johnston, J., *A Hundred Commoners*, London, Herbert Jenkins, 1931

Jones, T., *Diary With Letters 1931–1950*, Oxford, Oxford University Press, 1954

Klugman, J., *History of the Communist Party of Great Britain*, London, Lawrence and Wishart, 1948

Koestler, A., *The Invisible Writing*, London, Hutchinson, 1954

Laski, H., *Reflections on the Constitution*, Manchester, Manchester University Press, 1951

Lee, J., *The Great Journey*, London, MacGibbon and Kee, 1963

———, *My Life with Nye*, London, Cape, 1980

Lockett, T.A., *Three Lives*, London, University of London Press, 1968

Mahon, J., *Harry Pollitt*, London, Lawrence and Wishart, 1976

Manning, L., *A Life for Education*, London, Gollancz, 1970

Margach, J., *The Abuse of Power*, London, W.H. Allen, 1978

Middleton, L. (ed.), *Women in the Labour Movement*, London, Croom Helm, 1978

Middleton, M. and Weitzman, S., *A Place for Everyone*, London, Gollancz, 1976

Millar, J.P., *The Labour College Movement*, London, NCLC Publishing Society, 1979

Mitchell, H., *The Hard Way Up*, London, Faber and Faber, 1968

Morris, M., *The General Strike*, London, Penguin, 1976

Morrison, Lady, *Memoirs of a Marriage*, London, Muller, 1977

Morrison, Lord, *An Autobiography*, London, Odhams Press, 1960

Mowat, C.L., *Britain Between the Wars (1918–1940)*, London, Methuen, 1955

Nesbitt, C., *A Little Love and Good Company*, London, Faber and Faber, 1975

Nicolson, H., *Diaries with Letters 1930–39*, London, Collins, 1966

Oxford, Margot (ed.), *Myself When Young*, London, Muller, 1938

Pakenham, F., *Born to Believe*, London, Longford, 1953

Pankhurst, E., *My Own Story*, London, Eveleigh Nash, 1914

Pankhurst, E. Sylvia, *The Suffragette Movement*, London, Longmans Green, 1931

Parkinson, M., *The Labour Party and the Organisation of Secondary Education (1918–1965)*, London, Routledge and Kegan Paul, 1970

Phillips, M., *Women and the Miners' Lockout*, London, Labour Publishing Company, 1927 (pamphlet)

Pimlott, B., *Labour and the Left in the 1930s*, Cambridge, Cambridge University Press, 1977

Pimlott, J.A.R., *Toynbee Hall*, London, J M Dent, 1934

Priestley, J.B., *English Journey*, London, Heinemann, 1934

Pritt, D.N., *From Right to Left*, London, Lawrence and Wishart, 1965

Rea, V. (ed.), *Palmers Shipyard and the Town of Jarrow*, Jarrow, Bede Gallery, 1975

Rolph, C.H., *Kingsley*, London, Gollancz, 1973

Rowntree, B. Seebohm, *Poverty*, London, Nelson, n.d.

Rubinstein, D. and Simon, B., *The Evolution of the Comprehensive School (1926–1966)*, London, Routledge and Kegan Paul, 1969

Saville, J., *Dictionary of Labour Biography*, London, Macmillan, 1976, vol. 3

Sells, D., *The British Trade Boards System*, London, King and Son, 1923

————, *British Wages Boards*, Washington DC, Brookings Institution, 1939

Sherriff, R.C., *No Leading Lady*, London, Gollancz, 1968

Shinwell, E., *Conflict Without Malice*, London, Odhams, 1955

Simon, B., *The Politics of Educational Reform 1920–1940*, London, Lawrence and Wishart, 1974

————, *The Comprehensive Secondary School*, London, Lawrence and Wishart, 1955

Stocks, M., *Eleanor Rathbone*, London, Gollancz, 1949

Strachey, R., *The Cause*, London, G Bell and Sons, 1928

Strauss, P., *Cripps — Advocate and Rebel*, London, Gollancz, 1943

Sykes, C., *Nancy*, London, Collins, 1972

Thomas, H., *John Strachey*, London, Eyre Methuen, 1973

————, *The Spanish Civil War*, London, Eyre & Spottiswood, 1961

Thompson, E.P., *The Making of the English Working Class*, London, Gollancz, 1963

Trevelyan, G.M., *A History of England*, London, Longmans, 1926

Vallance, A., *Hire Purchase*, London, Nelson, 1939

Wade, E.C. and Phillips, G., *Constitutional Law*, London, Longmans, 1970

Wearmouth, R., *Social and Political Influence of Methodism in the 20th Century*, London, Epworth Press, 1957

• Webb, B., *Diaries — 1924–1932* (ed. M. Cole), London, Longmans Green, 1936

Weir, L. MacNeill, *The Tragedy of Ramsay MacDonald*, London, Secker and Warburg, 1978

Wilkinson, E., *Clash*, London, Harrap, 1929

———, *Peeps at Politicians*, London, P.A. Allen & Co., 1930

———, *The Division Bell Mystery*, London, Harrap, 1932

———, *The Town That Was Murdered*, London, Gollancz, 1939

Wilkinson, E. and Conze, E. *Why Fascism?*, London, Selwyn and Blount, 1934

Williams, F., *Fifty Years March*, London, Odhams, n.d.

———, *A Prime Minister Remembers*, London, Heinemann, 1961

———, *Nothing So Strange*, London, Cassell, 1970

———, *A Pattern of Rulers*, London, Longmans, 1965

Worswick, G.D.N. and Ady, P.H., *The British Economy 1945–1950*, Oxford, Oxford University Press, 1952

INDEX